CHRIST AND THE FUTURE

CHRIST AND THE FUTURE

―――――――――――

THE BIBLE'S TEACHING ABOUT THE LAST THINGS

CORNELIS P. VENEMA

THE BANNER OF TRUTH TRUST

THE BANNER OF TRUTH TRUST
3 Murrayfield Road, Edinburgh EH12 6EL, UK
P.O. Box 621, Carlisle, PA 17013, USA

*

© Cornelis P. Venema 2008

ISBN–13: 978 1 84871 008 5

*

Typeset in 10/14 pt Baskerville MT at
The Banner of Truth Trust, Edinburgh
Printed in the USA by
Versa Press, Inc.,
Peoria, IL

*

CONTENTS

PUBLISHER'S NOTE

*A*t the beginning of this millennium the Banner of Truth Trust published *The Promise of the Future* by Cornelis P. Venema. In the Foreword to that edition, Sinclair B. Ferguson wrote that 'Dr Venema's fine study is both comprehensive and careful.' While it has justly received acclaim from numerous reviewers, its size and weight may discourage the less experienced reader from taking it up and benefitting from its fine contents. The publishers, therefore, are grateful to Dr Venema for kindly agreeing to produce this abridgement of his original edition, and are now delighted to offer it to a wider readership in this smaller, paperback format.

THE PUBLISHERS
Edinburgh
August 2008

AUTHOR'S PREFACE

*W*hen The Banner of Truth Trust first proposed the preparation of an abridgment of my book, *The Promise of the Future*, I was initially somewhat reluctant to embrace the proposal. Not only would it require a considerable reduction in the length of the original (whose every word was thought by the author to be indispensable!), but it also might cause the reader to forego the fuller study altogether.

My initial hesitancy was overcome, however, for two reasons. First, the publishers indicated that it was their desire to see the abridged version serve as a kind of introduction to the longer, more substantial volume. Whether readers will find their appetite whetted for the larger book by reading this abridgment remains to be seen. But it remains the publisher's and my hope that this will occur. And second, Glenda Mathes, a freelance writer from Pella, Iowa, graciously consented to assist in the project. Glenda contributed significantly to the daunting task of abridging the original manuscript. I hereby wish to acknowledge and express my thanks for her considerable contribution to the abridgment of the earlier book.

Cornelis P. Venema
September, 2008

ix

1

THE FUTURE IS NOW

*P*eople have a keen interest in the future. That many 'itching ears' are ready to listen to any prophet (*2 Tim.* 4:3) is evidenced by the popularity of psychic hot lines, fortune-tellers and prognosticators of the future. Politicians make compelling 'campaign promises' for the future.

Interest in the future is especially pronounced in North America. Americans visiting Europe will notice how centuries of tradition continue to influence Europeans. North Americans are more oriented to the future, and interpreters of American culture generally agree that North Americans today are far more preoccupied with the future than previous generations.

Christians share this heightened interest in the future, but are confused as to what to believe. This may reflect cultural confusion, but it also reflects the myriad of pronouncements from differing voices within the Christian community. These pronouncements often arise from a dispensationalist perspective, and many authors are especially adept at seizing upon uncertainty about the future.

FOUR IMPORTANT BIBLICAL THEMES

Confusion and heightened interest in the future call for careful study and reflection on the Bible's teachings. We need to examine the Scriptures to determine what we can know and believe regarding the future.

The only reliable antidote to speculation and fear is a disciplined study of what God promises in the Bible. As we begin examining the biblical promise of the future, we should bear four biblical themes in mind: the need to stay within the boundaries of God's word; Christ is the Lord of history; 'Paradise Regained' will surpass 'Paradise Lost'; and our hope is living and certain.

The most important rule believers must observe is to stay within the boundaries of God's word. Much current confusion results from failing to abide by this rule.

The future might be termed a mystery. We can consult a scrapbook or examine historical documents to determine the past, but the future is hidden from our view. We can conjecture, but we cannot predict.

Though we cannot predict the future, God can. In his word he reveals the things we need to know for our salvation, including precisely what we need to know about the shape of things to come.

The only antidote to speculation is listening carefully to God's promises regarding the future and disciplining ourselves not to go beyond them. This is the only safe course in a confused and disputed terrain. We must gratefully receive what God teaches in his word about the future, and humbly remain within the limits of this revelation.

One of the central themes God's word teaches us is that Christ is the Lord of history.

A common mistake believers make in considering the future is to become disoriented by focusing on themes, without seeing their biblical connections. We think of the millennium, the signs of the times, the return of Christ, and the resurrection of the dead, but our vision is unfocused. We see a confused complex of disconnected events looming upon the horizon.

Disorientation about the future occurs when we fail to see that all God's ways in history centre on Jesus Christ, who is 'the same yesterday, today and forever'. He is the one through whom we know the meaning and purpose of all history. In the Old Testament, the Lord's dealings with his people continually pointed to the future and particularly to one in whom his promises would be fulfilled. When Christ communed with the two disciples on the Emmaus road, he began 'with Moses and with all the prophets, [and] explained to them the things concerning himself in all the Scriptures' (*Luke* 24:27).

Just as Christ fulfils the Old Testament promises (*2 Cor.* 1:20), he also guarantees the future consummation of God's promises by his resurrection, session at the Father's right hand, and outpouring of the Spirit at Pentecost. Christ has been given all authority in heaven and on earth and will reign until all things have been subjected to him, including the last enemy—death (*1 Cor.* 15:25-26).

Christ as the Author, Governor, and Goal of history is explicitly affirmed in several New Testament passages. In Ephesians 1:9-11 Paul describes the 'mystery of God's will' as 'the summing up of all things in Christ, things in the heavens and things upon the earth'. In Colossians 1:16-17, we read, 'For by him [Christ] all things were created, both in the heavens and on the earth, visible and invisible, whether thrones or dominions or rulers or authorities—all things have been created by him and for him. And he is before all things, and in him all things hold together.' John's visions in Revelation describe Christ as 'the faithful witness, the first-born of the dead, and the ruler of the kings of the earth' (*Rev.* 1:5). Only the Lamb of God has authority to 'open the book and its seven seals', signifying his power to administer God's sovereign purposes in history (*Rev.* 5).

The biblical revelation regarding the future always fixes our attention on Christ. Just as God's ways with his people in times past have all met in Christ, so all of his ways in the future will meet in Christ. The great event on the horizon of the future, in biblical perspective, is Christ's return or 'Second Coming'. This event is the great future toward which all history is moving. It is the event that gives meaning to present history and which will consummate God's work of redemption. The entirety of the biblical teaching about the future is intimately linked to the coming of Christ at the end of the present age.

Another theme in the biblical revelation regarding the future is that of 'paradise lost, paradise regained'. To understand the biblical promises for the future, it is necessary to go back to the beginning, to God's original covenant fellowship with Adam and Eve in the Garden of Eden.

3

In these circumstances we see something of that communion with God for which humankind was created, and which will be restored in the new creation.

It is striking how closely the vision of Revelation 22 resembles the original paradise. The new heaven and earth is described, not only as the new Jerusalem, but also as a renewed garden of life: 'And he showed me', says John, 'a river of the water of life, clear as crystal, coming from the throne of God and of the Lamb . . . And on either side of the river was the tree of life . . . yielding its fruit every month; and the leaves of the tree were for the healing of the nations' (22:1-2). The 'first things' of creation are prophetic of the 'last things' of the new creation. Paradise regained, however, will bring more than Eden. The progress of history and the greater glory in redemption through Christ ensure that the new heavens and the new earth will surpass the old. Not only will God be acknowledged throughout the whole of creation as the Most Holy One, but he will also suffer no further rebellion or covenant unfaithfulness. The covenant communion of God's people before the face of God will be unbroken and unbreakable. It will not be threatened by a 'fall from grace' or defection among the redeemed.

The Bible's promises for the future are not to be confused with the modern practice of 'fortune-telling' or predicting a precise timetable for the future. There is much that God does not give us to know in his word. But what he has given us kindles in the believer a living and certain hope, a confidence that the redeeming work of Christ will not fail to be fully accomplished. Through the resurrection of Christ, 'we have been born anew to a living hope' (*1 Pet.* 1:3) that will not die.

The believer's expectation for the future is marked by a hope nurtured by the word and a lively expectation of the accomplishment of God's purpose in Christ. The future does not loom darkly on the horizon. It is eagerly expected and anticipated, bright with the promise of the completion and perfection of God's saving work.

It is true that many biblical exhortations relating to the future call God's people to watchfulness and sobriety, warning them against being found unprepared at Christ's coming (*1 Pet.* 4:7; *1 Thess.* 5:6; *Matt.* 24:42-

45). They often warn the church to remain faithful to the apostolic teachings and word of God (*2 Thess.* 2:15; *Heb.* 10:23). Biblical descriptions of Christ's coming starkly describe its frightening consequences for the wicked (*2 Thess.* 2:8; *2 Pet.* 3:12; *Rev.* 18:10).

But the chief note sounded in God's revelation regarding the future is one of hope. God's people eagerly await Christ's return because it promises the completion of God's work of redemption for them and for the whole creation. The future is bright because it is full of promise, the promise of God's Word.

OLD TESTAMENT EXPECTATION FOR THE FUTURE

Staying within God's boundaries, honouring Christ as Lord of history, understanding that the lost paradise will be more fully regained, and being confident of our certain hope, we can now examine more carefully the Old and New Testament teachings concerning Christ's first coming.

All of God's redemptive dealings with his covenant people, prior to the birth of Jesus in the 'fullness of time', kindled an expectation and anticipation of Messiah's (Christ's) coming. Consequently, restlessness pervades the Old Testament. Each new chapter in covenant history heightened anticipation of that future consummation. There is a dynamic to the history of the covenant in the Old Testament that would not permit believers to look only to the past, in remembrance of what the Lord had already done, but demanded that they also look to the future, in the hope of even better things to come.

The Old Testament expectation of the coming Messiah is the seedbed for all the other dimensions of the Old Testament's teaching about the future.

The first word of the Lord, spoken to our first parents after the Fall, announces the future birth of a Redeemer who will crush the head of the serpent and vindicate God's gracious rule within his creation. In Genesis 3:15, we find this 'mother promise', the first gospel announcement: 'And I [the Lord God] will put enmity between you and the woman, and between your seed and her seed; he shall crush you on the head, and you shall bruise him on the heel.' In this first gospel promise, the Lord announces that he will establish an opposition or antithesis between two kinds of seeds, representing the people at enmity with God and the people whom he befriends. This antithesis will serve God's gracious purpose for his people whom he will deliver and save through one born of a woman. This 'mother promise' is the fundamental promise in the old covenant, fixing the eye of faith of God's people upon the person of the coming Saviour.

The Lord renews and specifies this promise to Abraham through whom 'all the families of the earth' would be blessed (*Gen.* 12:3). The Lord assured Abraham that in his seed this promise would be fulfilled. Through the birth of Isaac, Sarah would become the mother of nations (*Gen.* 17:16); from Isaac would be born the seed in whom all the nations would enter into covenant blessing (*Gen.* 22:18; cf. 26:4; 28:14). Now the promise becomes focused upon Abraham's seed, the son in whom the promise of redemption will be realised. Later in the Old Testament, we learn that this promised son will be born of the tribe of Judah (*Gen.* 49:10) and of the family of David (*2 Sam.* 7:12-13).

With the progressive unfolding of the Lord's revelation to his covenant people, the expectation of this coming Saviour becomes further refined in the three special offices ordained by the Lord: prophet, priest, and king. The children of Israel were taught to expect one in whom these offices would be fulfilled. The Messiah or 'Anointed One' would be called of God and empowered by his Spirit to speak the word of the Lord as a prophet, offer sacrifice and intercession on behalf of his people as a priest, and rule in righteousness in the Lord's name as a king. Moses was a 'type' of an even greater prophet to come. We read in Deuteronomy 18:15, 'The Lord God will raise up for you a prophet like me [Moses] from among you, from your countrymen, you shall listen to him' (cf. *Acts* 3:22). The Aaronic priests who ministered daily at the altar were only a 'shadow' of an eternal priest, in the order of Melchizedek, who would offer himself once for all a perfect sacrifice for his people (*Psa.* 110:4; *Heb.* 5). Furthermore, the Lord promised David that he would

6

establish the throne of his son forever (*2 Sam.* 7:12-13; *Isa.* 9:7). In the offices of prophet, priest and king, Israel was given the promise of the Messiah who, commissioned and empowered by the Lord, would reveal the word of the Lord, make atonement for the sins of the people, and rule in righteousness over an eternal kingdom.

The person and work of the coming Messiah are described in the Old Testament as the coming of the Lord to dwell among his people, just as he had in the tabernacle. The Messiah's name will be Immanuel, 'God with us' (*Isa.* 7:14). He will also be the suffering servant of the Lord, who will take upon himself the sin of his people. Isaiah strikingly foresees the suffering of the Messiah, by which he will accomplish redemption: 'But he was pierced through for our transgressions, he was crushed for our iniquities; the chastening for our well-being fell upon him, and by his scourging we are healed' (53:5). But the Messiah will not only be Immanuel and the suffering servant, he will also be the heavenly Son of Man to whom God will give dominion and power to establish his kingdom and to destroy every enemy who resists God's rule (*Dan.* 7:13-14).

Though the Old Testament clearly reveals God to be the King over all (*Psa.* 103:19), the majestic Lord of heaven and earth whose will cannot be frustrated in any corner of his creation-kingdom, it also acknowledges that sin has disrupted it. Sin is rooted in rebellion against God's righteous rule. Nations and people are under the dominion of darkness and sin, captive to the kingdoms of this world and at enmity with God. Only Israel was to know and confess the kingdom of the true and living God.

One way in which the Old Testament portrays the future is in terms of *the final victory and re-establishment of God's kingdom over all creation.* Not only will the Lord continue to reign in majesty from heaven, but he will also be acknowledged as King in the whole realm of creation. All who have rebelled against him, all kingdoms that have resisted his dominion, will be brought into subjection. A dramatic prophecy about the future establishment of God's kingdom is found in Daniel 2, which speaks of a kingdom that God will set up in the 'latter days', that will never be destroyed and that will fill the whole earth. This kingdom is depicted as a 'little stone' that will crush the kingdoms of this world and grow until it fills the whole earth, a depiction that associates the realisation of this kingdom with the coming of the Messiah, the Son of Man.

In the Old Testament it becomes increasingly clear that what the covenant of grace promised did not come to full flowering because of the unfaithfulness of the covenant people. The history of the covenant is marked by a striking contrast between the faithfulness of the Lord and the unfaithfulness of his people. The children of Israel are finally sent into exile under God's judgement, and it almost seems that the Lord's way of grace with his people has ended in failure.

But the Lord remains forever faithful to his promises! Israel's disobedience will not frustrate his redeeming purpose for his chosen people. Even in their exile and subsequent restoration to the land of promise, the people of God are given further promises of a new and better covenant. The day will come, the Lord promises, when he will gather his people to himself and establish a new covenant with them, based upon better promises! The old covenant failed, partly because its promises were less rich than those of the new covenant, and partly because of the stubborn refusal of the children of Israel to live according to the covenant's stipulations (cf. *Heb.* 8). In the new covenant, however, the Lord promised to write his law upon the hearts of the people: "'But this is the covenant which I will make with the house of Israel after those days", declares the Lord, "I will put my law within them, and on their heart I will write it; and I will be their God, and they shall be my people'" (*Jer.* 31:33).

Another aspect of the Old Testament expectation for the future is the restoration of God's people. The dispersion of the Israelites before and during the exile seemed to imperil the unity and future of the people of God. In this setting, the Lord reveals a future in which there will be a new exodus (*Isa.* 11:11), a return to the land of promise and restoration of the people of God. As the Lord spoke through Jeremiah, "'Then I myself shall gather the remnant of my flock out of all the countries where I have driven them and shall bring them back to their pasture; and they will be fruitful and multiply'" (23:3). This restoration of a remnant would not exclude, however, the fulfilment of the promise that all the families of the earth would be blessed through the seed of Abraham. Many Old

Testament promises concerning Israel's restoration include the promise that the nations and peoples of the earth will come to the light and enjoy, in fellowship with Israel, the blessings of salvation (e.g. see *Jer.* 48:47; 49:39; *Isa.* 2:2; *Mic.* 4:1). The Lord would not fail to gather his people, and through them, all the families of the earth.

On what basis could the Lord assure the people of Israel of a future bright with promise, a future that would bring a new and better covenant and a new exodus? The answer is found in the promise of a new outpouring of the Spirit of God.

In Jeremiah 31, the Lord's promise of a better covenant is intimately joined to the further promise of the Spirit who will write the law of God, not upon stone tablets, but upon the fleshy hearts of his people (*Ezek.* 36:24-28). Similarly, in Ezekiel 37 the restoration of God's people is likened to the resurrection of dead and dry bones, into which the Lord breathes his life-giving Spirit. Just at the time Israel's prospects seem bleakest, then the Lord will graciously intervene in a mighty way by his Spirit, granting life from the dead. As the Lord spoke through Ezekiel, 'And I will put my Spirit within you, and you will come to life, and I will place you on your land. Then you will know that I, the Lord, have spoken and done it' (*Ezek.* 37:14). This future work of pouring out his Spirit upon his people is most dramatically disclosed in Joel 2:28-29, a passage to which Peter appealed in his Pentecost sermon (*Acts* 2): 'And it will come about after this, that I will pour out my Spirit on all mankind; and your sons and daughters will prophesy, your old men will dream dreams, your young men will see visions.'

In prophecies relating to Israel's restoration, the Spirit's outpouring, and the covenant's re-establishment, references increasingly emerge to the 'day of the Lord'. This 'day of the Lord' indicates the Lord's final visitation in grace and in judgement. Though it frequently emphasises God's wrath and judgement upon the wicked, it also promises salvation for the righteous.

Sometimes this day is fearsomely described as in the near future, when God will execute judgement against Israel's enemies (*Obad.* 15-16). Sometimes it is disclosed as a final day of the Lord's visitation, when he will deal with the world because of its sin (*Isa.* 13:9-11). Though the wrath of the Lord upon the wicked tends to predominate prophetic announcements of the coming of the Lord, some passages speak of the salvation for the Lord's people that will accompany it. The prophet Amos warns the children of Israel that this day will mean destruction for the wicked, even as it brings vindication to the righteous (*Amos* 5:18). The prophets Isaiah (2:12, 17) and Zephaniah (1:14-15) sound similar notes of wrath falling upon the disobedient in that day, while Joel (2:32) promises salvation to all who call upon the name of the Lord before the terrible day of his wrath predicted by Malachi (cf. *Mal.* 4:2-5).

One of the grandest aspects of the Old Testament's expectation regarding the future is the promise that the Lord will establish a new heavens and earth. More than any other promise, this one reminds the believer of the beginning. Paradise lost will become paradise regained. But the future reality will exceed the past.

When the Lord's redeeming work has reached its goal, the whole of creation will be purged of sin and brought to perfection. In Isaiah 65:17, the Lord declares, 'For behold, I create new heavens and a new earth; and the former things shall not be remembered or come to mind.' Just as the Lord fashioned man from the dust of the earth, so man will be restored to the fullness of life. When the earth is renewed, according to Isaiah, it will become a fruitful field, rather than a wilderness (32:15). The dry places will become springs (35:7). There will be no more conflict or disorder within the creation; all creatures will live together in harmony and peace. As the prophet so beautifully puts it, 'They will not hurt or destroy in all my holy mountain, for the earth will be full of the knowledge of the Lord, as the waters cover the sea' (11:6-9).

We conclude this sketch of the Old Testament's view for the future by considering the phrase 'the latter days'. This phrase captures the whole thrust of the Old Testament revelation regarding the future. Old Testament believers, nurtured by the word of the Lord, fixed their gaze upon the latter days.

The use of 'the latter days' varies considerably in the Old Testament, but it does have some characteristic features. Typically, this language focuses on the future destiny, not only of individuals, but also of all peoples and nations. It indicates the Lord's intention to bring salvation as well as judgement upon all people. In Daniel 2:28, the 'latter days' encompass the entire history in which the stone will destroy the kingdoms of this world and inaugurate God's eternal kingdom.

The latter days are consistently days of blessing for God's people and tribulation for his enemies. Often the theme of blessing and peace for the people of God is prominent (*Isa.* 2:2; *Mic.* 4:1, *Hos.* 3:4-5). However, this is balanced by the theme of tribulation and judgement upon those who reject God and oppress his people (*Dan.* 2:28). Furthermore, the blessing that will come to Israel will also mean blessing for all nations who come to Jerusalem and share in the salvation of the Lord (*Jer.* 48:47; 49:39).

All of these aspects of the Old Testament outlook upon the future are cumulative. They form a single mosaic of anticipation and expectation for the day, on the furthest horizon of history, when the Lord will visit his people in grace and his enemies in judgement. All the promises we have discussed—the coming of the Saviour, the establishment of the kingdom of God, the granting of a new and better covenant, the restoration of the people of God, the day of the Lord—point to a time in history when the Lord will bring to fruition and perfection all of his gracious purposes and covenantal ways with his people.

New Testament Fulfilment: The Future Is Now

Old Testament believers peered over the immediate present toward the future horizon and the approach of a new and better day. When this glorious future dawned at the birth of Jesus, we should not be surprised to find believers like Simeon rejoicing. When Joseph and Mary presented Jesus at the temple, Simeon took him in his arms and blessed God and said: 'Sovereign Lord, as you have promised, you dismiss your servant in peace. For my eyes have seen your salvation, which you have prepared in the sight of all people, a light for revelation to the Gentiles and for glory to your people Israel' (*Luke* 2:29-32, NIV). This event indicates that the future of Old Testament expectation has become the now of New Testament fulfilment in the birth of the Saviour.

Similarly, songs of Mary and Zacharias celebrate and praise God for his faithfulness. Notice how the Song of Mary, the *Magnificat*, links the birth of Christ with the promises of the covenant: 'My soul exalts the Lord, and my spirit has rejoiced in God my Saviour . . . He has given help to Israel his servant, in remembrance of his mercy; as he spoke to our fathers, to Abraham and his offspring forever' (*Luke* 1:46-47; 54-55). Zacharias views the coming of Christ in light of all that had come before:

> Blessed be the Lord God of Israel, for he has visited us and accomplished redemption for his people, and has raised up a horn of salvation for us in the house of David his servant—as he spoke by the mouth of his holy prophets from of old . . . to show mercy toward our fathers, and to remember his holy covenant, the oath which he swore to Abraham our father . . . (*Luke* 1:68-70, 72-73).

These familiar songs celebrate the Lord's fulfilment of his Old Testament promises and indicate the altered situation of New Testament believers. Whereas the Old Testament believer looked forward, the New Testament believer now looks backward *and* forward: back to the coming of Christ in the fullness of time, forward to the expected coming of Christ at the end of time.

The New Testament clearly trumpets the good news that with the coming of Christ, the history of redemption has entered a new and decisive epoch. The 'latter days' of Old Testament expectation are now upon us. The most fundamental dimension of the New Testament's outlook upon the future is, ironically, that the future is now. What Old Testament believers anticipated on the furthest horizon of redemptive history has become a reality in the person and work of Jesus Christ.

In Matthew's Gospel, Jesus' birth is described as a fulfilment of Isaiah's prophecy (*Matt.* 1:20-23). Other events in Christ's life fulfil Old Testament prophecy: Christ's birth in Bethlehem (*Matt.* 2:5-6; cf. *Mic.* 5:2); his rejection by his people (*John* 1:11; cf. *Isa.* 53:3); his flight into Egypt (*Matt.* 2:14-15; cf. *Hos.* 11:1); his triumphal entry into Jerusalem (*Matt.* 21:4-5;

cf. *Zech.* 9:9); his being sold for thirty pieces of silver (*Matt.* 26:15; cf. *Zech.* 11:12); his being pierced on the cross (*John* 19:34; cf. *Zech.* 12:10); the soldiers' casting lots for his clothing (*Mark* 15:24; cf. *Psa.* 22:18); the fact that none of his bones were broken (*John* 19:33; cf. *Psa.* 34:20); his burial with the rich (*Matt.* 27:57-60; cf. *Isa.* 53:9); his resurrection (*Acts* 2:24-32; cf. *Psa.* 16:10); and his ascension (*Acts* 1:9; cf. *Psa.* 68:18). Nothing is more emphatically taught in the New Testament than that Christ is the heir of the Old Testament prophecies concerning the coming Saviour.

The coming of Christ is also described in terms signifying the finality and epoch-making significance of his coming. Implicitly contrasting Christ's work with the priestly ministry of the old covenant, Peter declares, 'For Christ also died for sins once for all, the just for the unjust, in order that he might bring us to God, having been put to death in the flesh, but made alive in the spirit' (*1 Pet.* 3:18). The writer to the Hebrews makes this a major theme in his comparison and contrast of the old and new covenants. He notes that Christ 'does not need daily, like those high priests, to offer up sacrifices, first for his own sins, and then for the sins of the people, because this he did once for all when he offered up himself' (*Heb.* 7:27).

In the coming of Christ, the long-awaited coming of God's kingdom on earth is inaugurated. In the Gospels, both John the Baptist and Jesus announce that the kingdom of God 'is at hand' (literally, 'has drawn near', *Matt.* 3:2; *Mark* 1:15). When Christ cast out demons, he testified to the Pharisees that this was evidence that the kingdom of God 'had come upon them' (*Matt.* 12:28). The Gospel accounts of Christ's miracles and the authority with which he commissioned the disciples confirm that the Old Testament promise regarding the future coming of the kingdom was being fulfilled. Though this kingdom has not yet come in all of its fullness, it has come in the person and work of Christ, in his life, death, resurrection, and ascension to the Father's right hand, where he reigns until all his enemies have been subdued beneath his feet (*1 Cor.* 15:25).

The New Testament emphasises the presence of the future of Old Testament expectation through the terms 'last days', 'fullness of time', or 'end of the ages'. In Peter's sermon at Pentecost, he cites the prophecy of

Joel in Acts 2:17, '"And it shall be in the last days", God says, "that I will pour forth of my Spirit upon all mankind."' When Paul describes the birth of Christ, he declares, 'But when the fullness of time came, God sent forth his Son, born of a woman, born under the Law' (*Gal.* 4:4). This terminology, 'the fullness of time', speaks of God's appointed moment for the completion of his saving purpose. In 1 Corinthians 10:11 Paul remarks that Israel's disobedience has been recorded for the benefit of believers, 'upon whom the end of the ages has come'. Elsewhere the sacrifice of Christ is described as having been offered 'once at the end of the ages' (*Heb.* 9:26). The Apostle John also speaks, in his warning to beware the coming of anti-Christ, of this being 'the last hour' (*1 John* 2:18).

All of these passages confirm the New Testament teaching that the times in which we now live are the times in which Christ has begun to establish and ultimately will fully usher in the glorious future of promise.

We must be careful, however, not to draw too sharp a distinction between the Old and New Testaments. Though the New Testament resoundingly declares that the great complex of events in redemptive history has occurred, it also still teaches that something further lies on the horizon of history. One great event must still happen: the return of the glorified Lord Jesus Christ at the close of the present age. Only with Christ's return will the curtain be drawn on redemptive history and the consummation of God's kingdom be achieved.

What from the Old Testament vantage point appeared to be a single movement has in the New Testament become a two-stage movement. While the Old Testament saw only one future Messianic age, the New Testament reveals that the present Messianic age awaits its consummation at Christ's second coming. In New Testament writings, we often find passages indicating that though the future has drawn near in Christ, there remains an even greater future, a consummate future at the end of the age.

Christ contrasts the present age and the future age in several passages. In Luke 20:34-35, responding to a question about the resurrection, Jesus answers, 'The sons of this age marry and are given in marriage, but those who are considered worthy to attain to that age and the resurrection of the dead, neither marry, nor are given in marriage.' In Matthew 12:32 a similar contrast is drawn between the two ages when Christ announces, 'And whoever shall speak a word against the Son of Man, it shall be forgiven him; but whoever shall speak against the Holy Spirit, it shall not be forgiven him, either in this age, or in the age to come.' Christ encourages the disciples with the promise of kingdom blessings by making a similar point about these two ages: 'Truly I say to you, there is no-one who has left house or wife or brothers or parents or children, for the sake of the kingdom of God, who shall not receive many times as much at this time and in the age to come, eternal life' (*Luke* 18:29-30).

This same contrast is drawn between 'the last days' (plural) and 'the last day' (singular), or between the 'end of the ages' (plural) and 'the end of the age' (singular). Though we live in the last days, these days are not identical with the final termination of redemptive history, marking the point of transition to God's eternal kingdom. In John 6:39 Jesus promises that 'everyone who beholds the Son and believes in him, may have eternal life; and I myself will raise him up on the last day.' Clearly, here Jesus means to refer to an event in the future, an event still anticipated. Using similar language, Martha, in John 11:24, speaks of the resurrection of her brother, Lazarus, 'at the last day'. Jesus also speaks, in John 12:48, of the judgement that will befall those who reject his word 'at the last day'. These passages suggest that, though we are living in the 'last days', the *last day* is yet to come. An alternative expression, 'the end of the age', is used in several places in the New Testament (e.g., *Matt.* 13:39; 24:3; 28:20) to designate the definitive day that will mark the closure of redemptive history at the return of Christ.

Since Christ's first coming inaugurates the future and points to his glorious coming at the end of the age, believers who are joined to Christ already share in his victory. The blessings of salvation that come to the believer are tokens of the fullness of salvation to be experienced in the age to come. This can be seen in two outstanding ways: the resurrection of Jesus Christ and the outpouring of the Spirit at Pentecost. Both are end-time events—events that are prophetic of the future of which they are a pledge and guarantee.

The familiar description of Christ's resurrection in 1 Corinthians 15 illustrates that it is an end-time event, pledging the certainty of the believer's resurrection. Paul utilizes the metaphor of gathering the first-fruits and the remainder of the harvest. The one, end-time harvest is a two-stage event, encompassing the period between Christ's resurrection and the resurrection of believers at the end of the age. These are not two separate events, but two aspects of one great end-time harvest. As Paul describes it, 'But now Christ has been raised from the dead, the first fruits of those who are asleep. For since by a man came death, by a man also came the resurrection of the dead. For as in Adam all die, so also in Christ all shall be made alive. But each in his own order: Christ the first fruits, after that those who are Christ's at his coming' (*1 Cor.* 15:20-23).

We noted that the outpouring of the Spirit at Pentecost was understood as a fulfilment of Joel's prophecy regarding 'the latter days'. In the New Testament, however, the work of the Spirit is also regarded as pledging the fullness of salvation in the future.

In Romans 8:23, Paul speaks of the 'first-fruits of the Spirit', which promise the full harvest in the future: '[we] have the first-fruits of the Spirit . . . waiting for our adoption, to wit, the redemption of our body.' On several occasions, the Spirit is spoken of as a 'pledge' of the fullness of salvation that awaits the believer (*Eph.* 1:13-14; *2 Cor.* 1:22; 5:5; cf. *Eph.* 4:30). This term suggests that believers have in the Spirit a promissory, though partial, participation in the fullness of salvation that will be theirs at Christ's return. Ephesians 1:13-14 is typical of this emphasis: 'you were sealed with the Holy Spirit of promise, who is an earnest or pledge of our inheritance, unto the redemption of God's own possession, unto the praise of his glory.' Through union with Christ the believer already experiences a foretaste of unbroken communion with God through Christ, a resurrection life in a glorified body that will be a fit dwelling-place of God in the Spirit.

In this present age, the believer lives 'between the times'. What gives shape to the Christian life is the relation between salvation already experienced and yet anticipated. Christians live out of the reality of Christ's

16

first coming. They also live in fervent expectation of Christ's return, when the work secured by his resurrection and ascension is consummated.

This accounts for the frequent New Testament exhortations to believers to walk by faith and to live in hope. As Calvin said, believers embrace Christ 'clothed in his promises', knowing that the future of God's consummated kingdom has been guaranteed in the great events of Christ's resurrection and the outpouring of the Spirit.

Paul summarises the quality of the Christian's life 'between the times':

> If then you have been raised with Christ, keep seeking the things above, where Christ is, seated at the right hand of God. Set your mind on the things above, not on the things that are on earth. For you have died and your life is hidden with Christ in God. When Christ, who is our life, is revealed, then you also will be revealed with him in glory (*Col.* 3:1-4).

The promised future is already a reality in the person and work of Jesus Christ, the crucified, resurrected, and ascended Lord, but it is not yet fully present to the believer who must walk by faith not sight. The certainty of the Lord's coming, however, strengthens believers' confidence that it will come and quickens their desire for it.

2

THE FUTURE BETWEEN
DEATH AND RESURRECTION

*T*heology customarily divides the Bible's teaching about the future into two parts regarding the individual believer and the creation. These divisions are sometimes termed 'individual eschatology' and 'general eschatology'. The term 'eschatology' is a combination of *eschatos*, meaning 'last' or 'end', and *logos*, meaning 'word'. Eschatology is the study of (or word about) the last things or end times. Individual eschatology deals with death and immortality, while general eschatology deals with Christ's return and the final judgement.

Believers are anxious to know what the Bible teaches about their condition following death and prior to Christ's return. Pastors and elders cannot escape the obligation to provide answers to their questions. And any attempted answer must faithfully reflect the Bible's teaching.

This chapter deals with subjects of individual eschatology: physical death, immortality, and the intermediate state. Later chapters will address general eschatology.

THE BIBLE'S VIEW OF DEATH

Contrary to many modern myths about death, the Bible paints a stark and sobering portrait of this subject. Nowhere is death treated as natural or as a part of life. The Bible does not encourage us to minimise the fearfulness of our 'last enemy' (*1 Cor.* 15:26).

The biblical understanding of death begins with the Fall. Death is divine punishment for disobedience. Adam became liable to death through his act of disobedience, a liability that now falls to all humanity. Physical death, the loss of fellowship with God in the sphere of creation, is a picture of spiritual death.

In Romans 5:12-21 the inseparability of sin and death is underscored. Through the sin of the first Adam, all have become sinners and are subject to the reign of death. Death signifies humankind's being cut off from God's blessing and is described as the 'wages of sin' (*Rom.* 6:23). The sin of the first Adam, which leads to condemnation and death, finds its remedy only in the obedience of the second Adam, which leads to righteousness and life for all who believe (*Rom.* 5:17–21).

Through his resurrection, Christ overcame the death resulting from Adam's sin (*1 Cor.* 15:21). Christ has 'abolished death and brought life and immortality to light through the gospel' (*2 Tim.* 1:10). As death is the 'wages of sin', so 'the free gift of God is eternal life in Christ Jesus our Lord' (*Rom.* 6:23).

This does not mean that believers no longer have to die. Though death is not a satisfaction for sin, it remains inevitable. But believers do not fear death, for it brings a more intimate fellowship with the Lord (*Phil.* 1:21; *2 Cor.* 5:8). As the *Heidelberg Catechism* concisely puts it, 'Our death is not a satisfaction for our sins, but only a dying to sins and entering into eternal life' (Question 42).

Since death is inseparably joined in Scripture to sin and God's curse against it, it is not surprising that the ultimate hope for the individual believer is the resurrection of the body. The grace of God includes the promise of believers' future glorification when they share in the power of Christ's resurrection. Believers anticipate that, when Christ finishes his work and vanquishes the 'last enemy', they will share in the glory of his resurrection (*1 Cor.* 15:20–23).

The 'Immortality of The Soul'

We must be wary of falling into the common error of minimizing the victory over death by adopting an unbiblical view sometimes called the 'immortality of the soul'. It has long been customary among Christians to use the expression, 'immortality of the soul', to correctly express that believers who die do not cease to exist, but continue to enjoy personal communion with God in heaven prior to Christ's return and the resurrection of the body. In this sense, the 'immortality of the soul' is the biblical view of the believer's intermediate state.

But this expression is often used in an unbiblical way that minimizes the reality of death and hope for the resurrection. In church history, there has been a tendency to read the Bible through the lens of Greek philosophical thought which taught that each person is composed of two distinct substances: soul and body. The soul, as the higher aspect, was considered indestructible or immortal. The body, as the lower aspect, was considered destructible and mortal. In extreme expressions of this thinking, redemption is seen as the soul's release from its bodily imprisonment. Salvation actually comes through the separation of body and soul in death.

This view threatens two clear biblical truths. First, God alone, in the strict sense of indestructible life, is immortal. Any 'immortality' enjoyed by humans is a gift from God's hand. If we speak of the 'immortality of the soul', we must preserve this difference. In 1 Timothy 6:16 God is spoken of as one 'who alone possesses immortality and dwells in unapproachable light'. And in John 5:26 Jesus declares that 'just as the Father has life in himself, even so he gave to the Son also to have life in himself'. In this last passage, a clear contrast is drawn between the Father and the Son, who owe their life to nothing outside of themselves, and every creature, whose life is a gift from God.

Second, the Bible typically ascribes believers' immortality to the whole person, body and soul, which requires the resurrection of the body. Interestingly, when the Bible speaks of the believer's immortality, it normally refers to the immortality of the body. It is remarkable how the language of 'immortality', applied to human beings, typically refers to the believer's perfected state of resurrection glory.

1 Corinthians 15:54 affirms, 'When the perishable has been clothed with the imperishable, and the mortal with immortality, then the saying will come true: "Death has been swallowed up in victory"' (NIV). This passage clearly refers to the immortality of the believer in the resurrection state of glory. This is consistent with other passages that speak of 'immortality', not as the disembodied state of believers between death and resurrection, but as the future inheritance of the redeemed (cf. *Rom.* 2:7; *1 Cor.* 9:25; *1 Pet.* 1:4). It would be better to talk about the 'immortality of the believer' as understood to include the resurrection of the body.

The work of the Triune God in redemption only reaches its perfection in the full participation of believers in Christ's resurrection. Until this mortal puts on immortality, even the believer's intermediate state of provisional joy in the Lord's presence is incomplete. The believer's hope for the future remains fixed upon Christ's return and the resurrection of the dead.

THE INTERMEDIATE STATE

This cannot be stressed too much, particularly when the intermediate state is addressed, since an emphasis upon the intermediate state might detract from the central hope of the resurrection of the body. Remembering that this hope is central, there is no reason to deny the biblical teaching about the intermediate state. The term 'intermediate' acknowledges that it is a provisional and incomplete communion that falls between death and the resurrection of the body. Though it is the penultimate (resurrection being the ultimate) hope of the believer, it is not any less real.

What is the circumstance of the believer between death and resurrection? There has generally been unanimity in the historic Christian church that believers enjoy a provisional and intensified communion with Christ upon death, but there also have been minority opinions.

Two Unbiblical Views: Annihilationism and Soul Sleep

Two minority views on the intermediate state distort this biblical focus by wrongly concluding that there is no living fellowship with God between death and resurrection. The first view is annihilationism, and the second is soul-sleep.

As its name suggests, annihilationism teaches that death brings annihilation of body and soul and the cessation of human existence in any form. There is no state between death and the resurrection because, until the resurrection of the body, the believer ceases to exist. The resurrection of the body actually amounts to the re-creation of the individual.

The terminology of 'annihilationism' is used in at least three different ways. The first is a materialistic world-view that all individuals (believers or unbelievers) cease to exist at death and have no prospect of any future life. The second view is that all humans are naturally mortal, but some (believers) are given immortality as a gift of God's grace. This 'conditional immortality' view can take one of two forms: either believers cease to exist until the resurrection or they enjoy a provisional state of fellowship with the Lord before the time of the resurrection. The third view (annihilationism proper) is that all individuals are created immortal, but God annihilates those he does not save (unbelievers). Those who do not believe in Jesus Christ are liable to annihilation by a direct act of God's judgement in death.

Although different views exist, annihilationism properly refers to any view that teaches there is no existence after death before the resurrection of the body. This annihilationist view has had few advocates in the history of the church; however, it has increasingly gained advocates in the last century among Jehovah's Witnesses and the Seventh-Day Adventists, and also among Christians who exaggerate the importance of the resurrection of the body. Advocates of this view are convinced that the biblical teaching of each person as a 'living soul' (not a soul 'having' a body) requires the conclusion that death means annihilation.

The basic argument is that because Adam was created from the dust of the earth and became, after the Creator breathed into him the breath of life, a 'living soul' (*Gen.* 2:7), the soul could not survive the dissolution of the body. The unity of soul and body is so intimate that they are inseparable, even at death. Advocates of this annihilationist view contend that affirming the continued existence of the soul between death and resurrection is succumbing to Greek influence and is an unbiblical view of our created unity. Because human beings do not have a body that is distinguishable from the soul, there can be no prospect of life apart from the body, even in any intermediate state.

A second and more important view is often termed 'soul-sleep' or 'psychopannychy'. For some similar reasons, advocates of this view reject the doctrine of any conscious existence in an intermediate state. The state between death and resurrection is like sleep, an unconscious state with no relational or chronological experiences. Just as the time between falling asleep and waking seems virtually non-existent, so it will seem as though no time has elapsed between death and resurrection.

Advocates of this view have included: 1) a small sect of Christians in Arabia, referred to by the church historian Eusebius; 2) a number of more radical sects among the Anabaptist movement of the sixteenth-century Reformation; 3) some of the 'Irvingites' in nineteenth-century England; and 4) a number of contemporary Christians who dislike the doctrine of a conscious intermediate state, fearing it belittles the importance of the body.

The two primary arguments for this view are that the unity of body and soul is essential to human existence, and that the Bible often describes death as 'falling asleep'.

The first argument is reminiscent of the major argument of annihilationism. Since it stresses humans as a psychosomatic unity, it is inconceivable that they could enjoy an intermediate state apart from their bodies, which are indispensable to all meaningful human experience.

The second argument is more substantial because it appeals to biblical passages that describe death as a 'falling asleep'. Old Testament passages describe death as a kind of sleep, in which conscious experience is presumably lost (e.g., *Gen.* 47:30; *Deut.* 31:16; *2 Sam.* 7:12; *Psa.* 30:9; 6:5; 115:17; *Eccles.* 9:10; *Isa.* 38:18-19). This is more clearly affirmed in the

New Testament (e.g., *1 Cor.* 7:39; *1 Thess.* 4:13; *Matt.* 27:52; *John* 11:11-13; *1 Cor.* 11:30; 15:20; 15:51; *Acts* 7:60; *Luke* 8:52). Advocates of the soul-sleep position argue that these texts clearly teach that believers are in a state of unconsciousness in the intermediate state.

An additional argument is Scripture's silence on the issue. Another argument is that the believer or unbeliever's bliss or woe in the intermediate state would be a premature anticipation of final judgement.

These arguments may initially seem convincing, but they fail to stand under individual scrutiny.

The first argument is partially true, but overstated. The normal state of human beings is certainly one of 'inner' and 'outer' union, soul and body. Death abnormally tears apart what God joined together. But this does not mean that it terminates conscious experience; such a conclusion is not warranted by biblical evidence. Not only do angels experience conscious existence without bodily form, but believers also experience fellowship with the Lord, apart from their bodies, upon death (see *Heb.* 12:23; *Rev.* 6:9-11).

The second argument is not as formidable as it might first appear. None of the referenced biblical passages state that the 'soul' sleeps; it is the whole person (body and soul) who sleeps. One might even argue that, because death results from the dissolution of the body, it is particularly the body that sleeps. Also, the imagery of sleeping describes death euphemistically, showing that its sting and terror have been removed for the believer. Death is a 'falling asleep' only for those who are 'in Christ' (*1 Cor.* 15:18) or 'in Jesus' (*1 Thess.* 4:14), not for those who are outside of Christ. Additionally, the predominating ideas in this euphemism are resting from one's work and the struggles of this life, and entering into a state of peace and joy (cf. *Psa.* 37:37-39; *Isa.* 57:1-2; *Phil.* 1:23; *1 Thess.* 5:10; *2 Cor.* 5:8). The idea of a loss of consciousness is a biblically unjustified pressing of the metaphor that would contradict other biblical passages ascribing conscious experience to believers in the intermediate state.

The argument from silence is based on only a few Scripture references when the dead are brought back to life. From these few instances, we are not permitted to establish a universal rule. It may well be for good reasons that such experiences are not reported. Perhaps Paul's declaration in 2 Corinthians 12:4 applies to them, regarding 'things that man is not permitted to tell'.

The other argument concerning judgement day supposes that the intermediate state reveals for the first time the eternal destiny of individuals. This conflicts with Scripture's teaching that believers have even now a foretaste of 'eternal life' (cf. *1 John* 5:13; *John* 5:24; *Phil.* 1:28; *Rom.* 5:1; 8:1). It also confuses what is constitutive with what is declarative: the final judgement does not constitute or determine the destiny of believers and unbelievers, but only publicly declares that destiny.

THE BIBLICAL VIEW

The only antidote for these unbiblical views is the positive teaching of Scripture. The comfort of every believer who 'falls asleep' in Jesus is that they go to be 'with the Lord'. They enter a new phase of conscious fellowship with Christ and his people. This—not annihilation or soul-sleep—is the future prospect of believers in the intermediate state.

If the Bible rejects annihilationism or soul-sleep, what does become of the believer in the state intermediate between death and the resurrection?

Though we should not speculate unduly about what this state will be like, the Bible clearly teaches that believers, in their 'soul' or 'spirit', will enjoy a state of conscious and even intensified communion with the Lord.

The *Heidelberg Catechism*, in its answer to the question concerning the resurrection of the body, begins by referring directly to this intermediate state. Even though it does not elaborate upon this state, it clearly affirms continued communion with the Lord:

> Q. 57 *What comfort does the resurrection of the body afford you?*
> A. That not only my soul, after this life, shall immediately be taken up to Christ, its Head; but also that this my body, raised by the power of Christ, shall again be united with my soul, and made like unto the glorious body of Christ.

The biblical support for this beautiful confession is found in Old Testament foreshadowings and New Testament affirmations.

OLD TESTAMENT FORESHADOWINGS

The relation between Old Testament and New Testament teaching has often been described as progressive revelation. The history of redemption includes a history of revelation, in which the Lord discloses his will bit by bit. Some things clearly revealed in the New Testament were only dimly foreshadowed in the Old.

This is especially evident when it comes to the subject of the intermediate state. Some have argued that the intermediate state is revealed only in the New Testament. But there are some interesting Old Testament foreshadowings of the New Testament teaching.

First, the Old Testament's vigorous condemnation of communicating with the dead implies a widespread conviction of continued existence after death (cf. *Deut.* 18:9-12; *Lev.* 20:6; *2 Kings* 21:6; 23:24; *Isa.* 8:19-20; 19:3; 29:4; *1 Sam.* 28:6ff.). This is particularly instructive since the Old Testament uniformly views death as the result of God's curse.

Second, the Old Testament relates two extraordinary instances when godly believers did not die, but were immediately ushered into the presence of God. Enoch 'was not, for God took him' (*Gen.* 5:24), and Elijah 'went up by a whirlwind into heaven' (*2 Kings* 2:11).

Third, several passages, particularly Psalms, express the confident hope of life for the believer beyond the grave, in distinction from the wicked (*Job* 19:25-27; *Psa.* 73:24-26; 1:6; 7:10; 37:18). Despite the preponderance of references to '*Sheol*' simply as the grave, in some instances it indicates punishment upon the wicked, from which the righteous are ultimately delivered (*Psa.* 9:17; 55:15; 16:10; 49:14; *Prov.* 15:24).

Fourth, the Old Testament clearly expresses the expectation of the resurrection of the righteous and the wicked, respectively, unto weal and woe (*Hos.* 13:14; *Dan.* 12:2; *Isa.* 26:19).

And fifth, the covenant promises the fullness of life in unbroken communion with the Lord. It should not surprise us that Christ spoke of this

27

promise to the Sadducees: 'have you not read that which was spoken to you by God, saying, "I am the God of Abraham, and the God of Isaac, and the God of Jacob"? He is not the God of the dead but of the living' (*Matt.* 22:31-32). This affirmation of life beyond death expresses an awareness of the covenant promise.

Recognizing these Old Testament foreshadowings, it is clear that the Old Testament believer anticipated life beyond the grave in communion with the Lord of the covenant. The Old Testament also teaches a doctrine of punishment for the wicked and blessedness for the righteous after death. Only in the light of the fuller disclosure of new covenant revelation, however, are these foreshadowings confirmed.

NEW TESTAMENT AFFIRMATIONS

Several passages in the New Testament clearly reveal that believers and unbelievers upon death continue to experience existence. Although believers enjoy a life of provisional blessedness in the presence of the Lord, unbelievers experience a provisional foretaste of eternal punishment.

A striking passage in this connection is the well-known parable of the rich man and Lazarus in Luke 16:19-31. Jesus describes the contrasting states of the rich man and Lazarus before and after death. Though the rich man enjoyed a life of luxury, subsequent to death he is 'in Hades . . . in torment'. After death the poor man Lazarus rests in the bosom of Abraham. Jesus describes a 'great chasm' as fixed between these places, preventing passage from one to the other. This passage affirms that immediately upon death the righteous and the wicked enter two separate modes of existence. The righteous enter provisional blessedness in the presence of God; the wicked enter provisional and inescapable torment. 'Hades' and 'Abraham's bosom' do not describe two compartments of the realm of the dead, but two distinct places.

This striking affirmation of an intermediate state is confirmed in several other New Testament passages. When Jesus tells the criminal on the cross, 'Truly I say to you, today you shall be with me in Paradise' (*Luke* 23:43), he is affirming the criminal's fellowship with him immediately upon death.

In Revelation 7:9-17 John describes the saints 'before the throne and before the Lamb' in heaven as a great multitude 'clothed in white robes, and palm branches were in their hands'. These saints worship God and clearly experience conscious communion with him, though they do not yet experience the final state described in Revelation 21 and 22. This description parallels Revelation 6:9-10 where the 'souls of those who had been slain because of the word of God' cry out for God's judgement. It also corresponds to frequent descriptions of departed saints living in the presence of God and reigning with Christ in heaven (cf. *Rev.* 3:12, 21; 4:4; 19:14; 20:4).

Other passages speak of the wicked experiencing a state of provisional torment upon death. In Matthew 11:23, Christ declares that the unbelieving in Capernaum 'will go down to Hades' rather than to heaven. In this passage Hades is a place of punishment, reserved for the unbelieving, that anticipates the final punishment of the wicked in hell. This language also corresponds to 2 Peter 2:4 which describes God's judgement upon disobedient angels who are 'kept for judgement' after being 'cast' into hell by God.

These New Testament affirmations do not provide a great deal of detail and should not trigger unnecessary speculation about the intermediate state, but they warrant the general conclusion that believers experience provisional blessedness in fellowship with the Lord and that unbelievers experience provisional punishment under the wrath of God. The final judgement is anticipated for believers and unbelievers alike, when some will be welcomed into glory and others cast into hell.

Two further New Testament texts demand closer attention. These texts explicitly affirm an intensified communion with the Lord for believers and confirm their confidence of being immediately in the Lord's presence.

The first text, 2 Corinthians 5:1-10, immediately follows Paul's acknowledgement of death before the return of Christ (4:16-18). Though acknowledging the dissolution of the body as an 'earthly tent', Paul declares his hope for a 'building from God, a house not made with hands, eternal in the heavens' (5:1) and declares his confidence that death will not separate the believer from fellowship with the Lord. Indeed, death will bring a fellowship that is, in a largely unexplained sense, even greater than that presently enjoyed.

This verse's bold affirmation of an imperishable body troubles some interpreters due to its use of the present tense, suggesting an immediate reception of the resurrection body. Some have suggested that Paul is describing a provisional body, given to believers in the intermediate state. But neither an immediate nor provisional body finds support elsewhere in Scripture.

The use of the present tense is a way of describing a future that is absolutely certain. When the apostle says, 'we have a building from God', he uses this language to describe what is an 'assured possession', the resurrection body that will be given on the last day.

After acknowledging in verses 2-5 the diminishment that death brings, Paul directly addresses the intermediate state in verses 6-9.

The contrast between 'being at home in the body' and 'being away from the body', and between 'being away from the Lord' and 'being with the Lord', corresponds to the contrast between our present bodily existence and our subsequent bodiless existence. These verses affirm that death for the believer means being at home with the Lord. Subsequent to death and prior to the resurrection of the body, believers will enjoy an intensified communion with the Lord.

The comfort for believers who walk by faith and not by sight is they will not experience, even in death, a breaking of the communion with Christ that they now enjoy. Rather, death will bring a new and more intimate fellowship with Christ.

A second important text affirming an intermediate state is Philippians 1:21-23, in which Paul makes a bold declaration: 'For me to live is Christ, and to die is gain.'

Paul finds himself torn between two desires. On the one hand, he is pulled toward continued life in the flesh in which he can fruitfully work for the churches. But on the other hand, he is pulled toward wanting to depart to be with Christ.

The contrast in these verses is between life in the body and life (after death) apart from the body. Life in the body does not permit the more intensified communion with Christ that only death will bring. Though the expression to be 'with Christ' is not explained in any detail, it conveys a more intimate communion than that presently enjoyed and contributes to our understanding of the intermediate state.

When considering the biblical teaching about the intermediate state, we should remember Paul's citations from Isaiah in 1 Corinthians 2:9: 'Things which eye has not seen and ear has not heard, and which have not entered the heart of man, all that God has prepared for those who love him.' The danger is to go beyond what the Bible says and speculate in ways that are not helpful to God's people. There is much that God has not revealed about the intermediate state.

This should not prevent us from receiving with gratitude what God has been pleased to reveal in his word. Remembering that the great hope of the believer remains fixed upon the glory of Christ's work in the resurrection at the last day, when the first-fruits of the harvest issue in the full in-gathering, we need not shrink from confessing that not even death can separate us from the love of God in Christ Jesus. We may find comfort in knowing that believers who 'die in the Lord' are promised an immediate, unbroken, and intensified communion with the Lord in the state between death and resurrection.

Though death may be the believer's 'last enemy', believers have every biblical reason to comfort one another with the knowledge that those whose bodies are laid in the grave have gone to be with the Lord, which is far better.

This comfort is not a futile shaking of the fist in the face of the inescapable reality of death. It is not the last vestige of Greek thinking that remains within Christian truth. Rather, it is the confident hope of every believer who can say with Paul, 'For me to live is Christ, and to die is gain.'

3

THE FUTURE OF CHRIST

*W*e begin our discussion of general eschatology by focusing on the biblical teaching regarding the return of Christ. This is the great centrepiece of biblical hope and expectation for the future. All the other subjects we will discuss are like spokes on a wheel, each attached to this hub. The nature or timing of the millennium, the 'signs of the times', the resurrection of the body, the final judgement, and the final state, all find meaning in relation to this consummating event in the history of redemption.

BIBLICAL TERMINOLOGY

There are three common terms used to describe Christ's return: 'revelation' (*apokalupsis*), 'appearance' (*epiphaneia*), and 'coming' (*parousia*). The following sampling of references indicates their pervasiveness in the New Testament.

The term 'revelation' literally means the 'removal of a veil', disclosing an object concealed from view. Paul writes in 1 Corinthians 1:7-8, 'Therefore you do not lack any spiritual gift as you eagerly wait for our Lord Jesus Christ to be revealed. He will keep you strong to the end, so that you will be blameless on the day of our Lord Jesus Christ' (NIV). The apostle parallels the revelation of Jesus Christ with the 'end' or the 'day of our Lord Jesus Christ'. This revelation is vividly described in 2 Thessalonians 1:7, '. . . when the Lord Jesus is revealed from heaven in blazing fire with his powerful angels' (NIV). Christ's return as a revelation of glory and majesty is also found in passages encouraging the people of God to continue steadfast in the faith in hope of Christ's coming (cf. *1 Pet.* 1:5, 13; 4:13; 5:1; *2 Thess.* 2:3, 6, 8).

The coming again of Christ is also termed an 'appearing'. All people will visibly see Christ come as their judge. Christ himself, in Matthew 24:30, speaks of how 'the sign of the Son of Man will appear in the sky, and the nations of the earth will mourn. They will see the Son of Man coming on the clouds of the sky, with power and great glory.' When Paul encourages Timothy, he reminds him of the 'appearing of our Lord Jesus Christ' (*1 Tim.* 6:14). The description of the 'man of lawlessness' in 2 Thessalonians 2:8 concludes with the confident declaration that the Lord Jesus will destroy him 'by the appearance of his coming'. Frequently, references to the 'appearing' of the Lord are used to encourage believers to remain faithful to the end (cf. *2 Tim.* 4:8; *Titus* 2:13; *1 Pet.* 5:4; *Col.* 3:4; *1 John* 2:28; 3:2), or to warn of the judgement that awaits the unbelieving (*2 Tim.* 4:1).

The third term, 'coming', was used in pre-Christian literature to describe the formal visitation of a ruler or person of prominence, and it is often used in the New Testament to designate the return of Christ the King.

Christ uses this language several times in his Matthew 24 response to the disciple's question about the sign of his coming at the end of the age. It is also frequently found in the epistles of Paul. In 1 Corinthians 15, the 'coming' of Christ coincides with the believer's participation in the resurrection harvest, of which Christ's resurrection was the 'first-fruits' (verse 23). The coming of Christ heightens the exhortation to faithfulness while preparing for his coming (cf. *1 Thess.* 2:19; 5:23, *James* 5:7, 8; *1 John* 2:28). Like the earlier references to Christ's 'revelation' or 'appearing', the language of his 'coming' is also used to warn those liable to condemnation (*2 Thess.* 2:8; *2 Pet.* 3:12). Other passages employ this language as shorthand for the great event of Christ's return (cf. *1 Thess.* 4:15; *2 Thess.* 2:1; *2 Pet.* 1:16; 3:4).

This sample of biblical passages speaking of Christ's return provides

a basis for some preliminary conclusions, which are encapsulated in 2
Thessalonians 1:6-10:

> For after all it is only just for God to repay with affliction those who
> afflict you, and to give relief to you who are afflicted and to us as well
> when the Lord Jesus shall be revealed from heaven with his mighty
> angels in flaming fire, dealing out retribution to those who do not know
> God and to those who do not obey the gospel of our Lord Jesus. And
> these will pay the penalty of eternal destruction, away from the presence
> of the Lord and from the glory of his power, when he comes to be
> glorified in his saints on that day, and to be marvelled at among all who
> have believed—for our testimony to you was believed.

First, the return of Christ will be an event that will personally and
publicly display his splendour, honour, and authority. It is not first of all
an event that promises relief and comfort to the beleaguered people of
God in this world. It is first of all the revelation of the triumph and consummation of the reign of the mediatorial king, the Lord Jesus Christ (*1
Cor.* 15:25-28).

The unifying thread in the biblical terms commonly employed to
describe this event is this idea of the revelation of Jesus and what he has
done, in all his glory and power. God has given Christ a name which is
above every name, crowned him with glory and honour at his right hand,
and entrusted him with the authority to govern all history for his church-
gathering work. Christ's present mediatorial reign will conclude and his
glory and dominion will become public. Both those who love the Lord
and long for his appearing and those who are his enemies will see him in
all of his splendour and authority in that day (cf. *Acts* 1:11; *Rev.* 1:1).

For this reason, it is a profound deviation from biblical teaching to
detract from the truth that Christ's return will be personal and visible,
a real occurrence marking the end of the present epoch of history. The
'fundamentalists' were right in the early decades of the twentieth century, when they insisted that the bodily and literal return of Christ from
heaven was a fundamental doctrine of the Christian faith.

Second, to use an expression from Titus 2:13, the return of Christ
is the blessed hope of his church. God's true children are those who are

'looking for the blessed hope and the appearing of the glory of our great God and Saviour, Christ Jesus'.

Note that the revelation of Christ is described in 2 Thessalonians 1:7 as a revelation from heaven. This reminds us that the hope of every Christian ultimately lies not in any religious, political, economic, or educational program or strategy, but only in the Lord who will bring full redemption from heaven to earth. That is why the *Heidelberg Catechism* speaks of the believer as one who 'with uplifted head' looks for the coming of his Saviour from heaven.

Perhaps this is the reason for so little talk about the return of Christ in many contemporary churches. Many churches convey a triumphalism that says, 'we will bring in the kingdom of God by our own efforts.' Or a horizontalism that says, 'we will expand the kingdom through social justice.' A humble awareness of the church's weakness is often absent. That awareness compels believers to look for their King to come from heaven to destroy his and his people's enemies and to take 'all his chosen ones to himself into heavenly joy and glory'. Admittedly, the expectation of Christ's return from heaven could give birth to passivity in the face of this world's ills. Nevertheless, from a biblical perspective, the return of Christ must always be the ultimate focus of the believer's hope for the establishment of God's kingdom.

Third, the biblical descriptions of Christ's return often undergird urgent exhortations to constant wakefulness and eager expectation. Believers who might be tempted to despair under the weight of persecution are encouraged by the prospect of Christ's return. Believers who might lag in their zeal are warned to live worthy of their calling, recognising that Christ will come to judge the living and the dead (*2 Cor.* 5:10). These frequent exhortations, buttressed by the certain prospect of Christ's return, strike a fine balance between words of encouragement in the midst of present distress and words of warning in the context of the temptation to despair. They stress the truth that the Christian life is framed by Christ's ascension on one hand and his coming again on the other (*Acts* 1:11).

Fourth, the promise of Christ's return, which brings encouragement to the believing child of God, brings a fearful prospect for the wicked. When Paul encourages the church in Thessalonica with the promise of Christ's revelation from heaven, he describes the returning Christ as coming with 'his mighty angels in flaming fire, dealing out retribution to those who do not know God and to those who do not obey the gospel of our Lord Jesus'. The return of Christ is awe-inspiring and terrible in its consequences for the impenitent and unbelieving. As John describes it in Revelation 1:7, 'Behold, he is coming with the clouds, and every eye will see him, even those who pierced him; and all the tribes of the earth will mourn over him.' This lends great urgency to the preaching of the gospel and the call to faith and repentance.

Christ's return is the great centrepiece of biblical expectation for the future when all lines of history converge. Though few Christians would dispute this claim, perhaps no area of biblical teaching is as disputed as the circumstances of his return.

Two Disputed Themes

Two areas of dispute relate directly to the expectation of Christ's return. The first of these has to do with whether Christ's return is a consummating event. Will Christ's return be accompanied by the resurrection of the dead and the judgement of all people (cf. *John* 5:28-29)? Or will it be an event that only inaugurates a new phase in the history of redemption, possibly a millennial period of 1,000 years in which Christ reigns on earth?

The second area of dispute deals with the time of Christ's return. If the return of Christ is at the centre of biblical expectation for the future, can we know when it will occur? Throughout the history of the Christian church, there have been repeated attempts to date the precise time of Christ's return. The question is whether such attempts are misguided or are warranted by the teaching of Scripture.

A CONSUMMATING EVENT

Why do some Christians maintain that the return of Christ is not a consummating event at the end of the age? Those familiar with the Apostles Creed know that it speaks of Jesus Christ being presently seated at the right hand of the Father, 'whence he shall come to judge the living and the dead'. The straightforward understanding is that Christ's return will mark the close of the history of redemption, when Christ will judge everyone and the eternal state of God's kingdom will commence. Christ's return is commonly taken to be a consummating event that closes the present age.

This is strongly disputed by the premillennialist and dispensationalist views of the history of redemption. These views share the conviction that Christ's return will inaugurate a millennial kingdom before the close of the present age. Both views are premillennialist in the sense that they regard Christ's return as an event that will precede a historical millennium on earth.

In dispensationalism, this premillennial conception has often included the view that Christ will first come secretly 'for the saints', and only after a period of tribulation will Christ be publicly revealed at his coming 'with the saints'. In this view, Christ's return will be a distinctly two-phased event and even the second phase of his return will not conclude present history, but commence a new millennial phase.

Both of these views are at odds with the teaching of the Bible. The conviction that the return of Christ marks the close of the present age not only enjoys favour among many Christians, but also remains the best understanding of the Bible's teaching. Several strands of biblical evidence, when woven together, constitute a compelling case for viewing this as an end-time event in the strict sense.

First, in the New Testament Gospels, Christ's coming again is viewed as an open, public event, when the future kingdom of God and the salvation of his people will be realised. In Matthew 24:27 and Luke 17:24, Christ warns his disciples against deceivers who will come proclaiming to be Christ or declaring that he is 'here or there'. The disciples should not be deceived because his coming will be as public and visible as the lightning striking across the sky from one end to the other. The Gospels use the terms of Christ's 'coming' and his 'revelation' as synonyms for the same event (*Matt.* 24:37-40; *Luke* 17:30). There is no hint that these terms describe different aspects of Christ's return that allow for an intervening period of tribulation or a literal reign of Christ for a thousand years. Christ's teaching about his return includes the promise that it will signal the inauguration of God's eternal kingdom and the full redemption of all his people (*Matt.* 24:33; *Luke* 21:27-28, 31).

Second, at the coming of Christ, there will be an immediate and simultaneous judgement of both the just and the unjust. In 2 Thessalonians 1:6-10, we find one of the more vivid accounts of the return of Christ and its consequences for believers and unbelievers. Paul promises the beleaguered believers of Thessalonica that they will be granted 'rest' at the revelation of Christ from heaven. However, he will 'deal out retribution to those who do not know God and to those who do not obey the gospel of our Lord Jesus'. The different consequences of Christ's revelation for the believing and unbelieving make it quite evident that Christ's return will close the present age and introduce the final state.

Third, the return of Christ is described in the New Testament as the termination or ultimate end point of the believer's hope for the future. Frequently, when the final hope of Christian believers is described in the New Testament, the event referred to is Christ's return. In 1 Corinthians 1:7-8, Paul presents the certainty of Christ's revelation as the object of the believer's hope for the future. He describes the believers in Corinth as those who are 'awaiting eagerly the revelation of our Lord Jesus Christ, who shall also confirm you to the end, blameless in the day of our Lord Jesus Christ'. Whether called 'the day of Christ Jesus' (*Phil.* 1:6,10), the 'coming' of Christ (*1 John* 2:28), 'that day' (*1 Tim.* 4:8), or 'His appearing and kingdom' (*2 Tim.* 4:1), the future event in the believer's line of vision is Christ's return. To suggest that Christ's return only initiates a new phase of his ongoing work in history would be to belie all these promises about the coming again of Christ.

Fourth, at the coming of Christ, there will be a 'rapture' of the living and the dead leading to the resurrection transformation of all believers. 1 Thessalonians 4:13-18 speaks of believers being 'caught up' with Christ when he comes from heaven with those saints who died or 'fell asleep' before his coming. These departed saints, together with all saints who are alive at his coming, 'will meet the Lord in the air'. 'Thus', says Paul by way of conclusion, 'we shall always be with the Lord.' This text confirms that Christ's return will consummate the present course of history, inaugurating the final state for all believers, those who have fallen asleep before Christ's coming as well as those who are still alive.

And fifth, the return of Christ will bring a number of accompaniments, not the least of which is God's creation of a new heavens and earth. In 2 Peter 3:3-13, the sudden and unexpected coming of Christ is directly linked with a fiery purification of the earth, a judgement that will befall all people, and the consequent creation of a new heavens and a new earth. In Romans 8:17-25, Paul describes believers (and even the creation itself) as waiting for the full deliverance from sin and its effects. This expectation is joined with expressions like: the believer's being 'glorified with Christ' (verse 17), the 'glory about to be revealed unto them' (verse 18), 'the revelation of the sons of God' (verse 19), 'the freedom of the glory of the children of God' (verse 21), and 'the adoption, the redemption of the body' (verse 23). All of these expressions show that the fulfilment of the believer's hope—and that of the whole creation's—will occur simultaneously, at the time of that great event that concludes the history of redemption, the return of Christ.

Believers have every biblical reason, therefore, to hold to the simplest understanding of the article in the Apostles Creed, 'whence he shall come to judge the living and the dead'. This article echoes biblical teaching and links Christ's coming with the judgement of all human beings at the close of the present age. Believers should anticipate the return of Christ as an event that will mark the end of the present period of history and inaugurate the final state. All that believers hope for the future is focused in this consummating event, an event that will fulfil all the promises of God that have their 'yes' and 'amen' in Christ.

DATING CHRIST'S RETURN

A strong impulse to date the return of Christ exists among many students of the Bible's teaching about the future. May we legitimately attempt to determine when Christ's return will take place? What constitutes a biblical position on this question?

Many misguided interpreters of the Bible have projected specific dates for Christ's return. Others have argued that the New Testament contains evidence for a delay of Christ's coming. These interpreters sometimes argue that there are contradictions within the New Testament; that Jesus himself taught he would return within the lifetime of his disciples, only to be proven wrong by the subsequent course of events. Paul similarly is said to have changed his view on the time of Christ's return; though his earlier epistles taught Christ's return within his lifetime, some of his later epistles express a different point of view.

Considering several passages in the Gospels and in Paul's epistles will test this claim of contradiction. Generally three types of passages speak of the time of Christ's return: those that speak of it as imminent, those that speak of it as delayed until certain prerequisites occur, and those that speak of it as unknowable.

IMMINENCE OF CHRIST'S RETURN

Among the passages that speak of it as imminent, three are especially important: Mark 9:1, Matthew 24:34, and Matthew 10:23.

In Mark 9:1, Jesus says to his disciples, 'Truly, I say to you, there are some standing here who will not taste death before they see the kingdom of God come with power.' Parallel statements are found in Luke 9:27 and Matthew 16:28.

Those who speak of a 'delay' of Christ's coming typically argue that Christ is teaching that he will return within the lifetime of many to whom he spoke. They claim that when Christ speaks of his 'coming with power', he is speaking of the great event of his return at the end of the age. Since

Christ did not return within the lifetime of those to whom he first spoke these words, he was mistaken.

Since Christ cannot be mistaken, it would be better to consider this text and its parallels in light of Christ's resurrection, ascension and outpouring of his Spirit at Pentecost. In each of these events, there was a dramatic demonstration of the power of Christ and his kingdom, and in each of them Christ's powerful and living presence with his people was manifested. Since these passages speak particularly of the coming of the kingdom of God within the lifetime of those to whom Jesus' words were spoken, it is best to understand them as references to these events in which the power of Christ was disclosed (cf. *Rom.* 1:4).

This does not exclude the possibility that the 'coming' of God's kingdom referred to in this text also includes the great event of Christ's second coming when the kingdom of God will be fully realised. The events of Christ's resurrection, ascension and Pentecost, all of which occurred within the lifetime of those to whom this promise was first made, form one complex with the great event of Christ's return at the end of the age. The resurrection is in the strictest sense an 'end-time' event, representing the 'first-fruits' of the resurrection harvest which is yet to come (*1 Cor.* 15).

The second passage where the imminence of Christ's return seems to be taught is Matthew 24:34: 'Truly, I say to you, this generation will not pass away until all these things take place' (parallel in *Mark* 13:30). This passage is said to show clearly that Jesus believed his coming again would occur within the lifetime of that present generation.

In answer, some Reformed interpreters have pointed to two important features of Christ's words in their context. First, the language, 'this generation', might be translated as 'this kind of generation'. Because Jesus elsewhere qualifies 'this generation' as an 'evil' (*Matt.* 12:45; *Luke* 11:29) or 'adulterous' (*Matt.* 12:39; 16:4) generation, he may have been saying that his coming would not take place until the evil generation of his day—as well as ours—had passed away and all things been fulfilled. The reference to 'this generation' may include all generations that share the quality of being 'evil' or 'adulterous'. Second, when Jesus speaks of 'all of these things' taking place, he seems to be referring to all the events that must occur before the event of his second coming. Because 'all of these things' include such things as the preaching of the gospel to all the nations, it does not seem likely that Jesus would have meant his words to be restricted to the generation alive when these words were first spoken.

The difficulty with this resolution of the problem, however, is that 'this generation' most likely refers to the generation living at the time Jesus first spoke these words. At least three reasons commend this reading. First, though it may be true that the language of 'evil' or 'adulterous' generation is used in other passages, this language is not used in Matthew 24 or Mark 13. Second, if the reference were to a kind of generation of people who live throughout history, then the term would have been *genos*, meaning 'kind' or 'race', rather than *gennea*, meaning 'generation'. And third, in most of the instances of the expression 'this generation' in the New Testament, the reference is clearly to the then-existing generation. For these reasons, it does not seem possible to escape the clear implication that Jesus was speaking of 'all these things', including his coming, and that he believed they would occur during the lifetime of the generation to whom he was speaking.

Some interpreters of this passage, therefore, have offered a different answer to the charge that Jesus was mistaken about the time of his coming. According to these interpreters, Jesus was teaching his disciples that his coming would occur during their lifetime, during which 'all of these things'—that is, all the signs and events described in the Olivet Discourse of Matthew 24 or Mark 13—would transpire. According to their reading of this text, the things referred to, including the coming of Christ, took place in the past during the first century. Sometimes termed a 'preterist' reading of this passage, this interpretation takes this to be a reference to the events of the destruction of Jerusalem in A.D. 70. Though these were not the events of Christ's final coming at the end of the age, Jesus was correctly predicting a coming in judgement upon Jerusalem that did occur in the first century.

Though this second answer to the radical claim that Jesus was mistaken has much to commend it, another understanding is more plausible. It acknowledges that 'this generation' most likely refers to those to whom

Jesus originally spoke. But because his Olivet Discourse answers a twofold question (When will the temple in Jerusalem be destroyed? and, What will be the sign of his coming and the 'end of the age?), this interpretation maintains that Christ answers both questions. Two parts are woven together; one answering the first, another the second. John Murray, representing this reading of the passage, notes in his *Collected Writings* that 'it is reasonable to suppose that in Matthew 24:34 (cf. *Mark* 13:30; *Luke* 21:32) Jesus is answering the first part of the disciples' question, that pertaining to the destruction of the temple'. The 'signs of the times' described in Matthew 24:1-14, and the 'day and hour' no one knows (verses 29-31, 36) refer to Christ's return. Because the 'all things' of verse 34 refers only to the events surrounding the destruction of Jerusalem rather than the specific time of Jesus' coming at the end of the age, the claim that he was mistaken is without basis.

Admittedly, the interpretation of this passage is notoriously difficult. But our survey of three responses to the radical claim that Jesus was mistaken, two of which are highly plausible, shows that the higher critics' position is itself open to the charge of prejudice.

The third text in which the imminence of Christ's return seems to be taught is Matthew 10:23. In this passage, which describes Christ's commission of the twelve disciples to preach the gospel to the lost sheep of Israel, Christ promises them, 'Truly, I say to you, you will not have gone through all the towns of Israel, before the Son of Man comes.' Here again, those who propose an unanticipated delay in the return of Christ insist that Christ is teaching that he would return within the timespan of the disciples' preaching, soon after his resurrection and ascension to heaven.

In the context of Matthew 10, however, some sayings clearly refer to future activities that will take place after Christ's ascension into heaven (verses 16-22). Some of these activities include circumstances that would be appropriate to the Christian church throughout history (verses 24-25, 26-39). Furthermore, the reference to the coming of Christ need no more be limited to the second coming of Christ than in Mark 9:1, already discussed. It is conceivable that in this passage Jesus links together circumstances that would precede his coming in power at his resurrection and his final coming at the end of the age. Whether the coming of the Son of Man refers to Christ's resurrection or second coming, it is clear that his disciples will not have 'gone through all the towns of Israel' before this event occurs.

THE DELAY OF CHRIST'S RETURN

In addition to these passages that seem to speak of the imminence of Christ's return, others speak of a delay before Christ's return. They indicate that some events must occur before Christ's coming, events whose fulfilment cannot take place without a considerable period of time elapsing.

In Matthew 24:14, Christ teaches that 'this gospel of the kingdom will be preached throughout the whole world, as a testimony to the nations; and then the end will come.' The preaching of the gospel to the nations is called one of the 'signs of the times', one of those signals of Christ's present work in the world pointing to his coming again. This sign has to be fulfilled before Christ comes again, a fulfilment that strongly suggests an extension of time for it to occur.

A similar passage is Mark 14:9 in which Jesus, describing the woman who anointed him with perfume, declared that 'wherever the gospel is preached in the whole world, what she has done will be told in memory of her'. The presumption is that the gospel will be preached in the whole world, not only in Israel, before Christ returns.

Many of Jesus' parables indicate a period of time elapsing before the end will come. These parables speak of the growth of the kingdom requiring a period of maturing and ripening. The parable of the pounds in Luke 19:11 speaks of those 'who supposed that the kingdom of God was to appear immediately', but whose belief Jesus corrected in part by the parable. In the well-known parable of the talents, Jesus uses language that assumes a considerable period of time before the day of judgement (*Matt.* 25:19). The same suggestion of delay is found in the parables of the ten virgins (*Matt.* 25:5, 'as the bridegroom was delayed'), the servants

(*Luke* 12:41-8, 'my master is delayed in coming'), the tares, mustard seed, and the leaven (*Matt.* 13).

A balanced reading of the Gospels reveals a double emphasis. Some passages emphasise the 'soon-ness' or imminence of Christ's coming; others suggest something of a delay. The best understanding of them, therefore, is one that acknowledges the certainty of Christ's return (it is 'soon' in the perspective of the history of redemption, since it is the only event remaining on the horizon that marks the conclusion of God's saving work), but does not draw the improper conclusion that little or no time remains before it will occur. Within the framework of a clear and lively expectation of Christ's coming again, the believer learns that a great deal is being accomplished, indeed must be accomplished, before all things are fulfilled and the great day of Christ's return arrives.

A similar conclusion can be drawn from the writings of Paul. Though it is true that some passages emphasise the 'soon-ness' of Christ's return, other passages emphasise events that must precede his coming. Some passages speak of Christ's return as though it were immediately 'at hand': in Romans 13:11-12 we read that 'the night is far gone; the day is at hand'; in 1 Corinthians 7:29 the apostle declares that 'the appointed time has grown very short'; and in Philippians 4:5, it is said that 'the Lord is at hand'. In two passages Paul speaks of 'we' in a way that suggests he might still be alive at the time of Christ's coming (*1 Thess.* 4:15; *1 Cor.* 15:51-52). However none of these passages actually teaches that Christ's return will occur within the apostle's lifetime. At most, this possibility is suggested. Other passages in the epistles clearly indicate something of a delay before Christ comes again (cf. *1 Thess.* 5:9-10; *2 Thess.* 2:1-12).

The New Testament contains no evidence, then, for the existence of any real contradictions on the subject of a delay of Christ's return. Some passages emphasise its imminence. Other passages emphasise the events that will precede its occurrence. Each kind of passage is understandable within the perspective of the history of redemption. Because Christ has already come, his coming in glory at the end of the age is 'at hand'. Because Christ has already come, the gospel must be preached to all the nations and all things be made ready for his triumphant return.

No One Knows The Day or The Hour

The more familiar question is its precise timing. If the return of Christ has the significance that we have suggested, it is not surprising that many have been tempted to determine how near or far we are from this event. Even Jesus' disciples were anxious to know the 'day' and the 'hour' of Christ's coming again.

The biblical answer to this question is expressed in the sixteenth- and seventeenth-century confessions of the Reformed churches. In the *Belgic Confession*, Article 37, when the certain event of Christ's return and the final judgement is described, it is almost noted in passing that 'the time appointed by the Lord . . . is unknown to all creatures.' Similarly, the *Westminster Confession of Faith*, Chapter 33:3, speaks of the day of Christ's return and the final judgement as one which Christ himself will have 'unknown' to all men. The biblical wisdom and truth of these two confessions becomes readily evident from the following considerations.

In several instances in the New Testament, we are told that no one knows the day or the hour of Christ's return. When Jesus instructs his disciples in Mark 13 concerning the signs that would alert them to his return, he clearly declares that 'of that day or hour no one knows, not even the angels in heaven, nor the Son, but only the Father' (verse 32). This remarkable saying has often raised questions among believers who wonder how it is possible that even the Son of God does not know the time of his coming again. We need only note that Jesus could not make the unknowability of the time of his return more emphatic—no one knows, not even the Son himself, the day or the hour!

Similar words are found in Matthew 25:13, where Jesus, warning his disciples, says, 'Watch, therefore, for you know neither the day nor the hour.' In Luke 12:39-40, we read that 'the Son of Man is coming at an hour you do not expect.' And, if these texts were not enough, we find in Acts 1:7 that Jesus answered his disciples' question whether he was about to restore the kingdom to Israel by saying, 'It is not for you to know times or epochs which the Father has fixed by his own authority.'

In addition to these texts that explicitly speak of the unknowability of the time of Christ's return, several also speak of it as an event that will come unexpectedly (*Luke* 12:39-49), even like the coming of a 'thief' in the night. Though these passages must be carefully considered and their differences acknowledged, they commonly teach that the return of Christ is essentially unpredictable.

For example, in Matthew 24:43-44, Jesus compares the head of a household's need to be alert because of the possible coming of a thief in the night with his disciples' need to be alert in the face of his own certain, but unknown time of coming. In Revelation 16:15, Christ announces his coming with the solemn words, 'Behold, I am coming like a thief. Blessed is the one who stays awake and keeps his garments, lest he walk about naked and men see his shame.' In this passage, not only is Christ's coming like that of a thief in its unknowability, it is also like that of a thief in that it will mean judgement for the unwashed and unclothed.

This is a feature of 1 Thessalonians 5:2, in which Paul notes that the believers in Thessalonica 'know full well that the day of the Lord will come just like a thief in the night'. The day of the Lord will be like the coming of a thief to the unbelieving, because it will bring destruction when they least expect it. Paul contrasts this with believers who 'are not in darkness, that the day should overtake you like a thief'. Here the point is not that believers will know the exact time of Christ's coming, but that this coming will not overtake them as those who are unprepared or fearful of Christ's return.

It should be apparent from all these biblical considerations that no one knows or may legitimately seek to know the exact time of Christ's return. Some passages remind us of the certainty, even the 'soon-ness' within the perspective of the timeline of the history of redemption, of Christ's coming. But others remind us of those events that must take place before Christ's return, which permit us to speak of God's 'patience' in calling the nations to repentance (*2 Pet.* 3:3-4). Several passages clearly forbid any attempt to know the day or the hour of Christ's second coming.

Christian believers are duty-bound to be cautious about the time of Christ's return. We must live expectantly, knowing the time is short and Christ's return is certain. But we must also live responsibly, carrying on with the work demanded of us in the interim between Christ's ascension and coming again. Such responsible living demands that we resist the temptation to predict the time of Christ's return. Those who attempt to set a timetable for the return of Christ disobey the teaching of God's word and risk bringing the gospel of our Lord Jesus Christ into disrepute.

Our duty is the same as that given by Paul to the Thessalonians: 'But since we are of the day, let us be sober, having put on the breastplate of faith and love, and as a helmet, the hope of salvation. For God has not destined us for wrath, but for obtaining salvation through our Lord Jesus Christ' (*1 Thess.* 5:8-9).

4

THE FUTURE MARKED BY THE 'SIGNS OF THE TIMES'

*W*e have seen that the return of Christ is the great event on the horizon of redemption's history, but that its time is unknown to us. Everything in the biblical picture concerning the future focuses upon Jesus Christ, the exalted Lord, who is seated at the Father's right hand 'whence he shall come to judge the living and the dead' (Apostles' Creed). We will now consider what are commonly termed 'the signs of the times'. Despite the rather common use of the expression, it is found in only one place in the New Testament and does not refer there to future events. In Matthew 16:1 the Pharisees and Sadducees came to Jesus asking him to show them 'a sign from heaven'. Jesus responded, 'Do you know how to discern the appearance of the sky, but cannot discern the signs of the times?' Jesus is referring to the works of God that disclose his will and purpose, like the deeds listed in Matthew 11:5, confirming that Jesus was the promised Christ: 'The blind receive their sight and the lame walk, lepers are cleansed and the deaf hear, and the dead are raised up, and the poor have good news preached to them.'

Though the Scriptures do not speak of 'the signs of the times' to signify Christ's return, it is not difficult to understand how the expression came to be used that way. Just as signs in the history of redemption disclosed and confirmed God's purpose, so signs in this present age point to Christ's coming again.

'The signs of the times' are, therefore, all those events revealed in

51

the word of God confirming that history is moving towards the day of the Lord. They are indicators that Christ will come as he promised and reminders that he is seated at the Father's right hand, ruling all things for the sake of his church, and bringing history to its appointed end.

IDENTIFYING THESE SIGNS

Even with this understanding, we need to guard against mistaken views. One mistaken notion is that the signs refer exclusively to events that will occur immediately prior to Christ's return. On the timeline of history, they are understood to be a cluster of events that will take place in a short period just before the end.

The problem with this approach should be obvious. The Bible refers to a variety of signs, many of which span the whole period between Christ's ascension into heaven and his coming again. Some of these clearly took place at the time of the destruction of Jerusalem in A.D. 70. The rich diversity of signs mentioned in Matthew 24, Mark 13, and Luke 21 cannot be accommodated by the idea that they all must occur in the period shortly before Christ's second coming.

Another similar notion maintains that 'the signs of the times' enable us to date the exact time of Christ's return. As soon as believers detect one or more of these signs, the conclusion is swiftly drawn that we must be living in 'the last days' and that the return of Christ is imminent.

This temptation involves a misreading of biblical prophecies. Too often these passages are read as though they were newspaper reports on events in the future, written as though they were already in the past. The signs of the times are not intended to afford an exact timetable for Christ's return.

One other notion that often plagues our understanding of 'the signs' is the idea that they are always abnormal, catastrophic, and spectacular. The tendency is often to think of unusual circumstances that will characterise history before Christ's return such as wars, rumours of wars, earthquakes, the Antichrist, and Armageddon.

It should be noted that the Bible expressly warns against this kind of identification. In Luke 17:20-21 Christ says, 'The kingdom of God is not coming with signs to be observed; nor will they say, Lo, here it is! or There! for behold, the kingdom of God is in the midst of you.' The Scriptures warn that 'the man of lawlessness' will deceive many with 'pretended signs and wonders' (*2 Thess.* 2:9; *Rev.* 13:13-14). Many of the signs refer to ordinary events that belong to this period of history as it prepares for Christ's coming. Because these mistaken ideas are so influential, it is important to understand scriptural teaching on this subject. The Bible highlights certain characteristics of 'the signs of the times'.

First, while these signs are often thought of as pointers to the future, many of them refer as much to the history of God's dealings with his people in the past and have antecedents in the Old Testament. Many signs are presently occurring. All of them call the people of God to constant vigilance and a hope-filled anticipation of the future under the plan and purpose of God. It is nonetheless appropriate that we should associate these signs with Christ's return. Whenever New Testament passages speak of various events that will take place during the course of history, they speak of them as indicators that the end is drawing near. They remind the believer that history is moving toward its appointed goal, the revelation of Christ.

Second, another feature often present in the Bible's delineation of 'the signs of the times' is the stress upon the antithesis between the kingdom of God and the powers of evil. As history moves forward under the lordship of Jesus Christ, this antithesis becomes increasingly evident and the certain triumph of Christ's cause is foreshadowed.

Finally, 'the signs of the times' remind believer and unbeliever alike that today is the day of salvation. They call believers to constant watchfulness. Christ said to his disciples, 'Watch, therefore, for you do not know on what day your Lord is coming' (*Matt.* 24:42). These signs are a call to be prepared for the coming of the heavenly bridegroom, Jesus Christ, who will receive his bride unto himself and cast his enemies into everlasting destruction (*2 Thess.* 1:6-10).

It is helpful to consider the various signs according to specific categories. Similar to those found in Anthony Hoekema's *The Bible and the Future,* we will consider the following categories and their signs: first, signs of the present working and eventual triumph of God's grace (the preaching of the gospel, the salvation of 'all Israel'); second, signs of the antithesis, the intensifying conflict between the kingdom of Christ and the kingdom of the Antichrist (tribulation, the Great Tribulation, apostasy, the Antichrist); and third, signs of God's judgement anticipating the great judgement (wars and rumours of wars, famine and earthquakes, the battle of Armageddon).

This list demonstrates how much attention is given in the Bible to this particular subject and therefore how important it is, even though difficulties arise in attempting to understand it. Nothing in history may be divorced from the consummation of Christ's glorious kingdom.

SIGNS OF GOD'S GRACE

We first consider the two signs of God's grace at work in the world: the preaching of the gospel to all nations and the salvation of all Israel.

One indication that many Christians have an unbiblical view of the 'signs of the times' is the common failure to note the preaching of the gospel to the nations as a sign of the period between Christ's first and second coming. Much literature about 'the signs of the times' focuses upon catastrophic events. This distorted view fails to do justice to the note of triumph throughout the New Testament. Christ is king and has been granted all authority in heaven and on earth (*Matt.* 28:18–20). Nothing can stand in the way of the forward march of the gospel and the gathering and preserving of Christ's church. Not even the gates of hell can prevail against the church (*Matt.* 16:18). Christ will come again to judge the living and the dead, and so the consummation of God's kingdom will bring present history to a close.

THE PREACHING OF THE GOSPEL

It should not surprise us that one of the great signs of the times is the preaching of the gospel to the nations. This sign confirms the promise that Christ has been exalted to the Father's right hand and given a name above every name (*Phil.* 2:9; *Eph.* 1:21).

To appreciate the importance of preaching as a sign of the times, it is critical that we go back to the Old Testament promise concerning the Messiah. This promise included the anticipation of an age when the gospel would go to all nations.

From the beginning of the Lord's dealings with his covenant people, his promise of salvation included blessings for all the families and nations of the earth (*Gen.* 12:3). This passage is commonly regarded as describing the formal establishment of the covenant of grace and harks back to the Lord's original promise to Eve that her seed would crush the head of the serpent (*Gen.* 3:15). Later, Abraham was promised a great reward (*Gen.* 15:1), an heir through whom the Lord's grace would extend to all peoples. When Abraham was ninety-nine years old, the Lord promised, 'I will establish my covenant between me and you, and I will multiply you exceedingly . . . for I will make you the father of a multitude of nations' (*Gen.* 17:2-4).

The Lord's gracious dealings with Israel set the stage in the history of redemption for the eventual extension of gospel blessings to all families of the earth. However much this scope of God's saving purpose may have been sinfully suppressed among the Old Testament people of God, it is basic to an understanding of redemptive history leading up to the sending of the Messiah. Not only is the promise of salvation for all people repeated subsequently in the book of Genesis (see *Gen.* 18:18; 22:18; 26:4; 28:14), but it is also illustrated throughout the Old Testament by the inclusion of non-Israelites into the people of God (Rahab, Ruth, household servants and foreigners).

It is remarkable to see how the inclusion of the nations is celebrated throughout the Psalter (for example, *Psa.* 8; 19:1-4; 67:4; 103:19). Psalm 24:1 declares that 'the earth is the Lord's, and all it contains, the world, and those who dwell in it.' The rule of the promised king in the line of David will be a rule over all the earth (see 72:19). The worship of the Lord included frequent rejoicing in his certain triumph over all his enemies (47:2; 77:13; 136:2), the call to make him known among the nations (9:11; 108:3), and the invitation to the nations to join in the worship of the Lord (50:4; 87; 98:4; 113:3; 117). Among these invitations, none is more powerful than Psalm 96:7: 'Ascribe to the Lord, O families of the peoples, ascribe to the Lord glory and strength.' The language of the Psalter echoes and re-echoes the promise that the Lord intends to make himself known among all the nations and extend his covenant blessings to every people.

The announcement of the Lord's coming clearly surfaces in the prophetic writings of the Old Testament. Though there are many facets to this announcement, all are centred in the conviction that the Lord will come to judge the nations in righteousness and grant salvation to all peoples (*Psa.* 59:5; 82:1, 8; 96:13). The day of the Lord, though variously described and understood, promises the outpouring of the Spirit of the Lord upon all flesh (*Joel* 2:28). Isaiah eloquently announces that 'in the last days, the mountain of the house of the Lord will be established as the chief of the mountains . . . and all the nations will stream to it. And many peoples will come . . .' (*Isa.* 2:1-4; 44:8; 66:19). Zechariah proclaims a similar announcement (*Zech.* 8:18-23). A new day is promised in which all the nations will see the glory of the Lord and enter into the enjoyment of full salvation. The seed of the woman, the son of Abraham, will come; and in him the blessings of the covenant will be imparted to every family and people.

Only within this Old Testament setting is it possible to appreciate the significance of the New Testament fulfilment. The preaching of the gospel to the nations, mandated by Christ (*Matt.* 28:18-20), is an end-time fulfilment of the Lord's earlier promise. Though this is not often adequately appreciated, it is really a striking development in the history of redemption. The preaching of the gospel that is 'the power of God for salvation to everyone who believes, to the Jew first, and also to the Greek' (*Rom.* 1:16), is one of the clearest signs that we live in the last days of redemptive history, days in which God's promises are being fulfilled and the triumph of his covenant grace in Christ is being manifested.

This is explicitly taught in the New Testament Gospels. In Matthew 24, we are told that the disciples came to Jesus and asked what would be the signs of Christ's coming and the end of the age. Jesus mentioned a number of signs, among them wars and rumours of wars, famines and earthquakes, and tribulation and apostasy. Especially prominent among these signs, however, is the preaching of the gospel: 'And this gospel of the kingdom', Christ announces, 'shall be preached in the whole world for a witness to the nations, and then the end shall come' (verse 14; see also *Mark* 13:10). Jesus clearly affirms that preaching is a sign that must precede the end of the age and the return of the Son of Man.

The New Testament preaching of the gospel of the kingdom is linked with the Old Testament promises of blessing for all nations in the end times. Notice how the Great Commission of Matthew 28 breathes the spirit of the Lord's original covenant promise with Abraham. When Christ tells the disciples to go and make disciples of all the nations, this is certainly a fulfilment of the promise to Abraham. The same emphasis upon the preaching of the gospel to all the nations is seen in parallel passages in the Gospels of Mark (16:15-16) and Luke (24:46-49).

That the preaching of the gospel marks off this period as the last days is also evident in the book of Acts, which records Christ's ministry through the apostles in establishing the New Testament church. At Pentecost, the promised outpouring of the Holy Spirit was expressed especially in the powerful preaching of the gospel of Christ (*Acts* 2). Acts traces the marvellous advancement of the gospel in the power and presence of the Spirit, beginning at Jerusalem but extending to the uttermost parts of the earth (*Acts* 1:8). Similarly in the New Testament epistles, it is evident that the apostles understood their preaching in this way (see *1 Pet.* 2:6-10). Frequently, the preaching of the gospel, though to the world a thing of foolishness and weakness, is regarded as a demonstration of the Spirit and of power (*1 Cor.* 1:18-31; 2:4-5). Consequently, the apostles in their preaching exhibited not a spirit of fear and timidity but a Spirit of power (*1 Cor.* 4:20; *1 Thess.* 1:5; *2 Cor.* 4:7). The mystery of Christ, hidden through the centuries but now revealed in the fullness of time, includes God's invincible purpose to save an elect people from every tribe and tongue and people and nation (*Eph.* 1:3-14). This purpose will be fulfilled through the ministry of the gospel of reconciliation in Christ.

These aspects of the witness of the New Testament, understood within the context of their Old Testament background and promise, show that the preaching of the gospel is perhaps the single most important sign of the times. It is the evidence of the triumph of God's gracious purposes in history, preparing the way for the coming again of the Lord of glory, much as John the Baptist did for his first coming.

In many churches today there is a decline of respect for and emphasis upon the preaching of the gospel. It is evidenced in the trend to disparage the importance of preaching in worship. It is also exhibited in the argument that preaching is only one among a variety of legitimate 'kingdom callings' and so ought not to be given any special emphasis. Sometimes it is reflected in Christian parents' unwillingness to encourage their children to consider the ministry as a high and holy calling.

This decline in esteem for the office and calling of preaching the gospel reflects a loss of biblical insight and conviction about preaching. Many believers have lost the biblical view of the central place of preaching in this period of redemptive history, which exists for the preaching of the gospel to the nations.

This loss of understanding has been accompanied by a corresponding loss of confidence in the power of the preached word to bring salvation and advance Christ's kingdom. Sometimes it is even thought that the kingdom of Christ can better be advanced through political means.

Those with a biblical view of the power of preaching should not fall prey to any spirit that diminishes it. It is by means of preaching that Christ's kingdom advances, his name is proclaimed, and his people are discipled. Nothing should restore the confidence of God's people in preaching more than the realisation that it is a sign of the last days, days of opportunity and salvation.

THE SALVATION OF 'ALL ISRAEL'

In the preaching of the gospel to the nations, what does the Bible teach about God's purpose with respect to his peculiar people, Israel?

Views of the millennium will be considered in a subsequent chapter, but the specific question of God's saving purpose regarding Israel cannot be postponed because it relates directly to the preaching of the gospel to the nations in this present period.

A brief review of some Old Testament promises regarding the restoration and salvation of Israel will provide a context in which Romans 9-11, the most important New Testament passage about God's purposes regarding Israel, can be studied.

The Old Testament promise was not that God would forsake his people Israel, substituting the other nations as the object of his saving love, but that he would include all the nations under the canopy of his saving mercy. Through Israel, not apart from her, the promise would be extended to all peoples. This promise was confirmed whenever non-Israelites or aliens were gathered into the people of God. However particular the Lord's dealings may have been with Israel, his purpose was never limited to this nation.

The Lord's promise regarding a future gathering of the Gentile nations was joined to his promise of the salvation of Israel. When Psalm 22 speaks of the future day in which 'all the ends of the earth will remember and turn to the Lord, and all the families of the nations will worship before thee' (verse 27), this will be in the company of 'all [the] descendants of Jacob . . . [and] the children of Israel' (verse 23). The blessing that falls upon Israel will be the means whereby the Lord's salvation will be made known among all the nations (*Psa.* 67). The announcement of salvation to Zion will take place in the sight of all the nations, that all the ends of the earth may see the salvation of our God (*Isa.* 52:7, 10). In the future day of the Lord's coming to save his people, the nations are described as coming to the light of Zion, and kings are said to come to 'the brightness of [her] dawn' (*Isa.* 60:1-3).

The story in Acts, tracing the gospel's testimony as it is preached first in Jerusalem and then to the remotest part of the earth (*Acts* 1:8), was already promised in the Old Testament. Paul's well-known declaration, 'I am not ashamed of the gospel, for it is the power of God for salvation to everyone who believes, to the Jew first and also the Greek' (*Rom.* 1:16), corresponds perfectly to the promise that salvation for the Gentiles would be effected through Israel and not apart from her.

But in addition to these promises of the salvation of the nations, many promises are made of Israel's future restoration. These promises, which often received initial fulfilment in the Old Testament, also point to a great restoration yet to come. Frequently the Lord spoke of how he would restore his people Israel to favour and salvation after a period of judgement and disfavour, provided they turned to him in repentance and faith (see *Deut.* 10:10; *1 Kings* 8:46-52; *Jer.* 18:5-10; 31:31-34; 29:12-14; *Ezek.* 36:33; *Hos.* 11:10).

The future held for Israel the prospect not only of the gathering of the nations and peoples to Zion, but also of her restoration to renewed fellowship and favour with the Lord. These Old Testament promises bring us to Romans 9-11 and to Paul's great question: 'God has not rejected his people, has he?' (11:1).

To understand the argument of these chapters, it is necessary to have a clear understanding of the problem posed in Romans 9:1-6. Put briefly, the problem is whether the word and promise of God regarding Israel have failed.

This problem arises within the setting of Paul's resounding conclusion and confident affirmation in Romans 8. Having set forth the mercy and grace of God in the salvation of his people, the apostle exults that nothing will be able to separate those called according to God's purpose (*Rom.* 8:28-39) from his love in Christ Jesus. This song of confidence in God's grace and redemptive purpose seems almost to be the conclusion to which the entire argument in Romans 1-8 has been leading. The conclusion of Romans 8 is a climactic affirmation of the victory of God's grace in Christ for all who believe.

This raises an inescapable problem for Paul. How can he exult in the triumph of God's grace in Christ, when this grace seems to be of no effect among the people of Israel? If God's promises regarding Israel have terminated in failure, how can he say that the gospel is the power of God unto salvation to the Jew first and also to the Greek? Indeed, if God's word has failed with Israel, can he (and we) have confidence that God's promises will not likewise fail in regard to the Gentiles? This question presses in upon the apostle at the outset of Romans 9.

To this troublesome question, Paul answers with a resounding 'No'. The word of God has in no wise failed. Rather, just as had been the case in the previous history of redemption, God's purpose according to election has been and is being realised (9:11). Just as election discriminated between some who were children of Israel according to the flesh and others who were true children according to the promise, so election continues to be realised in the salvation of some and not others.

It is evident that Paul addresses the question of Israel's apparent unbelief from the standpoint of God's electing purpose. Consequently, he cites in chapter 11 the history associated with the prophet Elijah. Though many children of Israel disbelieved during his day, God had not rejected his people. Even during this relatively low point, there remained a remnant according to God's gracious choice (11:5).

In the course of redemptive history, God has been fulfilling his electing purpose. This purpose is the only basis for the salvation of some from the entire number of Israel in the past. It is also the only basis for the salvation of any, Jew or Gentile, in the present and the future. We can be certain of one thing: the apostle insists that God's purpose of election has not failed in the past, is not failing in the present, and will certainly not fail in the future. All those whom God has chosen to save in Christ will unfailingly be saved.

That is only the general resolution to the question that Paul offers in this passage. His specific resolution of it takes the form of his inspired understanding of the rich depths of the wisdom and knowledge of God (11:33) in his respective purposes for Israel and the Gentiles.

In God's redemptive purpose, the unbelief of many children of Israel has been the occasion for preaching the gospel to the Gentiles. Paul describes this as cutting off the natural branches of an olive tree, that is, the children of Israel, and engrafting believing Gentiles (11:17-24). The poverty of Israel has thereby in God's wisdom been the occasion for the riches of the Gentiles (11:12).

But this is not the end of the story. The riches of the Gentiles, their response by God's electing purpose to the preaching of the gospel, will be the further occasion by which Israel will be provoked to jealousy and her 'fullness' be saved. This is the climactic conclusion of the argument in Romans 11:25-26:

> For I do not want you, brethren, to be uninformed of this mystery, lest you be wise in your own estimation, that a partial hardening has happened to Israel until the fullness of the Gentiles has come in; and thus all Israel will be saved; just as it is written, The Deliverer will come from Zion, he will remove ungodliness from Jacob.

The gifts and calling of God are irrevocable (11:29), the apostle concludes, and therefore the unbelief of Israel will not be permanent and universal. The time is coming when the preaching of the gospel to the Gentiles will occasion the turning of Israel in faith to Christ.

THREE VIEWS OF 'ALL ISRAEL'

How are we to understand 'all Israel'? There have been primarily three views on this in the history of the church.

The first view takes this phrase to refer to the people of Israel as a totality (though not necessarily every individual Jew) to be converted at some time after the fullness of the Gentiles has been gathered. Among those who take this view, three distinct forms of it are often defended: (1.) dispensational interpreters link this conversion of Israel with God's plan for the Jews in the future millennium; (2.) premillennial interpreters who are not dispensationalists understand it to refer to a future conversion of the Jewish nation; and (3.) some interpreters who are neither dispensationalists nor premillennialists take it to refer to a future conversion of Israel, not as a separate nation, but as a large company of Jewish people. All forms of this view maintain that the fullness of Israel must refer to the special people of God who will be converted in the future, as they are provoked to jealousy by the salvation of the Gentiles.

The second view takes this phrase to refer to the salvation of all the elect, Jew and Gentile alike, gathered through the preaching of the gospel in the whole course of the history of redemption. John Calvin took this position and argued that Israel here refers, not to a distinct people among the peoples of the earth, but to the people of God in the general and comprehensive sense, embracing Jew and Gentile alike.

The third view takes this phrase to refer to the total number of the elect from among the people of Israel. According to this view, the fullness of Israel refers to all elect Jews who constitute the remnant of believers gathered throughout the history of the church until the time of Christ's second coming.

Though these views and the arguments for them are quite diverse and at times complicated, the third form of the first view is the best understanding of the phrase 'all Israel'.

'Israel' in this phrase must refer to the special people of God, not all the elect, gathered throughout the entirety of redemptive history. This is because the term is used no less than eleven times in Romans 9-11, and in every instance it refers to the people of Israel. It is hard to see why Romans 11:26 should be an exception.

To take 'all Israel' as a reference to the total number of the elect among the people of Israel throughout all of the history of redemption would be anti-climactic and largely irrelevant to Paul's interest in Romans 9-11. In these chapters, the apostle is dealing with the mystery of God's will for the salvation of the people of Israel. Were the reference only to all the elect of Israel, it would not answer to the argument that Paul specifically develops in this passage.

The argument of this passage is that the hardening of the people of Israel will occur after they have been provoked to jealousy by the conversion of the Gentiles. Through their being provoked to jealousy, the fullness of Israel (11:12) will come to salvation. This fullness is the equivalent in Romans 11 of what is variously described as the acceptance of Israel (11:15), the grafting in of Israel (11:23-24), or the 'all Israel' of this phrase (11:26).

63

Though the expression 'and so' that is used in Romans 11:26 refers primarily to the manner in which all Israel will be saved—that is, as Israel is provoked to jealousy by the conversion of the Gentiles—its temporal aspect cannot be suppressed. In Romans 9-11 Paul is describing a sequence of events in redemptive history: the unbelief of Israel leads to the preaching of the gospel to the Gentiles; the conversion of the Gentiles leads to the jealousy and subsequent conversion of the fullness of Israel. Within this sequence of events, the phrase 'and so all Israel shall be saved' most naturally seems to mean that after the fullness of the Gentiles is engrafted, the time will come when the people of Israel will be converted and God's purposes of redemption be accomplished in them. The main point of Romans 11:25 seems to be that the hardening of Israel will come to an end and Israel will be restored. This point would be undermined, were we to understand 'all Israel' of Romans 11:26 only as the total number of elect Israel throughout the history of redemption.

This does not mean necessarily that every individual member of the people of Israel will ultimately be saved, or that all members of this people will be converted at some future time. The fullness of Israel need not mean the salvation of every member of this people any more than the fullness of the Gentiles means the salvation of every Gentile. It does suggest, however, that Paul taught the time will come in which a fullness of Israel will be converted, an engrafting again of Israel as a people, a restoration of this special people of God to gospel blessing.

If this understanding of the future salvation of the fullness of Israel through the preaching of the gospel is correct, then two corollaries deserve to be mentioned.

The first is that there is but one way of salvation for Jew and Gentile alike: the way of faith in response to the preaching of the gospel (*Rom.* 10: 1-17). Paul's argument in Romans 9-11 is that all are saved only as they are grafted into the one olive tree, in fellowship through faith with the Saviour. Nowhere in the word of God do we have a clearer repudiation of any teaching that suggests different pathways for Jews and Gentiles. This idea is often taught in the form of a 'two-covenant theology', the one covenant unique to the people of Israel, the other unique to the Gentile nations. Though Romans 9-11 suggests that God's purposes of redemption include a purpose uniquely suited to Israel, it stands opposed to any such two-covenant position. All who will be saved will be saved through faith in response to the same gospel and within the fellowship of the one people of God (*Eph.* 2:11-22).

The second corollary is that believers should have a keen interest in the preaching of the gospel to the people of Israel. Rather than concluding that God's purposes have ended for them, we should evangelise in expectation that his calling of Israel will terminate in her fullness being saved. This should encourage preaching the gospel to the Gentiles as well as to the Jews. Any presumption that God has wholly abandoned Israel to her unbelief is just that: a presumption without biblical warrant.

Let the gospel be preached to the Jew first and also to the Gentile, for God's purposes of salvation will not fail.

5

THE FUTURE MARKED BY SIGNS OF ANTITHESIS AND OF IMPENDING JUDGEMENT

*A*s history moves toward the time of Christ's return, the conflict in history intensifies between the truth and the lie, the kingdom of God and the kingdom of this world. This intensification confirms that all things are ripening for judgement and the consummation of history at Christ's return.

SIGNS OF OPPOSITION TO GOD

Several signs of the times reflect this intensified conflict as the end draws near. These are: tribulation, the Great Tribulation, apostasy, and the coming of Antichrist(s).

A number of general references in the New Testament clearly teach that struggle and difficulty are the common circumstance of believers in the present period of history. Such tribulation is not limited to a specific time either in the past or future; it spans the period between Christ's first and second coming and will not cease before Christ's revelation at the end of the age (*2 Thess.* 1:6-8).

In the Sermon on the Mount, Jesus taught his disciples that they should expect suffering as a consequence of their discipleship. Matthew 5:10-12 is well known:

> Blessed are those who have been persecuted for the sake of righteousness, for theirs is the kingdom of heaven. Blessed are you when men cast insults at you, and persecute you, and say all kinds of evil against you falsely, on account of me. Rejoice, and be glad, for your reward in heaven is great, for so they persecuted the prophets who were before you.

This suggests that persecution will be the normal consequence of seeking to be faithful to Jesus Christ.

Other New Testament passages contain similar warnings. When Christ was teaching his disciples in the Upper Room prior to his crucifixion, he declared, 'Remember the word that I said to you, A slave is not greater than his master. If they persecuted me, they will also persecute you' (*John* 15:20). The Lord issues a comparable warning in John 16:33, 'These things I have spoken to you that in me you may have peace. In the world you have tribulation, but take courage; I have overcome the world.' In 2 Timothy 3:12, Paul notes that persecution will be the experience of all believers: 'And indeed, all who desire to live godly in Christ Jesus will be persecuted' (cf. *Acts* 14:22).

THE 'OLIVET DISCOURSE'

One of the most important New Testament passages for understanding 'the signs of the times' is recorded in Matthew 24, with parallels in Mark 13:37 and Luke 21:5-36. This passage is known as the Olivet Discourse because it records the words of Jesus Christ to his disciples while he was sitting on the Mount of Olives (*Matt.* 24:3). The disciples had pointed out the temple buildings to Christ, and he had responded by declaring, 'Do you not see all these things? Truly I say to you, not one stone here shall be left upon another, which will not be torn down' (verse 2). This response provoked a twofold question from the disciples: 'Tell us, when will these things be, and what will be the sign of your coming, and of the end of the age?'

Christ responds by mentioning a number of signs that will characterise the present age before the end comes (verses 4-14). These signs will include such things as 'wars and rumours of wars', 'famines', 'earth-quakes', 'false prophets', 'lawlessness', and the preaching of the gospel 'in the whole world for a witness to all the nations'. Among these signs will also be the experience of tribulation: 'Then they will deliver you to tribulation, and will kill you, and you will be hated by all nations on account of my name' (verse 9). These verses seem to speak generally of signs that will characterise the age between the time of Christ's first and second comings.

In what follows, however, especially verses 15-28, the focus of Christ's words seems to be upon the events that will precede or accompany the destruction of the temple in Jerusalem. Many of the signs in this section of Matthew 24 may refer primarily and immediately to the destruction of the temple in Jerusalem in A.D. 70. However, there are several reasons we may also interpret these signs in the broader context of Matthew 24 to refer as well to events that will mark the entire period before Christ's final coming at the end of the age.

To say that all the events described in Matthew 24 took place before or during A.D. 70 does not do full justice to the disciples' question and the expression 'the end of the age'. This and the language about the coming (*parousia*) of Christ, used elsewhere in this passage (verses 27, 30, 42-44), commonly refer to the second coming of Christ (e.g., *Matt.* 28:20). In no other New Testament passage does the expression 'the end of the age' refer to an event prior to Christ's second coming.

As was previously discussed regarding the preaching of the gospel, only with difficulty can this sign be said to have been fulfilled prior to A.D. 70. This sign and the language Christ employs (verse 6) suggest that some time will elapse before all will have been fulfilled (see *Luke* 19:11).

In verses 29-31, Jesus seems to be speaking of his second coming, an event that can hardly to be said to have already occurred in A.D. 70. He speaks of a visible advent in verse 30b that parallels other New Testament descriptions (*Matt* 16:27; *Mark* 8:38; *Luke* 9:26; *Acts* 1:9-11; *1 Thess.* 4:17; *2 Thess.* 1:7; *Rev.* 1:7). The reference to the sign of his coming echoes the language used by the disciples in the second part of their question, and the language of the great trumpet and the angels in verse 31 is characteristically used of Christ's return at the end of the age (*1 Cor.* 15:52; *1 Thess.* 4:16; *2 Thess.* 1:7).

The teaching in verses 36-44 that no one knows the day or the hour can best be understood of Christ's second coming, not the destruction of Jerusalem in A.D. 70. This language also has New Testament parallels that uniformly refer to the second coming of Christ (*Matt.* 25:13; *Mark* 13:32; *Luke* 12:39-40; *Acts* 1:6-7; *1 Thess.* 5:2; *Rev.* 16:15).

Finally, it should be noted that Chapters 24 and 25 belong together. They are joined by the series of parables that illustrate the nature of Christ's coming and the need for preparedness in the light of its certainty. The language of Matthew 25:14-46 suggests that the Lord is still speaking of those events that will precede or accompany his coming at the end of the age.

OBSERVATIONS ON TRIBULATION

Accordingly, since Matthew 24 seems to describe signs of the times that are characteristic of the whole period leading up to the coming of Christ at the end of the age, it confirms the previous references to tribulation as the experience of the believer in this present age. Some observations about the nature and occasion of tribulation may help explain what this sign means.

First, the most common New Testament term for tribulation, *thlipsis* in Greek, describes the trouble or distress that results from the believer's commitment to Christ, his word, and his kingdom. In 2 Thessalonians 1:6-8, the tribulation presently suffered by the believer is contrasted with the rest or peace that will result from Christ's coming at the end of the age. The contrast in this passage between the present and future circumstance of believers indicates that the tribulations of the present life are those which make the Christian's present pilgrimage difficult and which fall short of the future peace.

It is crucial to notice that this tribulation results from believers' commitment to Christ. It is not just any circumstance of trouble, but it specifically results from faithfulness. Many references to the persecution in the present age use language that closely joins the experience of tribulation with the believer's relationship with Christ. Nowhere is this language bolder than in Colossians 1:24, where Paul speaks of his joy in suffering and sharing in filling up that which is lacking in Christ's afflictions. This passage should not be understood to teach that there was any lack in Christ's atoning work, but it does speak clearly of a participation on the part of the church in the afflictions of Christ. One important way in which the church has fellowship with Christ is suffering affliction for his name's sake. Consider Christ's confrontation of Saul on the way to Damascus: 'Saul, Saul, why are you persecuting me?' (*Acts* 9:4) So intimate is the communion of the believer with Christ that the affliction of the believer is a participation in Christ's affliction.

Second, tribulation in the life of the believer can take many forms. Often it takes the form of open hostility from those who reject the gospel of Jesus Christ (*1 Thess.* 1:6; *2 Thess.* 1; *2 Tim.* 3:12-13; *Acts* 14:22; *Rev.* 1:9). It can mean imprisonment, which the apostles and many believers have experienced (*Acts* 20:23). Sometimes it means ridicule (*Heb.* 10:33), poverty (*2 Cor.* 2:4), illness (*Rev.* 2:22), or inner distress and sorrow (*Phil.* 1:17; *2 Cor.* 2:4). Whether a believer lives in a society friendly or hostile to the gospel, some form of tribulation cannot be escaped. Tribulation attests the genuineness of the believer's fellowship with Christ, as well as commitment to him and his gospel.

Third, tribulation—like the other signs—testifies not to the uncertainty of Christ's cause, but to its certain victory. In Revelation 12:7-12 we are given a vision of Michael and his angels casting down the dragon and his angels. This victory is accomplished because of 'the blood of the Lamb and because of the word of their [the believers'] testimony' (verse 11). It is striking how the defeat of Satan results in his intensified persecution of the church on earth, knowing that his time is short and his defeat certain. The suffering of the church witnesses to the victory of Christ's cross in the purposes of God. Far from being a fearful prospect, it reminds the believer that God's kingdom will prevail.

Fourth, the circumstance of tribulation in the life of the believer is often an occasion for growth in discipleship. Only in affliction does the believer come to realise the depth and the extent of his fellowship with Christ. Tribulation serves as a constant reminder of the centrality of the cross of Christ, not only as the means of atonement, but also as a call to self-denying patience under circumstances of suffering (*1 Pet.* 2:21-25). As Paul declares: 'We also exult in our tribulations, knowing that tribulation brings about perseverance; and perseverance, proven character, and proven character, hope; and hope does not disappoint, because the love of God has been poured out within our hearts through the Holy Spirit who was given to us' (*Rom.* 5:3-5).

Believers should count their trials 'all joy' and 'the testing of the faith' an occasion for growth in the Christian life, growth that produces maturity and completeness (*James* 1:2-4). In the midst of the trials of this life, the Christian is like a child disciplined by a father (*Heb.* 12:6), like gold refined through fire (*1 Pet.* 1:7), or like the vine pruned by the gardener (*John* 15:1ff.).

The tribulation of the present age, like all of the Bible's other teaching about the future, serves to nurture the believer's hope. It reminds him of the triumphant words of Paul at the end of Romans 8:

> But in all these things [tribulation, distress, persecution, famine, nakedness, peril, the sword] we overwhelmingly conquer through him who loved us. For I am convinced that neither death nor life, nor angels, nor principalities, nor things present, nor things to come, nor powers, nor height, nor depth, nor any other created thing, shall be able to separate us from the love of God, which is in Christ Jesus our Lord' (*Rom.* 8:37-39).

A 'GREAT TRIBULATION'

Having considered the sign of tribulation generally, we now look at what is often called the 'Great Tribulation'. The question is: does the Bible teach that the tribulation of the present age will issue in a circumstance of intensified tribulation, a great tribulation, prior to the return of Christ? The subject of the great tribulation has been especially prominent among Christian believers who are dispensational premillennialists. Since in Dispensationalism the rapture of believers will precede the period of great tribulation (usually thought to be for a period of seven years), this position is often known as Pre-tribulationalism. A minority position among dispensationalists, known as Mid-tribulational Premillennialism, has taught that the rapture would occur in the middle of the great tribulation. Non-dispensational premillennialists teach that Christ will return only after the great tribulation; this position is known as Post-tribulational Premillennialism.

These various views within Premillennialism are mentioned because they illustrate the bearing a certain view of the great tribulation has upon the various millennial views. They cannot be wholly ignored, since any position concluding that believers will experience the great tribulation is incompatible with the traditional view of Dispensationalism. The position we will defend could be compatible with some forms of Premillennialism, but not with classic Dispensationalism.

The most important passage that speaks of a great tribulation is again Matthew 24, in which Jesus speaks of a coming period of great tribulation. Because of the importance of this passage and its specific description of this great tribulation, it will be useful to quote it at some length:

> Therefore when you see the ABOMINATION OF DESOLATION which was spoken of through Daniel the prophet, standing in the holy place (let the reader understand), then let those who are in Judea flee to the mountains; let him who is on the housetop not go down to get the things out that are in his house; and let him who is in the field not turn back to get his cloak. But woe to those who are with child and to those who nurse babes in those days! But pray that your flight may not be in winter, or on a Sabbath; for then there will be a great tribulation, such as has not occurred since the beginning of the world until now, nor ever shall. And unless those days had been cut short, no life would have been saved; but for the sake of the elect those days shall be cut short (verses 15-22).

Here Christ clearly teaches that one of the signs that will precede the destruction of the temple is a period of intensified tribulation. He also associates this period of great tribulation with the fulfilment of Daniel's prophecy regarding the destruction of the temple, which occurred in the year A.D. 70.

As noted before, the primary and immediate reference in these verses is to events that took place in the period of the generation to whom Jesus first spoke these words. The question remains, however, whether they might not also have reference to further great tribulation that will occur prior to the end of the age.

It is not necessary to repeat the reasons for applying the signs of the times in Matthew 24 to the entire period between Christ's first and second comings. Just as the prophecy of Daniel regarding the desecration of the temple had an earlier and initial fulfilment in the time of Antiochus Epiphanes (before the first coming of Christ), and then a subsequent and further fulfilment at the time of the destruction of the temple in Jerusalem, so we may understand our Lord's prophecy in Matthew 24 to foreshadow a further and final fulfilment at the end of the age. According to this understanding, the tribulation that characterises the circumstance of the faithful church in the interim between Christ's first and second advent will reach its most intensified expression in the period preceding his second coming. Several additional biblical references suggest a period of intensified tribulation prior to Christ's coming at the end of the age.

In Revelation 2:22, in the letter to the angel of the church in Thyatira, Christ warns that he will 'cast her [the woman Jezebel] upon a bed of sickness, and those who commit adultery with her into great tribulation, unless they repent of their deeds'. Though some interpreters have sought to restrict this warning to the church in the first century, it would seem more appropriate to regard it as including a solemn warning to the church during the entire age prior to Christ's return. Similarly, in Revelation 7:9-17 John describes his vision of that 'great multitude, which no one could count . . . clothed with white robes' (verse 9) which is composed of those 'who are coming out of the great tribulation' (verse 14). This passage seems to use the language of 'great tribulation' to describe an ongoing experience of the saints in this present age. If such language can be employed to describe what is common to the period between Christ's first and second comings, it seems appropriate that it should also be applicable to the period just prior to his return.

Though the term 'great tribulation' is not used in Revelation 20, this passage speaks of Satan's little season at the end of the period of one thousand years during which Satan is bound so as not to deceive the nations. It seems most likely that this little season corresponds to that period of intensified opposition to the gospel that will characterise the close of the age prior to Christ's return.

Another similar and important passage is 2 Thessalonians 1:1-15, which describes the coming of 'the man of lawlessness' prior to the coming of Christ. In this passage, which follows one in which Christ's revelation from heaven will bring rest to the beleaguered believers (*2 Thess.* 1), it is evident that the coming of 'the man of lawlessness' will be accompanied by persecution of and apostasy within the church. This passage bears a striking resemblance to the references in Daniel 9 and Matthew 24 to 'the abomination of desolation'. One of the features of this 'man of lawlessness' will be his effort to exalt himself above every object of worship, so that he takes his seat in the temple of God, displaying himself as being God (verse 4).

It appears that Satan's opposition to Christ will come to acute and final expression in a short season of more severe tribulation. In none of the passages we have considered is it taught that believers will be snatched away prior to the great tribulation. Rather, the consistent emphasis seems to be the call to patient endurance in the expectation of Christ's certain return and triumph, which will bring rest to the beleaguered church (see *2 Thess.* 1). The Bible's teaching about the prospect of a great tribulation shortly before the return of Christ ought not to be understood to allow any prediction of the time of Christ's return. No one should be so confident of his understanding of the Bible's teaching about the great tribulation that he concludes Christ could not return in the near future. The Bible's teaching about the church's tribulation in this present age and in the period shortly before Christ's return does not permit any confident conclusions about the precise nature and course of a great tribulation that might be yet to come. Consequently, no one may be too sure or dogmatic about these things.

One thing is absolutely certain: whatever the present trial and distress, whatever the future intensity of opposition to Christ's gospel and cause,

Christ must reign until he has put all his enemies under his feet (*1 Cor.* 15:25). Tribulation, even great tribulation, cannot and will not separate us from the love of Christ (*Rom.* 8:35-39).

APOSTASY

The Old Testament contains a remarkable account of Jeremiah prophesying God's judgement upon the city of Jerusalem. This prophecy is striking, in that it was spoken within the sanctuary and it pronounced the Lord's curse upon the church of Jeremiah's day, and not the enemies of the Lord and his people.

We should not be surprised, therefore, to read that the response of the people was one of shock and anger. How could the prophet speak judgement against the house of the Lord? The priests and the prophets spoke to the officials and to all the people, saying, 'A death sentence for this man! For he has prophesied against this city as you have heard in your hearing' (*Jer.* 26:11).

This account reminds us that apostasy and unfaithfulness among the people of God is a sign of the times. The Bible teaches that God's judgement begins with the house of God (*1 Pet.* 4:17) and that apostasy has always been a feature of the church's life. The prophecy of Jeremiah should alert the church to the continuing threat of apostasy and its significant role in our Lord's teaching.

In the New Testament's teaching regarding the signs of the times, apostasy among the people of God often figures prominently. It is also implicit whenever the church is warned against unfaithfulness, in appeals often buttressed by the example of the apostasy of the Old Testament people of God.

In the Olivet Discourse, Christ prophesies that 'many will fall away, and betray one another, and hate one another. And many false prophets will arise and lead many astray. And because wickedness is multiplied, most men's love will grow cold' (*Matt.* 24:10-12; cf. *Luke* 8:13; *1 Tim.* 4:1). Christ adds that 'false Christs and false prophets will arise and show great signs and wonders, so as to lead astray, if possible, even the elect'

(*Matt.* 24:24). These verses present a sobering, even terrifying, picture of the church being assaulted, not simply by external enemies, but also by enemies within. Some of those who claim to speak for Christ within the church will actually be 'anti'-Christ. And some numbered among the visible people of God will, in truth, be opposed to the gospel of our Lord Jesus Christ. In his first letter to Timothy, Paul warns that in later times some will fall away from the faith (*1 Tim.* 4:1). The pressure of the world's hostility to the gospel may occasion this departure, as the apostle adds in his second letter to Timothy, 'in the last days difficult times will come' (*2 Tim.* 3:1).

Many of the words of exhortation, warning and encouragement in the New Testament indicate that apostasy will plague the people of God in this present age. In 2 Peter, believers are exhorted to be on guard so as not to be carried away by the error of 'lawless men' (3:17). The book of Hebrews is pervaded by the theme of the temptation to fall away from the truth, a falling away that would make it impossible for believers to be restored again to repentance (*Heb.* 3:12; 6:6).

This possibility of apostasy also underlies the promise that God will preserve and keep his people from falling. Thus, Jude 24, that well-known doxology with which the epistle concludes, praises God as the one 'who is able to keep [his people] from falling and to make them stand in the presence of his glory, blameless with great joy'. It also lends urgency to Peter's exhortation: 'Therefore, my brothers, be all the more diligent to make certain about his calling and choosing you, for as long as you practise these things you will never stumble' (*2 Pet.* 1:10). It becomes evident in these passages that the people of God will be severely tried in their allegiance to Christ and the truth of God's word. This testing will prove the faith of some, while exposing the unbelief of others. Even leaders and office bearers of the church will fall away from the way of truth. Apostasy directly involves and affects the people of God. It is a sign of internal opposition to Christ by those who claim to be God's people, not of external opposition by those who make no boast of being God's people. This should surprise no one. It has always been a feature of the church's existence, and it will most certainly be a feature of the church's existence during this present period between Christ's first and second advent.

Does the Bible teach that, just as tribulation will issue in a period of great tribulation before Christ's return, so apostasy will issue in a period of great apostasy before the end comes? 2 Timothy 3:1 suggests this, and is paralleled in 1 Timothy 4:1, which warns that 'the Spirit explicitly says that in later times some will fall away from the faith, paying attention to deceitful spirits and doctrines of demons.' The language in both passages seems to indicate that, as the end approaches, apostasy will become ever more evident among the people of God.

The clearest example of this emphasis is 2 Thessalonians 2, in which Paul seeks to allay the anxiety of some in Thessalonica who have been shaken by the report that the day of the Lord has come (verse 2). The apostle warns the church that the day of the Lord will not come until 'the apostasy comes first, and the man of lawlessness is revealed, the son of destruction' (verse 3). The language used in this text, coupled with the description offered of 'the man of lawlessness' intimates there will be a period of substantial falling away within the church before the coming of Christ. The apostle warns believers against any premature conclusion that the day of the Lord has come; this day will not come until the apostasy occurs and the man of lawlessness is revealed.

The most likely conclusion to be drawn from these passages is that the sign of apostasy will reach an intensified expression in the period prior to the return of Christ. Just as the sign of tribulation will issue in great tribulation, a period of more acute distress for the people of God, so the sign of apostasy will also issue in a period of great apostasy.

If apostasy within the church is a sign of the times, and if the threat of it may become more pressing as the time of Christ's return approaches, then there are some inescapable consequences for the people of God and the church of Jesus Christ.

First, this sign reminds us that the church's greatest enemy arises not from the world without, or even from the wily devices of the devil himself, but from within her own ranks. Some people naively believe that the church is immune from the danger of real apostasy. They are unwilling to believe that those who claim to speak in the name of Christ, even leaders and office bearers among the people of God, may be deceived and in serious error.

Such naivety is clearly exposed in the word of God as foolish. Anyone who reads the record of Israel's repeated apostasies or listens carefully to the New Testament warnings against unfaithfulness must realise that the danger of falling away is ever present. Indeed, apostasy functions as a signal within the unfolding purpose of God that the day of the Lord is at hand.

Second, no one who takes seriously the biblical teaching about this sign of apostasy can afford the luxury of being 'at ease in Zion', blithely confident that the church is a safe haven of rest in the midst of the storm and fury of history. The antithesis sometimes cuts across lines within the church as much as it separates the church from the world.

One of the deadliest temptations facing the church of Jesus Christ is institutionalism or denominationalism. Both of these 'isms' express a blind and unyielding loyalty to organisations and agencies that takes precedence over loyalty to Christ and his word. Whether rooted in nostalgia, sentiment or wishful thinking, such blind loyalty has no place in the life of a believer. Christians are not to place their trust in princes, least of all ecclesiastical princes, nor in institutions. Their trust is in the Lord who alone will preserve his church by the working of his Spirit and word. The Lord of the church stands ready to remove the candlestick from any church that falls away from the faith (see *Psa.* 118:8-9; *Rev.* 2:5).

And third, only that church which remains resolute and vigilant in the preservation of the faith has the right to claim the promise that the gates of hell will not prevail against her. The sign of apostasy serves as a clarion call to the church to be on guard against the temptation to fall away, to let go her rich inheritance in the word of God and the gospel.

Christendom is littered with the dead remains of once strong and vibrant churches. Many churches that once offered sturdy and uncompromising testimony to the truth of the gospel are today no more than empty shells, or merely social clubs for people with particular political views. Such churches witness to the truth of the Lord's words regarding apostasy within the church.

This sign of the times ought to be a sufficient deterrent to any complacency. There is no room in a true church of Jesus Christ for smugness. When Paul speaks of the coming apostasy, he hastens to encourage the church to stand firm and hold to the traditions that they were taught (*2 Thess.* 2:15). Unless the church remains vigilant and careful to hold fast to the apostolic word, it risks becoming apostate and falling away from the truth.

The sign of apostasy speaks a word of warning and a word of encouragement. It warns the church against complacency, alerting it to the dangers faced within and without. But it also reminds the church that Christ will preserve a faithful people. Those who make their calling and election sure need not be afraid, for Christ will keep them in his care.

THE 'ANTICHRIST'

Of all 'the signs of the times' mentioned in the Scriptures, none is better known nor more commonly the subject of speculation than the sign of the coming Antichrist. The temptation to go beyond the clear teaching of Scripture and to fall prey to an unbiblical curiosity about God's purposes in history is nowhere more acute than in respect to this particular sign.

It is remarkable to notice that in those biblical texts that speak expressly of an Antichrist, however, none fix exclusively upon one person or speak of the Antichrist as of a figure of political power. Rather, they speak of various antichrists whose defining characteristic will be their anti-Christian teaching. In only four places in the epistles of John are the terms 'antichrist' or 'antichrists' used. In the now familiar passage on the signs of the times in Matthew 24, the language used is that of 'false' or 'pseudo' Christs who are associated with 'false' or 'pseudo' prophets: 'Then if anyone says to you, Behold, here is the Christ, or There he is, do not believe him. For false Christs and false prophets will arise and will show great signs and wonders, so as to mislead, if possible, even the elect. Behold, I have told you in advance' (verses 23-25; cf. *Mark* 13:21-23). These words are a solemn warning that the coming of Christ will be preceded by the emergence of false Christs, figures who will claim to be or to speak for Christ, even performing signs and wonders, but enemies of Christ and the gospel.

In 1 John 4:2-3, we find an extensive reference:

> By this you know the Spirit of God: every spirit that confesses that Jesus Christ has come in the flesh is from God; and every spirit that does not confess Jesus is not from God; and this is the spirit of the antichrist, of which you have heard that it is coming, and now it is already in the world.

This passage speaks of false teaching, the spirit of the Antichrist, which denies the coming of Christ in the flesh. According to John, this anti-Christian denial of Christ's incarnation was already present in the early history of the church.

A similar thought is conveyed in 1 John 2:22: 'Who is the liar but the one who denies that Jesus is the Christ? This is the antichrist, the one who denies the Father and the Son'; and in 2 John 7: 'For many deceivers have gone out into the world, those who do not acknowledge Jesus Christ as coming in the flesh. This is the deceiver and the antichrist.'

None of these three passages speaks of a specific Antichrist. However, in 1 John 2:18, we read: 'Children, it is the last hour; and just as you heard that antichrist is coming, even now many antichrists have arisen; from this we know that it is the last hour.' Though this passage echoes earlier passages—that there are many antichrists, some manifest already in the period of the early church—it adds the further thought of a specific person in whom this anti-Christian spirit would be embodied. It supplements the teaching of the other passages by speaking of a future personal Antichrist in whom the spirit of these antichrists comes to striking expression.

If these general passages speaking of 'Antichrist' and 'antichrists' are considered together, then at least three preliminary conclusions may be drawn.

First, as with the signs of the times considered previously, this sign may not be relegated to some brief period just prior to the end of the

age. The references to the antichrists we have considered all refer to figures contemporaneous with the New Testament. They are figures of the
past though they continue to be typical of new figures arising throughout
history to deny the gospel of Jesus Christ. These passages clearly teach
that we live in that period of history known as the 'last hour', characterised by opposition to the gospel and the emergence of figures hostile to
the gospel, even at times from within the fellowship of the church itself.
Any teaching about the Antichrist that misses this emphasis cannot be
said to be faithful to the teaching of the Scriptures.

Second, there are several antichrists. It is frequently taught today
that the Antichrist is to be understood only as a single figure and as one
who could not have been known to the writers of the New Testament.
Much of the New Testament's emphasis regarding the Antichrist or
antichrists, however, aims to arouse the people of God from their complacency. The teaching is not intended to provide an occasion for arm-
chair reflections or the writing of many books, most of whose content is
unbiblically speculative. This teaching aims to warn the church not to
be deceived. Not all those who bear Christ's name are truly his servants.
Some are wolves in the garments of sheep. Some may even be antichrist,
that is, opposed to the truth regarding the person and work of Christ.

And third, the telltale evidence of the presence of antichrist is the
presence of anti-Christian teaching, not the exercise of political power.
The predominant emphasis in the New Testament is upon the false doctrine associated with the Antichrist. Those who deny the incarnation of
Christ, who call into question the deity of Christ and the doctrine of the
Trinity, are as likely to fit the biblical portrait of the Antichrist as figures
wielding political power in opposition to the cause of the Christian gospel.

Does the Bible also teach that one particular person is coming who
will be the Antichrist? This is commonly believed by many Christians, but
where is this taught, and what is the nature of the Bible's teaching regarding this figure?

We have seen already in 1 John 2:18, that reference can be made in
the New Testament to a particular figure who is, in some unique sense,
the Antichrist. Moreover, in another important passage usually taken to

refer to the Antichrist, 2 Thessalonians 2, Paul speaks of the coming of 'a man of lawlessness'.

This passage has antecedents in the Old Testament and calls to mind some of the description in Matthew 24 regarding the 'abomination of desolation' that will be set up in the temple in Jerusalem. In Daniel, two passages speak of an 'abomination that makes desolate' or 'causes desolation'. The first speaks prophetically of the coming of those who will 'desecrate the sanctuary fortress and do away with the regular sacrifice. And they will set up the abomination of desolation' (11:31). The second speaks similarly of how 'from the time that the regular sacrifice is abolished, and the abomination of desolation is set up, there will be 1,290 days' (12:11). Many interpreters of Daniel take these two passages to refer to the profaning of the temple in Jerusalem by Antiochus Epiphanes.

In Matthew 24, however, Christ speaks of the destruction of the temple in Jerusalem as a fulfilment of Daniel's prophecy regarding 'the abomination of desolation'. Certainly Christ is speaking about the events that occurred in A.D. 70, at the time of the destruction of the temple in Jerusalem by the Roman emperor Titus and his conquering legions.

These earlier fulfilments of prophecy, both at the time of the destruction of the temple in Jerusalem by Antiochus Epiphanes and later by the emperor Titus, may be prefigurements of a coming event in which the temple of the Lord, the church, will be invaded by another figure and the house of the Lord will once more be profaned. This seems to be the teaching of 2 Thessalonians 2, in which Paul employs language reminiscent of Daniel 11 and 12 and Matthew 24 to describe the coming of another 'man of lawlessness'.

The importance of the description of this 'man of lawlessness' in 2 Thessalonians warrants quoting the passage at some length:

> Now we request you, brethren, with regard to the coming of our Lord Jesus Christ, and our gathering together to him, that you may not be quickly shaken from your composure or be disturbed either by a spirit or a message or a letter as if from us, to the effect that the day of the Lord has come. Let no one in any way deceive you, for it will not come unless the apostasy comes first, and the man of lawlessness is revealed,

the son of destruction, who opposes and exalts himself above every so-called god or object of worship, so that he takes his seat in the temple of God, displaying himself as being God. Do you not remember that while I was still with you, I was telling you these things? And you know what restrains him now, so that in his time he may be revealed. For the mystery of lawlessness is already at work; only he who now restrains will do so until he is taken out of the way. And then that lawless one will be revealed whom the Lord will slay with the breath of his mouth and bring to an end by the appearance of his coming; that is, the one whose coming is in accordance with the activity of Satan, with all power and signs and false wonders, and with all the deception of wickedness for those who perish, because they did not receive the love of the truth so as to be saved (2 *Thess.* 2:1-10).

Several general observations regarding this passage have a direct bearing upon the question of the identity and nature of the Antichrist.

First, the coming of this 'man of lawlessness' is associated with the period of great apostasy that will plague the church immediately before Christ's return. This sign of the Antichrist not only belongs to those signs that bespeak opposition to Christ and his cause, but it also expresses the intensification of those signs as the end approaches. As with tribulation and the great tribulation, so with this sign; there will be many antichrists, and toward the end of the age an Antichrist.

Second, this passage suggests that the Antichrist will be a particular person in history. He is called '*the* man of lawlessness', '*the* son of perdition', and '*the* one who opposes God and exalts himself against every object of worship'. This language implies the emergence of a single person in whom the spirit of Antichrist will be pre-eminently displayed.

Third, one of the striking features of this man of lawlessness will be his claim to divine status and worship. Just as with earlier fulfilments of Daniel's prophecy, so the coming of this man of lawlessness will be evident in his profanation of the true temple of the Lord, the church of Jesus Christ. Like those before him, this Antichrist will be a deceiver and an impostor, one who pretends to be a friend of Christ though in reality he will be Christ's deadliest enemy. His appearing and work will be aimed at the people of God themselves, from among whom he will arise and whom he will seek to lead astray.

Fourth, the man of lawlessness will test the church's loyalty to Christ and his word. As with the other signs of the times, the sign of the Antichrist will be an occasion for the church to stand its ground, to resist temptation, and to persevere in faithfulness. What will make this testing peculiarly poignant is that the Antichrist will perform many powerful signs and wonders in an attempt to deceive even the elect. For this reason, Paul in 2 Thessalonians stresses the church's obligation, in the face of the temptations of this Antichrist, to hold fast the [apostolic] traditions she has received.

And fifth, despite much unsatisfactory speculation about the identity of that which restrains or he who restrains the man of lawlessness, his eventual defeat is certain. Like the other signs of opposition to the cause of Christ, the sign of the Antichrist is a sign—not of defeat—but of sure victory for Christ and his people. Not for one moment should the church fear that the Antichrist will be able to frustrate the fruition of God's purposes in Christ.

Therefore, the Bible appears to teach that the Antichrist, a person in whom the growing opposition to the gospel will be concentrated, will appear prior to Christ's return at the close of this present age. While during this 'last hour' there will be many antichrists, figures falsely claiming to represent Christ but denying the truth concerning his person and work, toward the end of this age one person will emerge in whom these antichrists will find their archetype.

In a pattern we have observed before, the Scriptural teaching regarding the Antichrist calls the church not only to vigilance, but also to renewed hope. The true people of God do not tremble at the prospect of the Antichrist. Rather, they remember the encouraging words of Paul, written to comfort and steady the church, that when the man of lawlessness is revealed, Christ will return and 'slay him with the breath of his mouth and bring [him] to an end by the appearance of his coming' (*2 Thess.* 2:8).

SIGNS OF GOD'S JUDGEMENT

Now that we have considered the signs of God's grace and the signs of the antithesis, only the third category remains, those signs dealing with God's judgement in anticipation of the great judgement to come.

These signs of God's judgement are reminders that God's work of redemption in Christ has not been concluded, but that it soon will be. Furthermore, they remind us that God's kingdom will triumph over all of his enemies and all the unrighteousness of sinful creatures will come under the judgement of God. Like those signs already considered, they indicate the tension of this period between the time of Christ's first and second advents. They not only speak of the conflict in history that continues between the work of Christ and his enemies, but they also point forward to the consummation of the ages, the great Day of Christ's coming in glory to judge the nations and peoples in righteousness.

As with many other signs of the times, these signs of God's judgement are prominent in Christ's Olivet Discourse in Matthew 24:

> And you will be hearing of wars and rumours of wars; see that you are not frightened, for those things must take place, but that is not yet the end. For nation will rise against nation, and kingdom against kingdom, and in various places there will be famines and earthquakes. But all these things are merely the beginning of birth pangs (verses 6-8).

The language of the parallel passage in Mark 13:7-8 is virtually identical to that of Matthew 24. In another parallel passage in Luke 21:11, there are two slight differences in language. The earthquakes mentioned are said to be great and, in addition to the sign of famine, the sign of plagues or pestilence is mentioned.

Since so much misunderstanding about these familiar signs exists, it will be useful to make a number of interpretive comments.

All of these signs have antecedents in the Old Testament. When the Lord Jesus Christ speaks of nation rising up against nation and kingdom against kingdom, he is using the language of Isaiah 19:2 and 2 Chronicles 15:6. Earthquakes frequently occur in the Old Testament as a signal of God's direct working in history (*Judg.* 5:4-5; *Psa.* 18:7; 68:8; *Isa.* 24:19;

29:6; 64:1). The signs of plagues and famines are also evident in the preceding history of the Lord's dealings with the nations in general and Israel in particular (*Exod.* 7-11 [the plagues upon Egypt]; *Deut.* 28:15ff.; *Jer.* 15:2; *Ezek.* 5:16-17; 14:13). None of these signs, therefore, is new. They continue what might almost be termed a pattern of the Lord's dealings with the nations.

This pattern indicates the presence of the Lord in history judging the sinful rebellion of the nations and his own people. These judgements do not imply that all who suffer them are personally guilty and the special objects of God's wrath (*Luke* 13:43). They illustrate that the world still lies under the curse of God (*Gen.* 3:17) and remind us that the wrath of God continues to be revealed from heaven against all the ungodliness and wickedness of men (*Rom.* 1:18). As signs of God's just displeasure with the sinfulness of the nations, they prefigure and anticipate the great day of judgement to come, when the justice of God will be manifested in the judgement exercised by Christ (*Acts* 17:31). As such they are a continual reminder that the judge is at the door (*James* 5:9).

Another interesting feature of this group of signs is that they do not promise, in the strictest sense, that the end of the age has come. In Matthew 24:4, Christ adds to his words about these signs, 'For the end is not yet.' Then, in a phrase that characterises all of these signs, he remarks that these are 'the beginnings of the birth pangs' (verse 8). Like the other signs we have considered, these are not to be relegated to a brief period just prior to the end of the age. Nor should they be cited as clear evidence that the return of Christ is imminent, as is so often done.

Rather, these signs designate features of the Lord's dealings with the nations that will characterise the entire period between Christ's first and second advents. Even the mention of birth pangs reminds us that the travail of this present period will be prolonged. This language is reminiscent of Romans 8:22, where Paul speaks of 'the whole creation . . . groaning as in the pains of childbirth right up to the present moment.' So long as Christ remains seated at the Father's right hand, his dominion over the nations will take the form not only of the gathering of his people, but also of the exercise of judgements which prefigure and anticipate the great day of judgement.

By no biblical measure are these signs to be contemplated as evidence of failure or uncertainty respecting the coming of God's kingdom. They are, rather, one clear body of evidence for its presence and eventual triumph.

ARMAGEDDON

When addressing the wars associated with the end times, the battle of Armageddon cannot be ignored because it has been the object of much speculation, and because it is one of those signs portending the consummation of the present age.

This battle is only explicitly mentioned in Revelation 16:16: 'Then they gathered the kings together to the place that in Hebrew is called Armageddon.' In this context, the battle of Armageddon occurs after the sixth angel has poured out the sixth bowl of wrath on the Euphrates (verse 12). The kings are gathered under the leading of demonic spirits in opposition to God and his people (verses 13-14). We are also told that they gather for the great day of God, the Almighty (verse 14), prior to the pouring out of the seventh and last bowl of God's wrath in anticipation of the final victory of the Lamb of God (*Rev.* 17). Remarkably, this great battle occurs in the midst of a series of events in which God's just wrath is being poured out upon the nations, accompanied by such signs as famines, pestilence, earthquakes, and the like. The setting and meaning of this sign, therefore, fits well with this group of signs and relates to God's judgement prior to the end of the age.

Though this is the only instance in the New Testament where the battle of Armageddon is expressly mentioned, a number of passages in the book of Revelation speak of the war or the battle that will take place prior to the final victory of Christ and his people over their enemies (*Rev.* 17:14; 19:19; 20:8). This language is apocalyptic, describing end-time events in language drawn from earlier scriptural prophecies, and therefore ought not to be pressed too literally. But the language nonetheless underscores the present reality and future intensification of opposition to the Lord and his church, opposition whose futility and certain defeat is symbolised in the great victory to be won in this final battle. The battle of Armageddon fits well with the biblical teaching that opposition to his rule will intensify, but be definitively overcome in the day of the Lord's appearing.

It should not be overlooked that this theme of a great and final conflict echoes prophetic passages in the Old Testament. In Joel 3:2 we are told that when Jerusalem is restored, all the nations will be gathered together against it in the valley of Jehoshaphat. In Zechariah 14:2, the Lord declares that in the future he will gather all the nations to Jerusalem to fight against it. Similarly, Ezekiel 38 and 39 contain references to a great battle on the mountains of Israel in which Gog, chief prince of Meshech, will be defeated (passages to which allusion is made in *Rev.* 19:19 and 20:8). These passages intimate that the conclusion of God's redemptive working in history will be signalled by a great warfare between himself and his enemies, the end of which will be the latter's utter destruction.

Perhaps this helps to provide a context for the specific reference to this final battle of Armageddon. This may be a reference to Mount Megiddo, a site on the great plain of Esdraelon in Issachar, near the valley of Jezreel (see *Judg.* 5:19).

The battle of Armageddon may hark back to the great battle recorded in Judges 4 and 5, in which the Lord led his people to victory over her enemies. Mount Megiddo was a strategic military stronghold at which many important battles were fought in Israel's history (cf. *Judg.* 6:33; *1 Sam.* 31; *2 Sam.* 4:4; *2 Kings* 23:29-30; 9:27). In Judges 4 and 5, we are told that the people of God were oppressed by the Canaanite King, Jabin, and his general, Sisera. Israel was, humanly speaking, in an impossible position. How could she stand against nine hundred chariots of iron, when she did not even have a spear or a shield (*Judg.* 5:8)? And yet the Lord, through the judges Deborah and Barak, led his people in a marvellous victory over their enemies.

If we take these Old Testament antecedents into account, the meaning of the language of the battle of Armageddon in Revelation 17 becomes clearer. The battle of Armageddon is a reminder that as the end approaches, opposition to the gospel and the kingdom of Christ will intensify. This opposition will issue in a final battle, signifying the Lord's judgement upon the nations and the certain triumph of his cause in the earth. Even as things appear most hopeless for the people of the Lord, suddenly and dramatically Christ will come to his people in triumph to crush both his and their enemies under his feet.

It is fitting that we conclude our treatment of all the signs of the times, including this group signalling God's judgement in history upon his enemies, with the sign of the battle of Armageddon. For this sign confirms the one grand theme interwoven throughout the Scriptural teaching regarding the signs of the times: as the present age draws to a close, and as the antithesis intensifies, the certainty of God's redemptive purposes becomes all the more clear. Nothing, not even the combined opposition of the nations against the Lord's anointed and his people, will be able to prevent Christ's dominion from reaching its appointed end, the subjection of all things to him and the defeat of all his enemies, including the last enemy, death (*1 Cor.* 15).

6

THE FUTURE OF THE KINGDOM: FOUR MILLENNIAL VIEWS

*T*he title of a book by Stanley Grenz, *The Millennial Maze: Sorting Out Evangelical Options*, captures the difficulty of sorting out the differing views found among Christian believers on the subject of the millennium. The person attempting to make sense of these views faces a challenge not unlike a bewildering maze. Before beginning our treatment of these views, it will be helpful to consider briefly the meaning of the term 'millennium'. It will also be useful to recognise that among the maze of differing viewpoints, there are ultimately only two major types of millennial views. The four major millennial views normally considered are variations on one or other of these types.

'Millennium' is a Latin word, the equivalent of two Greek words used six times in Revelation 20:1-7, which mean 'a thousand years'. The thousand years in Revelation 20, clearly denotes a period in which Christ reigns subsequent to the binding of Satan. When we speak of various millennial views, therefore, we are referring to differing interpretations of this thousand-year period. Does it describe a future period in which Christ will reign upon the earth? Or does it describe the period between Christ's first and second advent? Will it be a literal one thousand years' period? Or are we to understand the millennium as a protracted period in history, when the reign and rule of Christ will be almost universally acknowledged by the nations and peoples of the earth?

In this chapter, we will summarize and evaluate the four represent-ative millennial views. The simplest way of identifying and classifying mil-lennial views is in relation to Christ's return. All the millennial views place the millennium either before or after the second coming of Christ. Con-sequently, there are two major types of millennial positions: those that are postmillennial (Christ comes after the millennium) or premillennial (Christ comes before the millennium). Premillennialism has two primary versions: Historic Premillennialism and Dispensational Premillennial-ism. Postmillennialism also has two primary versions: golden age Postmil-lennialism and Amillennialism.

HISTORIC PREMILLENNIALISM

Historic Premillennialism has had adherents throughout the history of the Christian church. Some defenders of Premillennialism argue that it has been the predominant view of the Christian church throughout the centuries. Though this is an overstatement, a number of church Fathers advocated a form of premillennial teaching.

When Saint Augustine adopted a view of the millennium as the present age of the church and gospel proclamation, the influence of Premillennialism began to wane. There was a resurgence of interest in a premillennialist view during the Protestant Reformation among the Ana-baptists, but most of the churches of the Reformation rejected Premillen-nialism. Even the Reformed tradition, however, has had notable advo-cates of premillennialist teaching.

Although Premillennialism has not been the predominant view of the church throughout its history or the view of the Reformed churches, it enjoyed a renewed popularity in the nineteenth and twentieth cent-uries, largely in the form of Dispensationalist Premillennialism, and has become the prevalent viewpoint among conservative Protestants today.

Premillennialism insists that the return of Christ will introduce a mil-lennial period during which Christ will be bodily present upon the earth for an extended period of time (commonly one thousand years). Reigning over the nations from the earthly seat of his kingdom in Jerusalem, Christ will usher in a period of peace and prosperity in which the earth and its inhabitants will enjoy unprecedented blessedness.

Another feature that stands out in Historic Premillennialism is its insistence that the return of Christ will come suddenly and cataclysmically, after a period of intensified opposition to the people of God. Tribulation, apostasy among the people of God, the coming of the Antichrist—these events will immediately precede Christ's return. For this reason, Historic Premillennialism is often referred to as post-tribulationalism, in distinction from the pre-tribulationalism that is commonly a feature of Dispensational Premillennialism.

Although Historic Premillennialism teaches that there is ultimately only one people of God, the church, comprised of Jewish and Gentile believers alike, it reserves a special place in God's kingdom for the Jewish nation and people. When Christ returns and the millennium commences, national Israel will experience a corporate conversion and receive a place of special prominence in the millennial kingdom. Though historic premillennialists reject many of the tenets of Dispensationalism—for example, that the sacrificial system will be reintroduced in Israel—they do maintain that the majority of Jewish people will be converted and find many of the special promises of God's word for them fulfilled in this period of the millennium.

One further feature of Historic Premillennialism is its insistence on two separate bodily resurrections, one occurring at the beginning and the other at the end of the millennium. Premillennialists appeal to Revelation 20 in defence of the view that believers will enjoy the first resurrection, to reign with Christ upon the earth during the millennium, and unbelievers will be raised in the second resurrection, to be judged and receive their just punishment in hell, which is the second death.

Premillennialists also appeal to Revelation 20 to support their view of the millennium. The language of this passage is interpreted to describe a millennial period during which the kingdom of Christ will be openly manifest and triumphant upon the earth. A straightforward reading of this text, it is claimed, leaves no other interpretation than this view of the millennial reign of Christ, and it also fits well with the understanding of a favourable future for the people of Israel. Another passage Premillennialists appeal to is 1 Corinthians 15:23-26:

> But now Christ has been raised from the dead, the first fruits of those who are asleep. For since by man came death, by a man also came the resurrection of the dead. For as in Adam all die, so also in Christ all shall be made alive. But each in his own order: Christ the first fruits, after that those who are Christ's at his coming, then comes the end, when he delivers up the kingdom to the God and Father, when he has abolished all rule and all authority and power. For he must reign until he has put all his enemies under his feet. The last enemy that will be abolished is death.

In this passage, premillennialists argue, we are taught that history has three distinguishable stages. The first is the age of the Christian church, during which Christ's reign is largely hidden. The second is the age of the millennium, during which Christ's reign is manifest. And the third is the age of the eternal kingdom when the kingdom reverts to God the Father.

Though premillennialists admit that the temporal sequence of these stages is not explicitly revealed in this passage, they claim that it is implicit. They believe the sequence of events in 1 Corinthians 15—Christ's resurrection, at his coming the resurrection of believers, at the end the turning over of all things to the Father—confirms the sequence of events in Revelation 20.

Historic Premillennialism, which has had advocates throughout Christian history, teaches that signs of opposition will intensify as Christ's return approaches. The age of the church will close with the coming of the Antichrist and great tribulation. However, Christ will suddenly come from heaven and utterly vanquish Satan, binding him for a period of one thousand years. During this period Christ will reign on earth with his saints, prominent among whom will be many Jewish people converted in the last days. This millennial period will be one of tremendous blessing, righteousness, and prosperity on the earth; however, it will close with a 'little season' of Satanic rebellion that Christ will put down. The rest of the dead, the unbelieving, will then be raised to be judged, and then the end will come with the inauguration of the eternal kingdom of God.

Dispensational Premillennialism

Unlike Historic Premillennialism, Dispensational Premillennialism is a newcomer to the millennial debate, beginning around 1825 with John Nelson Darby, a clergyman in the Church of England. Darby originated a meeting in Plymouth, England, giving rise to the name Plymouth Brethren. Darby was an influential Bible teacher and introduced many of the features of what would become Dispensationalism.

Though a number of influential ministers and Bible teachers followed Darby's interpretation of the Bible, the most important for the growth of Dispensationalism was Cyrus I. Scofield, a Congregationalist minister in the United States. Although Scofield's training was in law and not in theology, he prepared his own study Bible, known popularly as the *Scofield Reference Bible*. First published in 1909, it became the single most effective means in spreading dispensationalist teaching.

In addition to the influence of Darby and Scofield, the emergence of a number of fundamentalist Bible institutes in the early twentieth century greatly contributed to the spread of Dispensationalism. Many of the founders of these institutes opposed the liberalism of mainline church institutions and embraced a dispensational reading of the Bible, fortified by the conviction that alternative views came from an unbelieving approach to the Scriptures. Despite the recent development of Dispensational Premillennialism and some evidence of its waning popularity, it remains the majority opinion among many conservative Christians, especially in North America.

It is difficult to summarise the main features of Dispensationalism since there are so many varieties and since it has been modified in recent years. Some primary features, however, distinguish it as a particular view.

The term 'dispensation' derives from a biblical term from which we get the word 'economy' (see *Eph.* 1:10; 3:2; *Col.* 1:25), and refers originally to the manner in which a household is administered. In Dispensationalism, this term is used to describe the various arrangements in the history of redemption by which God regulates man's relationship with himself. Though dispensationalists debate the precise number and significance of these different dispensations, the most common position distinguishes seven dispensations or economies: the dispensation of innocence (from creation until humankind's expulsion from the garden of Eden); the dispensation of human conscience (from humankind's expulsion until the great flood); the dispensation of human government (from the time of the flood until the calling of Abraham); the dispensation of promise (from the call of Abraham until the giving of the law at Sinai); the dispensation of the law (from the time of Sinai until the crucifixion of Christ); the dispensation of the church (from the cross of Christ until his coming for his saints); and the dispensation of the kingdom (the millennium when Christ reigns over restored Israel on David's throne in Jerusalem for one thousand years). Each successive dispensation furthers God's purposes in a distinct manner to a particular people.

One question that arises in connection with the distinguishing of these various dispensations is whether there is one way of salvation during these different periods. Though the implication of the original definition of a dispensation—and the popular form in which Dispensationalism is often taught and believed—seems to be that there are several ways of salvation, official statements today typically deny this conclusion. There is also a tendency in recent expositions of Dispensationalism to modify the earlier division of the economy of redemption into distinct administrations.

Within the broad framework of this dispensational view of history, Dispensationalism insists upon the uniqueness of the church, especially its distinction from Israel and God's dealings with Israel before and after the dispensation of the church.

In its earliest expression, this view argued that Christ began his ministry upon earth after his first coming by preaching the gospel of the kingdom, offering to restore the fortunes of national Israel and assume the throne of David in Jerusalem. However, when the Jewish people of his day rejected him, the establishment of the kingdom of heaven was postponed and God commenced the dispensation of the church. This accounts for the description of the church dispensation as a parenthesis or intercalation in the course of redemptive history, a dispensation during which God's peculiar dealings and purposes for Israel have been suspended.

With the suspension of God's dealings with his earthly people, Israel, there is revealed, after the crucifixion and resurrection of Christ, what is often termed the mystery phase of the kingdom of God. This mystery phase unveils the peculiar purposes of God to gather a predominantly Gentile people, the church, through the proclamation of the gospel to the nations. This is the mystery of the gospel taught in a passage like Colossians 1:25-27. Though hidden from his people throughout all preceding dispensations, God has now made it known through the gospel that he has a heavenly people, the church, alongside his earthly people, Israel. This mystery phase of the kingdom of God coincides with the period between the sixty-ninth and seventieth weeks of Daniel 9:24-29, the period from Pentecost, the birth of the New Testament Gentile church, and the rapture of the saints at Christ's coming.

This significant feature of Dispensationalism, the sharp separation between God's earthly people and his heavenly people, informs an all-embracing method of reading and understanding the Bible.

According to Dispensationalism, the prophecies and promises of the Old Testament regarding Israel do not find their fulfilment in the dispensation of the church, but in the dispensation of the kingdom or millennium yet to come. Prophecies and promises dealing with earthly blessings (a new Jerusalem, a restored Davidic kingdom and throne, universal peace among the nations, economic and material blessing, the restoration of Israel to the land of promise) are interpreted literally. And since they have not and cannot be literally fulfilled in the present dispensation of the church, they must await their fulfilment when God's purposes for Israel recommence. Because the earthly, national, and political aspects of God's promises to Israel were not fulfilled at Christ's first coming—when his own people rejected him—they await their fulfilment during the dispensation of the millennium.

This insistence upon a literal hermeneutic or manner of reading the Bible's promises in the Old Testament is one of the most distinctive features of Dispensationalism and its approach to the interpretation of the Scriptures. If the Old Testament promises a rebuilt temple (*Ezek.*), the temple in Jerusalem must be rebuilt. If the Old Testament promises that David's Son will sit upon his throne (*2 Sam.*), this throne must be located in a literal Jerusalem still to come. If the Old Testament speaks of a renewed creation in which prosperity and peace will be enjoyed (*Isa.*), then this must be fulfilled during a literal, earthly period of Christ's reign upon this earth. It is simply inadequate to interpret these promises as having been or being fulfilled in the present age. Were that the case, so Dispensationalism argues, the language of Scripture would no longer be reliable.

The only solution is to treat the Old Testament prophecies and promises as directed to a future age in which God's purposes for his earthly people will be realised in history, the dispensation of the millennium. The fact that God's dealings with the church do not fulfil Old Testament expectation confirms that they are part of the mystery phase of the kingdom, which God had purposefully concealed from his Old Testament people, Israel.

If God's dealings with the church are a parenthesis or interruption of his dealings with Israel, the obvious question for dispensationalists is: How is it anticipated that God will resume his dealings with Israel in the future?

The dispensationalist argues that the church dispensation will be concluded at the time of the rapture, or Christ's coming for his saints. A distinction is often made between this rapture, in which Christ will come 'for' his saints, and a return seven years later, in which Christ will come 'with' his saints.

Most dispensationalists believe that the rapture referred to in 1 Thessalonians 4:17 will occur before the period of great tribulation, a view known as pre-tribulational rapturism. At the rapture, resurrected believers and transformed believers will be caught up with Christ in the clouds to meet him in the air. The raptured church will go with Christ to heaven to celebrate the seven years of the marriage feast of the lamb. Meanwhile, the seventieth week of Daniel 9 will commence on earth. This will be a period of tribulation on the earth, the latter half of great tribulation during the reign of the Antichrist. This great tribulation will witness the conversion of the elect Jews and conclude with Christ's final triumph at the Battle of Armageddon. The devil will be bound and cast into the abyss for a literal period of one thousand years.

As with Historic Premillennialism, Dispensationalism believes that the millennium will begin with the first of at least two resurrections, the resurrection of saints who died during the seven-year period of tribulation and the remaining Old Testament saints. These saints, together with the raptured church, will live and reign in heaven, while the Jewish saints on earth will begin to reign with Christ from Jerusalem for a period of one thousand years during a golden age of peace and prosperity. Two judgements will also occur at this time: the judgement of the Gentiles who persecuted the people of God during the seven-year period of tribulation (cf. *Matt.* 25:31-46) and the judgement upon Israel (cf. *Ezek.* 20:33-38). All believers, the church and Israel, will then enter into the final state, when the heavenly Jerusalem descends to the earth.

A contemporary movement within Dispensationalism known as 'progressive Dispensationalism' has introduced considerable modifications into the older, more classical form of Dispensationalism.

First, Progressive Dispensationalism argues that ultimately God's redemptive purposes bestow the same redemptive blessings upon the whole people of God, Gentile as well as Jew. Without rejecting the distinction between the dispensation of the church and the earthly kingdom or millennium, Progressive Dispensationalism denies that the dispensation of the church is an interruption in the course of redemptive history. In fact, the spiritual blessings of salvation granted to the church will be the portion of the entire people of God in the final state. There will not be a separation between an elite class of Jews, whose salvation is upon the earth, and a secondary class of Jews and Gentiles, whose salvation is in heaven. All the purposes and blessings of salvation, spiritual and material, will terminate upon one people of God.

Second, Progressive Dispensationalism, as its name suggests, emphasises the continuity of redemptive history. Though progressive dispensationalists still distinguish the various economies, they acknowledge that these economies represent the historical realisation of one kingdom purpose; the differences between the various covenants do not mitigate a genuine covenantal unity throughout the Scriptures.

Third, Progressive Dispensationalism has modified the older Dispensationalism's view of the Old Testament promises and their fulfilment. Rather than insisting upon the literal and exclusive fulfilment of these promises during the millennium, Progressive Dispensationalism allows the fulfilment of these promises to occur in progressive stages. Many promises, for example, of the Old Testament are fulfilled not only at one level during the dispensation of the church, but also find a further and related fulfilment in the dispensation of the millennial kingdom.

Fourth, and perhaps most decisively, Progressive Dispensationalism rejects the radical separation between two peoples and two purposes of God in the history of redemption. Ultimately, God has but one people, comprising Jew and Gentile alike, and one plan of salvation.

In many ways Progressive Dispensationalism represents a departure from the classic form of Dispensationalism and a return to Historic Premillennialism. It is hard to find any substantial difference between this modification of Dispensationalism and its older cousin, classical Premillennialism. This does not mean, however, that the older Dispensationalism has been abandoned or no longer has any viability. The advocacy of Progressive Dispensationalism has been largely an academic pursuit among scholars. The older Dispensationalism, only slightly modified, remains alive for many believers and their churches; however, such a substantial revision within the ranks of dispensationalists themselves may not bode well for the future vitality of the older Dispensationalism.

Postmillennialism

In our introduction to the subject of the millennium, we noted that the primary difference in millennial positions lies between a premillennial and a postmillennial conception of the return of Christ. It should be observed that the terms 'Postmillennialism' and 'Amillennialism', which are commonly used today, are of rather recent vintage. The term 'Postmillennialism' has until recently been used to describe all forms of the view that Christ's coming will follow the millennium, including those views which today are distinguished as postmillennialist and amillennialist. Though the differences between postmillennial and amillennial views have long existed in the history of the church, they were not until recently explicitly described with these terms.

As recently as the first half of the twentieth century, the term 'Postmillennialism' was still being used in a general way. Until about 1930, all those who rejected a premillennialist view were considered postmillennialists.

Some authors maintain that Postmillennialism has been the predominant eschatological position of the Christian church; others more cautiously maintain only that it has been a continuing and significant position in the Reformed tradition. It is undoubtedly true that the Reformed tradition has witnessed the most significant expressions of postmillennialist thought. John Calvin gave expression to some ideas that received greater emphasis in later Presbyterian and Puritan writers, who were more evidently postmillennialist in outlook.

Frequently, the beginnings of modern forms of Postmillennialism are associated with the name of Daniel Whitby, an Anglican, who published his *Paraphrase and Commentary on the New Testament* in 1703. However, even before the publication of this treatise, a number of Puritan writers were advocating a postmillennialist point of view. It is generally agreed that the *Savoy Declaration* of 1658, which modified the *Westminster Confession of Faith* for the congregational churches, gave expression to a postmillennialist outlook.

Perhaps the greatest flourishing of Postmillennialism occurred in North America, first in the writing and preaching of Jonathan Edwards and then in

101

the nineteenth and early twentieth centuries, when it was a dominant viewpoint in the influential Princeton tradition. Though especially prominent among many conservative Presbyterian theologians during this period, other influential writers held a basically postmillennialist view as well.

The twentieth century has seen a substantial decline in the influence of Postmillennialism. Some postmillennialist authors (J. Marcellus Kik, John Jefferson Davis, and Iain H. Murray) have continued to articulate traditional Postmillennialism; however, many recent advocates of Postmillennialism have been 'reconstructionists' or 'theonomists' (Rousas J. Rushdoony, Greg Bahnsen, Gary North, David Chilton, and Ken Gentry). Perhaps due to the rather controversial nature of the reconstructionist movement, Postmillennialism is today frequently regarded as a fringe position, despite its having enjoyed considerable support among able and conservative Reformed writers for many centuries.

Since the dispute regarding the predominance of Postmillennialism in the Christian tradition depends so much upon the definition of Postmillennialism that is being used, it is vitally important to come to a clear understanding of this position and its main features.

The most obvious feature of all postmillennialist positions is the insistence that in the period of history prior to the return of Christ, the preaching of the gospel will triumph on the earth and bring about the conversion of the nations.

Many postmillennialists distinguish this triumph of the gospel from the optimism of the old 'social gospel' teaching of liberalism in the nineteenth and early twentieth centuries, as well as the theory of historical progress often associated with evolutionism. The growth of the church will be through spiritual means, the preaching of the gospel in the power of the Spirit of Pentecost, and not by worldly strategies.

With the triumphant spread of the gospel and the conversion of the nations, a golden age will emerge in history prior to the return of Christ. Though sin will still be present and this millennium will not be a period of absolute perfection and righteousness, it will be a time during which the standards and precepts of the gospel and the word of God will prevail on the earth and among the nations.

Among postmillennialists, differences regarding this golden age exist. Some interpret 'one thousand years' more literally than others, though most take it in a symbolic sense to refer to a period of long duration within the purpose and will of God. Some anticipate that this golden age will emerge almost imperceptibly as the gospel progresses and the church grows among the nations. Others believe that the introduction of this golden age will occur suddenly. Though Postmillennialism historically regarded this golden age as a period in the future, some recent postmillennialists have suggested that it is coterminous with the period of time that began with the destruction of Jerusalem in A.D. 70.

Allowing for some divergence among advocates of Postmillennialism, the general sequence of events is as follows: the gospel progressively advances and the nations are converted, whereupon the millennium commences; at the close of this millennial age, Satan is released for a 'little season' of rebellion, only to be defeated decisively by Christ at his second coming; Christ's return will coincide with the general resurrection of the righteous and the unrighteous and the final judgement; and, with the conclusion of the final judgement, the final state will commence, in which the wicked will be consigned to hell and the righteous will enter everlasting life in the new heavens and earth.

Though this sequence bears considerable resemblance to that of Amillennialism, the significant difference is the relegation of many of the signs of the times to the period before the millennium. Differences of viewpoint exist among postmillennialists, however, some of whom acknowledge these signs re-emerging during Satan's little season after the millennial age.

One less obvious feature of Postmillennialism relates to the conversion of the Jews. Though most postmillennialists expect the large-scale conversion of the Jewish people, some who affirm this expectation do not advocate postmillennialism. Consequently, though the teaching of the conversion of the Jews prior to the return of Christ may be a tell-tale evidence of Postmillennialism, it is not a sufficient condition for identifying someone as a postmillennialist.

Historic representatives of Postmillennialism have taken the position that the Bible teaches (especially in *Rom.* 11:11-32) that most of the Jewish people will be converted through the preaching of the gospel prior to Christ's return. This conversion will be a distinctive feature of the millennial age, though it will not occur in the same way as it is understood in premillennialist views (especially the dispensationalist view). Postmillennialism rejects the sharp lines of distinction drawn between Jew and Gentile in most forms of Premillennialism.

The advocates of Postmillennialism often insist that the triumph of the gospel and the emergence of the millennium at some point in history prior to Christ's return are necessary implications of Christ's universal dominion as king. Christ's reign at the Father's right hand must come to visible expression on the earth prior to his return. Since the other millennial views do not confidently see the prospects for the gospel and the church in this present age, they really amount to a denial of Christ's present dominion.

A recent form of Postmillennialism has given a peculiar expression to this view of Christ's dominion. Within the Reformed—especially conservative Presbyterian—tradition, a movement has developed which is called variously Christian reconstructionism, dominion theology, or theonomy. Though not all present-day postmillennialists are reconstructionists, all reconstructionists are postmillennialists.

According to the chief representatives of this movement, the dominion of Christ will come to expression in the reconstruction of society along biblical norms. Christ's millennial reign in history requires that Christian believers seek to bring all aspects of life—economic, social, and political as well as ecclesiastical and familial—under the lordship of Jesus Christ. The terminology of 'theonomy' is used to insist that the biblical laws, including the Old Testament case laws and their prescribed capital punishments for various offences be applied in exhaustive detail by governments today. The laws for the governance of Israel, including the judicial laws, should also be the standard for governments and their judicial instruments today.

When critics of Postmillennialism point out the decline of the church and the increase of secularism, postmillennialists are frequently unimpressed.

They rightly argue that the debate is fundamentally about the teaching of the word of God.

If this is the case, what biblical reasons are most often cited in support of Postmillennialism?

One of the most common arguments for Postmillennialism is the biblical promise of universal covenant blessing. It is noted that, when the Lord covenanted with Abraham, he promised that in him all families will be blessed. The number of Abraham's descendants was promised to be as innumerable as the dust of the earth (*Gen.* 13:16; cf. *Gen.* 15:5, 6; 17:6; 22:17-18; *Num.* 23:10). When Christ gave the Great Commission to his disciples, he mandated that they make disciples of all the nations (*Matt.* 28:18-20). Christ himself, when asked whether few would be saved, confidently asserted that 'they will come from north, south, east and west' (*Luke* 13:29). Reading these and other passages, especially those that speak of the surprising growth of the kingdom (*Matt.* 13:31-33), postmillennialists insist that the biblical picture is one of a vast multitude who will be saved. Rather than suggesting a meagre, insignificant response to the gospel, these passages encourage an expectation of assured and amazing results.

These promises of a great ingathering of the nations into the kingdom of God are correlated, in the view of many postmillennialists, with the biblical understanding of the present authority and dominion of Jesus Christ. In the Messianic Psalms (e.g., *Psa.* 2; 22; 45; 67; 72; 110), the prophecies of Isaiah (e.g., *Isa.* 2:2-4; 9:6-7; 11:6, 9-10; 40:4-5; 49:6), and the New Testament descriptions of Christ's authority, we are presented with a picture of Christ the King who reigns in the midst of history, overcoming his enemies and subjecting all things under his feet (*1 Cor.* 15:25).

According to many postmillennialist authors, the biblical descriptions of Christ's present lordship are adequately appreciated only within the framework of Postmillennialism. If Christ is the reigning Lord, if he has been given all authority in heaven and on earth, if the nations are his by right of inheritance, if the power and works of the devil have been broken and defeated by his cross, resurrection, and ascension—then Postmillennialism is the only biblical view anticipates the success of Christ's church-gathering and kingdom-building work in history. The problem with alternative views, according to the postmillennialist, is that they spiritualise the concreteness of the biblical understanding of Christ's kingdom or relegate to the final state what is expected in the period of history prior to Christ's return.

One of the key arguments for Postmillennialism is the insistence that many signs of the times will be fulfilled prior to the establishment of the millennial kingdom in the present age. Though views differ regarding whether these signs of the times have already been fulfilled either in part or in whole, postmillennialists generally regard these signs to be virtually absent during the period of the millennium.

In Matthew 24, the passage that most comprehensively describes the signs of the times, postmillennialists typically find a description of those signs present before the destruction of Jerusalem in A.D. 70. The great tribulation and associated signs of opposition to Christ's kingdom will precede Christ's coming to establish his millennial kingdom. This understanding is often termed a preterist interpretation.

Though postmillennialists do not necessarily regard the millennium to be a literal period of one thousand years, most take the binding of Satan to be a description of his complete defeat and the introduction of a period in which his activity is not merely curtailed, but completely terminated.

Postmillennialism teaches that the millennium will occur before the return of Christ, when the cause of Christ and the gospel will prevail on the earth. A great period of time (a literal period of a thousand years or an indefinite period of many centuries) will see unparalleled righteousness, peace, and prosperity. Christian believers who live out Christ's lordship will populate the nations. Governments will govern in accord with the word of God. Though it has become more common among contemporary postmillennialists to maintain that the millennium roughly coincides with the entire Christian era, at least the period subsequent to the destruction of Jerusalem, the historic postmillennialist view regards the millennium as a future period.

106

Amillennialism

Since the term 'amillennial' literally means 'no millennium', it appears that Amillennialism rejects the idea of a millennium altogether, which is not the case. The term has been coined because this view rejects the specific millennial periods of the other major millennial views. Unlike both Premillennialism and Postmillennialism, it does not look for a golden-age millennium either before or after the return of Christ. Amillennialism regards the entire period of history between Christ's first and second coming as the period of the millennium. Because it rejects the idea of a distinguishable golden age at some point after early church history, this view has been given the name Amillennialism. In order to prevent misunderstanding of this view, some have suggested alternative terminology. However, and it is highly unlikely suggested alternatives will displace the traditional term.

Amillennialism has a long history of advocacy going back to the beginning of the Christian era. Since the fourth and fifth centuries, it has been the predominant position within the Christian church. Though Premillennialism has had its advocates throughout the history of the church and has enjoyed recent resurgence among conservative evangelicals in North America, it is safe to say that Amillennialism has been the consensus position of the largest portion of the Christian church.

It is generally agreed that Augustine was instrumental in establishing this as the predominant view. By treating the millennium of Revelation 20 as a symbolical description of the church's growth in the present age, Augustine gave impetus to the amillennialist contention that the millennium does not follow chronologically the early history of the New Testament church. With the exception of some exponents of Premillennialism, the tenets of amillennialist teaching prevailed throughout the Middle Ages and during the Reformation. The Reformers were aligned with this broad tradition, though soon after the Reformation advocates of Postmillennialism arose within the Reformed tradition.

However strong the influence of Postmillennialism may have been within the Reformed churches, especially in North America during the eighteenth and nineteenth centuries, the predominant view among Reformed churches today is Amillennialism.

Perhaps the most important way to distinguish Amillennialism from the other millennial views is to note that it teaches the present reality of the millennial kingdom. Amillennialism regards the millennium of Revelation 20 to be a symbolical representation of the present reign of Christ with his saints. During the period of time between Christ's first advent and his return at the end of the age, Satan has been bound in order to no longer deceive the nations. The millennium is not a literal period of one thousand years, but represents the complete period during which God has granted Christ the authority to receive the nations as his inheritance (see *Psa.* 2; *Matt.* 28:16-20).

Though opinions vary among amillennialists as to the nature of the millennium—some are more pessimistic and others more optimistic—amillennialists typically reject the postmillennialist conviction that the millennium will be a period of universal peace, the dominion of biblical principles in all aspects of life, and the subjection of the vast majority of the nations to Christ's lordship. Amillennialists believe that the biblical descriptions of the inter-advental period suggest that the world's opposition to Christ and the gospel will become more intense as history draws to a close.

Amillennialism commonly understands that the signs of the times are both present and future realities. The entire period between the ascension of Christ and his return at the end of the present age will see an ongoing conflict, sometimes more and sometimes less intense, between the church and the world, the kingdom of God and the kingdom of the evil one. Though there may be periods of peace for the church in different places at different times, there will never be a millennial period in which suffering will no longer be experienced by the church of Jesus Christ.

Most amillennialists read Revelation 20 as a passage which, in parallel with several sections of Revelation, describes a vision sequence that covers the entire period from Christ's first to his second coming. Unlike many postmillennialists who read Revelation 19 and 20 in chronological succession, amillennialists view the vision of the millennium as a symbolic portrayal of the period of the church's mission in the world. The binding of Satan is a picture of the restraint God has placed upon Satan, preventing him from deceiving the nations, and of the certainty of the church's success in discipling them.

Though opinions differ among amillennialists regarding the 'first resurrection' and the 'coming to life' of the saints who reign with Christ, most understand the first resurrection to be a spiritual one in which all believers participate, particularly the martyred and deceased saints who reign with Christ in heaven. By virtue of this first resurrection, believers are no longer subject to death and share in Christ's reign over all things. Only at the end of the period of Christ's gathering his church will he return, the dead be raised, and the resurrection of the body (the second resurrection) occur. Thus, Revelation 20 does not describe an earthly golden age in the postmillennialist sense, but the progress of Christ's kingdom upon the earth, as the gospel is preached to the nations and believers (especially those who are deceased—even martyred for the faith) reign with Christ in the expectation of his triumph at the end of the age.

Another distinctive feature of Amillennialism is its insistence that the great hope of the Christian for the future is the return of Christ at the end of the age. Though postmillennialists would regard Christ's return to be the final, consummating event at the end of this present age, they tend to deflect attention from this event to the expectation of a future millennial age. Amillennialists, on the other hand, anticipate that the victory of Christ and the triumph of his kingdom will occur only when Christ returns.

Often postmillennialists decry the amillennialist pessimism about the prospects of Christ's kingdom in this present age. Conversely, amillennialists criticise postmillennialists for being unjustifiably optimistic. Amillennialists are said to be too other-worldly in their expectations for the future; postmillennialists are said to be too this-worldly in their expectations.

One of the ways in which Postmillennialism and Amillennialism may be distinguished is that Amillennialism has a clearer expectation of the imminence (the 'soon-ness') of Christ's return than does Postmillennialism. Postmillennialism regards the return of Christ to be a distant reality, one whose fulfilment can only follow upon the millennium or golden age to come.

It is evident that Amillennialism is a form of postmillennialist teaching without the literal millennium of classic Postmillennialism. Amillennialism regards the millennium as the entire period of history between Christ's resurrection and ascension and his coming again. The amillennialist expects a continuing history of growth as well as struggle, of advance as well as of temporary retrenchment, for the church of Jesus Christ in this present age. Only at the end of the age, with the return of Christ in glory and power, will every enemy be subdued and Christ's reign be openly acknowledged in all the earth.

Having surveyed each of the four major millennial views, we must now evaluate them by the standard of the Scriptures.

7

THE FUTURE OF THE KINGDOM: REVELATION 20

*N*o biblical treatment of the subject of the millennium can avoid addressing the teaching of Revelation 20:1-11, especially verses 1-6. This is the one passage in the Bible that explicitly speaks of the millennium, six times using an expression that literally means a 'thousand years'. Because premillennialists are convinced that Revelation 20 is a definitive passage clearly teaching the millennial reign of Christ after his second coming, it will be helpful to give special attention to this passage before offering a general evaluation of the distinct millennial views.

THE PREMILLENNIALIST INTERPRETATION

We will begin with a summary of how this vision has been traditionally understood by premillennialists, and then examine the relation between Revelation 19 and 20. After dealing with these preliminary matters, we will consider the most important aspects of Revelation 20: the description of the binding of Satan (1-3), and the reference to a first resurrection of believing saints in distinction from an apparent second resurrection of the unbelieving (4-6).

In the premillennialist view, the sequence of visions in Revelation 19 and 20 should be read chronologically. It is as though John were saying, 'first this will occur . . . then this . . . then this.'

Most who hold this view regard Revelation 19:11-21 as a description of the second coming of Christ and his victory over all his enemies. There are several reasons for holding this view.

In the vision of Revelation 19:11-16, Christ is described as the divine warrior who comes to vanquish all his enemies. Riding a white horse, he comes to judge and wage war in righteousness (verse 11). His name is called 'The Word of God' (verse 13) and on his robe and thigh are written, 'King of Kings, and Lord of Lords' (verse 16). The weapon he uses to defeat the nations is a sharp sword protruding from his mouth (verse 15). The language seems to describe the return of Christ at the end of the age, when he will destroy both his and his people's enemies (see *2 Thess.* 1:6-10). Christ will win this victory, not with the armies of this world, but with the word of God that is 'living and active, sharper than any two-edged sword' (*Heb.* 4:12).

That this vision depicts the return of Christ is suggested further by the references in Revelation 19 to the marriage supper of the Lamb (19:7-10) and the defeat of the beast and the false prophet (19:17-21). The marriage supper symbolises the full and intimate communion between Christ, the Lamb, and his blood-bought bride, the church. The destruction of the beast and the false prophet represents the destruction of the Antichrist, whose person and work were earlier described in Revelation 13 and 17. Within the context of the visions of Revelation, it seems apparent that Revelation 19:11-21 constitutes a symbolic depiction of the second coming of Christ.

If Revelation 19 is a description of the return of Christ, then it is obvious why so much depends upon the relation between its vision and that of Revelation 20. If the vision of Revelation 20 follows the vision of Revelation 19, it seems natural to regard the return of Christ as being followed by the millennium of Revelation 20.

In Revelation 20:1-6, repeated reference is made to a period of one thousand years that commences with the binding of Satan. According to the premillennialist, this can be nothing less than a literal millennium, during which Satan is completely bound and prevented from exercising any deceptive influence among the nations.

Perhaps the most vital part of the premillennialist argument from Revelation 20, however, is the reference to a first resurrection. In verses 4-6, the first resurrection is described as follows:

> And I saw thrones, and they sat upon them, and judgement was given to them. And I saw the souls of those who had been beheaded because of the testimony of Jesus and because of the word of God, and those who had not worshipped the beast or his image, and had not received the mark upon their forehead and upon their hand; and they came to life and reigned with Christ for a thousand years. The rest of the dead did not come to life until the thousand years were completed. This is the first resurrection. Blessed and holy is the one who has a part in the first resurrection; over these the second death has no power, but they will be priests of God and of Christ and will reign with him for a thousand years.

For premillennialists, only believing saints come to life in this way and participate in the first resurrection. By contrast, the rest of the dead remain in the grave and do not come to life until the thousand years are completed, only to be cast forever into the lake of fire with the beast and the false prophet (verses 13-15). Since a close parallel is suggested between those who come to life in the first resurrection, and those who come to life in the second resurrection, the premillennialist reading takes both resurrections to be bodily resurrections, the one of believing saints before the millennium, the other of the unbelieving after the millennium.

If Revelation 19 is a vision of the second coming of Christ at the end of the present age, and if Revelation 20 describes events which occur after this event, then the primary claim of Premillennialism—that the millennium will commence after the return of Christ—would seem established.

THE RELATION BETWEEN REVELATION 19 AND 20

Though the premillennial claim on this point has an initial plausibility, there are several reasons—some more significant than others—why these passages should be read as parallel descriptions of the same time period. A careful study of these visions within the setting of the book of Revelation as a whole suggests that they describe the same period of history, but from differing vantage points.

The book of Revelation is structured according to a series of visions, several of which repeat or recapitulate events and periods of history covered in preceding or following visions. Each of these visions covers events that occur within the period between Christ's first and second coming. The visions overlap a great deal, and often jump from one set of events to another. Most interpreters agree that the book of Revelation should not be read as a historical novel, a preview of upcoming events listed in their order of occurrence.

William Hendriksen, in his overview of the book of Revelation, concludes that its structure is 'progressive parallelism'. He notes that the book can be divided into seven distinct sections, the first three sections describing events between Christ's first and second comings as they transpire upon the earth, the second four sections describing events between Christ's first and second comings as they transpire in heaven.

According to Hendriksen, the seven sections of the book of Revelation should be read as parallel descriptions of the period between the first and the second coming of Christ. They parallel and often re-capitulate events earlier described in preceding visions. As the book of Revelation proceeds, it progressively emphasises events that lie upon the furthest horizon of history. The book concludes with a grand vision of the state of consummation, the new heavens and the new earth.

Hendriksen's analysis of the structure of Revelation illustrates a commonly acknowledged feature of the book: it should not be read as a linear description of end-time events. The simple fact that one vision follows another vision in the book does not mean that it does so chronologically.

The visions of Revelation 19 and 20 need not be read as though they depicted events in sequence. If other clues in the text suggest that these visions are parallel or recapitulatory, then there is no reason to insist that they are in chronological order. Several features of the visions of Revelation 19 and 20 corroborate the thesis that they should be read not in sequence, but parallel to each other.

At least six such features are of particular significance.

1. The theme of angelic ascent and descent.

The vision of Revelation 20 begins with the descent of an angel from heaven in order to bind Satan for a period of one thousand years. In other instances in the book of Revelation where an angel's ascent or descent begins a new vision sequence, the vision portrays the course of events from the present time to the time of Christ's return at the end of the age (*Rev.* 7:2; 10:1; 18:1). The angel's descent in Revelation 20 would not only be consistent with the structure of the book, but it would also follow the pattern in which vision sequences that parallel each other are introduced by the announcement of an ascending or descending angel.

2. The discrepancy between Revelation 19:11-21 and Revelation 20:1-3.

The visions of Revelation 19 and Revelation 20 show an obvious discrepancy if they are read in chronological sequence. In Revelation 19:11-21, especially verses 19-21, Christ's victory over the nations is final. However, if the vision of Revelation 20 follows in time and sequence the vision of Revelation 19, it seems senseless to speak of the binding of Satan in order to prevent his deception of the nations. Premillennialists who recognise this discrepancy might suggest that the nations of Revelation 20 are survivors of the battle described in Revelation 19. But the language of the nations' defeat in Revelation 19 is too absolute to allow for the notion that some nations survive unscathed. Also, the terminology of 'the nations' in Revelation typically denotes nations in rebellion against the Lord's anointed. With the premillennialist construction, the nations of Revelation 20 would have a different reference from the nations mentioned in Revelation 19.

3. The use of Ezekiel 38-39 in these visions.

There are several striking parallels between Ezekiel 38-39 and Revelation 19 and 20. In Revelation 19:17-18, an angel issues an invitation to the great supper of God. This is almost an exact quotation of the invitation extended for the Gog-Magog conflict in the prophecy of Ezekiel (39:17-20). In Revelation 20:7-10, when John describes the great warfare that will conclude Satan's little season at the close of the millennium, the prophecy of Ezekiel regarding Gog-Magog is again drawn upon extensively. The nations in rebellion are termed Gog and Magog (verse 8; cf. *Ezek.* 38:2; 39:1, 6). The weapon used by God to destroy Gog-Magog is a fire coming down from heaven (verse 9; cf. *Ezek.* 38:22; 39:6). Therefore, it seems unlikely that the episodes described in these visions are different episodes in history, separated by a period of one thousand years. A much more plausible reading is that these visions describe the same event and are to be read as parallel descriptions of the same historical period.

4. The battle of Revelation 19:19 and 20:8.

The visions of Revelation 19 and 20 show a similar parallelism in their battle description. Three times in the book of Revelation, an end-time conflict in which Christ defeats the rebellious nations is described as '*the* battle'. The definite article suggests that this battle is a conclusive defeat, and the language describing the nations' revolt is virtually identical (see *Rev.* 16:14; 19:19; 20:8).

Interpreters of Revelation readily acknowledge the parallels between the battle description in Revelation 16:14-21 and the description in Revelation 19:19-21. The latter battle is regarded commonly as concluding the battle in Revelation 16. Fewer interpreters have noticed the similarities of language in Revelation 20:7-10. This is likely due to the assumption that the battle of Revelation 20:8 refers to a battle after the millennium rather than the battle before the millennium at the time of Christ's second coming.

If we consider the possibility of a parallel description of the same period of history in Revelation 19 and 20, then it is likely that the battle described in these passages is the same battle. Rather than replaying the earlier war that concluded history at Christ's second coming, it is more likely that these battles are the same battle described in visions that parallel each other.

5. The end of God's wrath.

Just as a discrepancy exists between the destruction of the rebellious nations in Revelation 19 and their continued presence in Revelation 20 (were these two visions describing events in sequence), so there is a discrepancy between the end of God's wrath in Revelation 19 and its further outpouring in Revelation 20.

Revelation 15:1 declares the end of God's wrath with the dispensing of the seven bowls of wrath by the seven angels. The last bowl of wrath is described in Revelation 16:17-21, a passage that concludes with the final defeat of the nations in Revelation 19:19-21. The vision of Revelation 19, therefore, represents the completion of history and the finishing of God's wrath upon the nations. The time frame for the outpouring of God's wrath in Revelation 15:1 is concluded by the vision of Revelation 19.

In a premillennialist reading of Revelation 19 and 20, however, the battle and pouring out of God's wrath in Revelation 20 comes one thousand years later than the battle and pouring out of God's wrath in Revelation 19. Thus, this reading conflicts with the teaching of Revelation 15:1, exceeding the deadline set for the completion of God's wrath. For this and the reasons already mentioned, it makes better sense to read the vision of Revelation 20 as a recapitulation of the period of history described in Revelation 19. Both visions would then be describing the same battle at the close of history with the final outpouring of God's wrath upon the nations.

6. The cosmic destruction of Revelation 19:11-21 and 20:9-11.

Finally, another parallel in the visions of Revelation 19 and 20 reflects the influence of Old Testament prophecy. Old Testament scenes of the Lord's judgements and triumphs among the nations often include the involvement of the created universe. Similarly, many visions of warfare in Revelation describe the shaking of the cosmos itself. This remarkable shaking accompanies the coming of Christ as king and the exercise of his judgement upon the nations (e.g., 6:12-17; 16:17-21; 19:11-21; 20:9-11). The last two instances of this association of Christ's victory and the earth's shaking occur in the visions of Revelation 19 and 20.

This confirms that these visions describe the same end-time event, but from a slightly different vantage point. Since the shaking of the earth at Christ's coming is the last instance of such shaking, after which nothing shakeable will remain to be shaken further (*Heb.* 12:26-27), it makes no sense to say that the shaking of the cosmos at Christ's second coming (*Rev.* 19) would still have to be followed by a further shaking at the end of the millennium (*Rev.* 20).

If these six features of Revelation 19 and 20 are recognized, the premillennial position is seriously compromised, if not refuted. Not only does Premillennialism enjoy little support from other portions of Scripture, but it also fails to provide a plausible account of the relation between the visions of Revelation 19 and 20. For if these visions are read as parallel accounts of the same period of history, then the millennium of Revelation 20 precedes rather than follows Christ's return at the end of the age.

We have every reason to believe that the millennium Revelation 20 describes is now. The millennium of Revelation 20 coincides with the period of history prior to Christ's return at the end of the age, prior to the day of Christ's final victory over his and his people's enemies, and prior to the last judgement and all the other events that will accompany the close of this present age.

THE BINDING OF SATAN (*REV.* 20:1-3)

The vision of Revelation 20 begins with a striking portrayal of the binding of Satan. The focus is fixed upon an angel laying hold of Satan (variously named 'the dragon, the serpent of old . . . the devil'). The angel seizes Satan, casts him into the abyss, and seals it over him. The language of sealing symbolizes complete and sovereign control exercised over Satan (cf. *Dan.* 6:17; *Matt.* 27:66). Thus, when Satan is released for a short time after the period of one thousand years, this will occur only by God's permission and under his complete control. This emphasis is underscored by the expression, 'after these things he must be released for a short time'.

The key question for the interpretation of this first section of the vision concerns the exact nature and implications of the binding of Satan. Historic and dispensational premillennialists as well as postmillennialists all concur that this binding must be understood as an action that completely curtails the actions of Satan. Though premillennialists argue that this millennial period commences after the return of Christ and postmillennialists argue that it occurs before, they agree in their insistence that the binding of Satan during the millennium cannot be identified with the entire period between Christ's first and second advents. Who would dare maintain that the present period of history is one in which the millennial binding of Satan is a reality?

Though this objection initially sounds powerful, upon further reflection it loses some of its punch. There are good biblical reasons to conclude that the present period of history—taking the vision of Revelation 20 as a description of the period between Christ's first coming and his second coming at the end of the age—represents the period of Satan's being bound so as not to be able to deceive the nations.

In the history of redemption, there is significant change from the old covenant to the new regarding the nations of the earth. In the old covenant, the Lord called Abraham from Ur of Chaldees and dealt primarily with the nation of Israel, while in the new covenant the gospel is being preached in the whole world (*Matt.* 24:14) and the nations are being discipled (*Luke* 24:47; *Matt.* 28:16-20). This difference in covenant administration does not affect the substance of the covenant of grace, but it does affect the way in which the good news is being preached to all the nations of the earth.

Compared to the extension of the kingdom of God in this present age, the nations prior to the coming of Christ remained predominantly under Satan's deception. Members of the new covenant church of Jesus Christ are apt to forget the greater richness of saving blessing that has

119

been poured out upon the nations in these last days. The light of the gospel that has shone among the nations of the earth in the present age contrasts vividly with the darkness in which the nations dwelt during the period of the old covenant.

It is important to note that the binding of Satan in Revelation 20 restricts his activity so that he 'should not deceive the nations any longer'. Satan is bound so that he can neither prevent the spread of the gospel among the nations nor effectively deceive them. This vision confirms the teaching that the period between Christ's first coming and his second coming is one in which the gospel of the kingdom will powerfully and effectively go forth to claim the nations for Jesus Christ. It confirms the confidence and authority with which Christ, after his resurrection, commissioned the disciples to go into all the earth and make disciples of the nations. This commission was given in the context of Christ's having been given all authority in heaven and on earth (*Matt.* 28:16). It was also concluded with the promise that Christ would be with his disciples until the end of the age. Consistent with Christ's confident declaration to his disciples that 'they will come from east and west, and from north and south, and will recline at table in the kingdom of God' (*Luke* 13:29), the vision of Revelation 20 declares that the great obstacle to the evangelisation of the nations—Satan's deceptive hold over them—has been removed.

Furthermore, if the vision of Satan's binding is interpreted in the broader context of the book of Revelation and the teaching of the Gospels, it corresponds quite closely to the biblical understanding of the present period in the history of redemption.

In an earlier vision in the book of Revelation, John saw a great war in heaven that was concluded with the casting down of the dragon, the serpent, to the earth (12:7-12). In this vision, Satan is described as the one who deceives the whole world. But now that Satan has been defeated in heaven and cast down, a loud voice in heaven is heard to say, 'Now the salvation, and the power, and the kingdom of our God and the authority of his Christ have come, for the accuser of our brethren has been cast down . . . And they overcame him because of the blood of the Lamb and

because of the word of their testimony, and they did not love their life
even to death' (12:10-11). Though the language of this earlier vision in
Revelation is different from that in Revelation 20, it seems to describe
the same realities: Satan's ability to deceive the nations and prevent the
coming of the kingdom of God has been effectively destroyed. Now has
come the kingdom of God. Now the nations are being discipled. Now the
power of Christ's gospel is being revealed in the earth.

The Gospel accounts of the preaching and teaching of the Lord Jesus
Christ find an echo in Revelation 20 and provide the biblical context
within which it becomes clear.

Matthew contains an account of Jesus healing a demon-possessed
man. When the multitudes hear of this miraculous healing, they are
amazed and wonder whether Jesus might be the Son of David (*Matt.*
12:23). However, the Pharisees declared, 'This man casts out demons
only by Beelzebul the ruler of the demons' (verse 24). In response to this
unbelief and blasphemy, Jesus notes that no kingdom divided against
itself can stand. He then claims that his power to cast out demons demonstrates the presence of the power and kingdom of God: 'But if I cast
out demons by the Spirit of God, then the kingdom of God has come
upon you. Or how can anyone enter the strong man's house and carry
off his property, unless he first binds the strong man? And then he will
plunder his house' (verses 28-29). The healing of this demon-possessed
man illustrates the presence of the kingdom and confirms that Satan has
been bound so that he is no longer able to prevent the plundering of
his house. It is interesting to observe that the word used to express the
restraint placed upon Satan, 'to bind', is the same word used in the vision
of Revelation 20 to describe the binding of Satan.

On another occasion in the Gospel accounts, we are told that Jesus
sent out seventy disciples, two by two, to proclaim the nearness of the
kingdom. Jesus commissions the disciples to go into the field of harvest
and heal those who are sick, and say to them, 'The kingdom of God has
come near you' (*Luke* 13:9). When the disciples return from fulfilling this
commission, they return with joy, reporting, 'Lord, even the demons are
subject to us in your name' (*Luke* 13:17). Jesus replies, 'I was watching

Satan fall from heaven like lightning. Behold, I have given you authority to tread upon serpents and scorpions, and over all the power of the enemy, and nothing shall injure you' (verse 19). In this and other Gospel passages, Christ's coming and ministry is a concrete realisation of the coming and presence of the kingdom of God, a kingdom that plunders and destroys Satan's household and releases those who are captive to sin and the demons.

In another significant passage in the Gospel of John, the coming of Christ is associated with a dramatic curtailment of Satan's activity. Predicting his death, Christ declares, 'Now judgement is upon this world; now the ruler of this world shall be cast out. And I, if I be lifted up from the earth, will draw all men to myself' (12:31-32). This passage speaks of a casting out in judgement of the ruler of this world, and it speaks of the crucified Christ who will draw to himself all men, Jew as well as Gentile, from among the peoples of the earth. In these ways it parallels the thought of the vision in Revelation 20, that the kingdom of Christ will be realised through the binding of Satan and the gathering of the nations. Furthermore, as was true of the passage in Matthew 12, the language employed to describe Satan's judgement is very similar to that in Revelation 20. In John 12, we read of the 'casting out' of Satan. In Revelation 20, we read of the 'casting down' of Satan.

If Scripture should interpret Scripture and an obscure passage should be interpreted in light of a more clear passage, the conclusion that best fits this evidence is this: the vision of Satan's binding in Revelation 20, so that he is no longer capable of deceiving the nations, represents the events coinciding with the coming of Christ in the fullness of time. Christ has come and won a decisive victory over the evil one. This victory is variously revealed to us in the Gospels and throughout the New Testament. With his victory over Satan's temptations in the wilderness, his declaration and exhibition of the power of the kingdom in casting out demons and plundering the enemy's stronghold, his vanquishing of sin and death upon the cross, his resurrection from the dead, his ascension to the Father's right hand, and his pouring out of the Spirit at Pentecost—in this entire complex of Christ's saving work—he has won a decisive vic-

122

tory over Satan. No longer is Satan able to deceive the nations. The promise of Psalm 2, that the nations will be given by God the Father to his Son as his rightful inheritance, is being fulfilled (verses 7-9). Between the times of Christ's first coming and his second coming, the millennial reign of Christ upon the earth is being manifested for all to see.

'ONE THOUSAND YEARS'

One of the intriguing features of the vision of Revelation 20 is its reference to a period of one thousand years. For most premillennialists, this must be taken literally as a reference to a distinct period in history after the return of Christ. Particularly within Dispensational Premillennialism, with its commitment to a literalistic reading of the Bible, the language of Revelation 20 is regarded as sufficient to prove the error of Amillennialism and Postmillennialism. To the objection that this is the only passage in Scripture which speaks of a one-thousand-year period, the premillennialist response is typically that one passage should be more than adequate to make the point.

Two general observations regarding this premillennialist claim should be noted. First, the insistence that the language of Revelation (and of all Scripture) be taken literally betrays a way of reading the Bible that we will critically evaluate further in the next chapter. However, if much of Revelation—with its rich symbolism and use of biblical types and figures—is clearly not literal, some reason must be given why this is the case with the 'one thousand years'. Second, no other passage of Scripture speaks of a literal period in history of one thousand years (whether before or after Christ's return). One of the great difficulties in the case for Premillennialism is the relative lack of support for its doctrine of the millennium from other passages in Scripture. Before we concede the claim that one thousand years must mean one thousand literal years, we should consider whether Scripture supports a different reading of this expression.

Those who argue that the thousand years is not to be taken literally often note that it is a perfect cube of ten, ten being a number of completeness. This suggests that the reference to a one-thousand-year period is symbolic of a perfect and complete number within the purpose of God. This is a plausible way of reading this language, but it tends to be too abstract. Do the Scriptures elsewhere use the number one thousand in a symbolic way which might cast some light upon Revelation 20?

Though in some instances the number may be quite literal (e.g., *Gen.* 20:16; *Ezra* 1:9-10) or possibly literal as well as symbolic (e.g., *Judg.* 15:15-16; *1 Chron.* 29:21), in other instances it has a clearly symbolic meaning. In Deuteronomy 7:9, the Lord is described as a 'faithful God who keeps covenant and mercy for a thousand generations with those who love him and keep his commandments'. In the summary of the law given in Exodus 20, a contrast is drawn between the Lord's judgement upon the third and fourth generations of those who hate him, and his 'showing loving-kindness to thousands' who love him and keep his commandments (*Exod.* 20:5-6). Similarly, in the Psalms we read that the 'cattle on a thousand hills' belong to the Lord (*Psa.* 50:10-11). The Psalmist also speaks of how a 'day in thy courts is better than a thousand' (*Psa.* 84:10). In the well-known words of Psalm 90, the believer confesses that 'a thousand years in thy sight are like yesterday when it passes by, or as a watch in the night' (verse 4). Responding to the mockers who mocked the promise of the Lord's coming, Peter notes that 'with the Lord one day is as a thousand years, and a thousand years as one day' (*2 Pet.* 3:8).

These passages illustrate that the number one thousand is often used in the Scriptures to refer to an extensive period of time. When interpreted against this background of symbolism, the use of one thousand years in Revelation is likely a reference to a period of fullness, completion and perfection in God's redemptive plan. This expression is not meant to teach that the millennium will be a period of not one more or one less than 365,000 days. Just as God's faithfulness is perfect and never failing (unto one thousand generations), so the times within his redemptive purposes are perfect and never failing. The most that can be concluded from the number one thousand in Revelation 20 is that the period of Satan's binding will be great and full, not small and empty, of years. That this is the sense of the vision is only reinforced by the contrasting language that describes Satan's season of rebellion as a little season, suggesting that it is a meagre and limited period of time within the will of God.

In this first section of the vision of Revelation 20, we have a representation of that period of history between the time of Christ's first coming and his return at the end of age, in which Satan has been bound. The millennium is now, the period in which Christ's kingdom is advancing by his Spirit and word and the nations are being discipled. This period is not literally one thousand years, but the entire period, perfect, complete and extensive, between the first and second comings of Christ. Compared to the vast expanse and power of the kingdom of Christ, the period of Satan's rebellion prior to Christ's return will be pathetically small and limited in scope.

THE BELIEVER'S REIGN WITH CHRIST (*REV.* 20:4-6)

The second part of the vision in Revelation 20:4-6 focuses on the reign of the saints with Christ during the millennium, particularly their participation in the first resurrection. Admittedly, this is even more controversial and difficult to interpret than the first part.

When considering the meaning of the reference to the first resurrection, two questions immediately come to mind: What is the location of the scene that John sees in this vision? Who are these saints whom John sees?

It is significant that John first notices thrones. He says, 'I saw thrones, and they sat upon them, and judgement was given to them.' The likeliest location of these thrones is in heaven. Heaven is the place of the throne of God and the Lamb in the book of Revelation. But it is also the place where the saints who have died or who have been martyred have a share in the reign of Christ. In all of the references to 'throne' in the book of Revelation (some 47 instances), only three refer to some place other than heaven (see 2:13; 13:2; 16:10). For example, in Revelation 3:21 we read this promise of Christ: 'he who overcomes, I will grant to him to sit down with me on my throne, as I also overcame and sat down with my Father on his throne.' Were the thrones of Revelation 20 located on the earth, taking the reign of these saints as not only over but also upon the earth, this would be inconsistent with the imagery of the book.

The fact that John speaks of the 'souls' of those who had been beheaded because of the testimony of Jesus adds to the likelihood that the scene is in heaven. This language is reminiscent of that used earlier in Revelation to describe 'the souls of those who had been slain for the word of God and for the witness they had borne' (6:9). These souls were seen by the apostle under the altar, before the throne of God in the heavenly sanctuary. Though the word 'souls' need not require that these saints are no longer dwelling in the body, the reference to their beheading implies that this is the case. When these saints are contrasted in verse 5 with 'the rest of the dead', it becomes increasingly certain that John is seeing a vision of the saints in glory.

It must be admitted that the location of these saints also depends upon the meaning of their participation in the first resurrection. If the first resurrection is a bodily resurrection, as premillennialists typically argue, then it seems to follow that their reign is from and upon the earth. In the understanding of Premillennialism, the vision of Revelation 20 is a picture of the resurrected saints reigning upon the earth during the entire period of the millennium. However, the natural reading of this vision certainly favours the position that these saints are reigning with Christ in heaven.

The second question—who are these saints?—is also disputed. Premillennialists commonly argue that John sees a vision of all the saints, believers who come with Christ to the earth after the tribulation period as well as believers who are alive at his coming, who reign with Christ upon the earth for a thousand years. Many postmillennialists and amillennialists regard these saints as the saints in glory, especially the martyred saints. However, some amillennialists say that these saints are only the martyred saints who enjoy a peculiar privilege during the millennium of reigning with Christ.

There are good reasons to take the saints in this vision to include all the saints in heaven, especially—but not only—the martyred saints.

Those who would restrict these saints to martyred Christians do so by insisting that the conjunction 'and' be translated in the sense of 'namely'. In such a translation, we would read this text to say, 'And I saw thrones, and they sat upon them, and judgement was given to them, namely, the souls of those who had been beheaded.'

Though this is a possible reading, it could better be read using 'and' in the sense of 'especially'. Upon this reading, the privileges enjoyed by the saints—judging, reigning with Christ, not being subject to the second death—are shared by all the saints in heaven. But the martyred saints' enjoyment of them is particularly emphasised. Not only does this reading fit well the natural meaning of the word 'and' in this text, but it is also consistent with a theme that runs throughout Revelation: that those who are faithful to the Lord and their testimony are more than conquerors through Christ (see 2:7b, 10-11; 2:17; 2:26-28; 3:11-12; 3:21; etc.). This reading does not require that these martyred saints enjoy exclusive privileges. They exercise judgement, reign with Christ as priests, enjoy immunity from the power of the second death—but these are privileges known to all those who belong to Christ (see *Eph.* 2:6; *Rev.* 5:9, 10; *Col.* 3:1; *1 Pet.* 2:9, 10; *John* 12).

The scene, then, that opens before John is of the saints in heaven before the throne of God and the Lamb. Among these saints, John singles out for special emphasis those who were martyred for their testimony and faithfulness. He sees them all enjoying a remarkable set of privileges: they are seated upon thrones, they are reigning with Christ, and they are serving as priests of God and of Christ.

THE 'FIRST RESURRECTION'

At this juncture in the vision of Revelation 20:1-6 the most contentious issue arises: what is meant by the 'first resurrection' enjoyed by the saints whom John sees? In the description of these saints, we read that 'they came to life and reigned with Christ for a thousand years. The rest of the dead did not come to life until the thousand years were completed. This is the first resurrection.'

The premillennialist takes this to be a reference to the bodily resurrection of all the saints at the commencement of the millennium. The language used in this passage for the 'coming to life' of these saints, especially the term 'resurrection', is taken to mean a physical resurrection of believers prior to the millennial reign of Christ on the earth. This resurrection is distinguished from a second resurrection, the bodily resurrection of the unbelieving, which will occur after the millennium. Believers who participate in the first resurrection are not liable to the second death; however, unbelievers who participate in the second resurrection remain liable to the second death. According to the premillennialist, nothing could more obviously confirm the idea of a literal millennial reign of Christ with his saints upon the earth after his coming at the end of the age. The postmillennialist and amillennialist position that this first resurrection is not a bodily resurrection but a spiritual reality with corresponding consequences is simply untenable.

However, a number of considerations lead to a different conclusion: that the first resurrection refers to the life and blessing reserved for the saints, particularly those who have died and will be raised on the last day. The first resurrection does not refer to the bodily resurrection of the saints, but to a spiritual participation in Christ that brings the blessings of living and reigning as priests with him, as well as immunity from the power of the second death. Among supporting considerations are the following.

First, if the first resurrection refers to the bodily resurrection only of believing saints at the commencement of the millennium, this resurrection would be separated by one thousand years from the resurrection of unbelievers at the end of the age. This separation in time between the resurrection of the just and the unjust, however, contradicts the teaching of Scripture elsewhere that these events will occur together as parts of one complex and consummating series of events at the end of the age. In John 5:28-29, Jesus Christ said to the disciples, 'Do not marvel at this; for an hour is coming, in which all who are in the tombs shall hear his voice, and shall come forth; those who did the good deeds to a resurrection of life, those who committed the evil deeds to a resurrection of judgement.'

At a point in time that coincides for all, the just and the unjust alike, a resurrection of life and of judgement will occur. A number of other passages suggest that the resurrection of believers and unbelievers will occur concurrently at the end of the age (see *Matt.* 16:27; 25:31-33; *Acts* 24:15; *2 Cor.* 5:10; *2 Thess.* 1:6-10; *Rev.* 20:11-15).

Second, though premillennialists correctly point out that the terms 'coming to life' and 'resurrection' are most commonly used in the New Testament for a bodily resurrection, this is not always the case. The verb translated in verses 4 and 5 as 'came to life' is used in several places for a life that is not a bodily resurrection. In Luke 20, for example, Jesus, speaking against the Sadducean denial of the doctrine of the resurrection, says that God is not the God of the dead, but of the living; for all live to him (verse 38). In several instances in the book of Revelation itself, this verb is used to describe God, who 'lives forever' (*Rev.* 4:9-10), who is the 'living God' (7:2), or who 'lives forever and ever' (10:6; 15:7). One especially interesting passage is found in Revelation 13. The vision here first describes the beast, one of whose heads was 'as if it had been slain' (verse 3). Then, in a subsequent description of this beast, we are told that the beast 'who had the wound of the sword . . . had come to life' (verse 14). This description indicates that the coming to life of the beast was not a bodily resurrection, but the healing of an apparently fatal wound. Consequently, when the vision of Revelation 20 speaks of the saints who 'lived', this word need not refer to a bodily resurrection.

Third, and perhaps most importantly, the New Testament speaks of the believer's fellowship with Christ as a resurrection that brings victory over the dominion of sin and death. This is evident in the well-known words of John 11:25-26, where Christ promises: 'I am the resurrection and the life: he who believes in me shall live even if he dies, and everyone who lives and believes in me shall never die.' Likewise, Paul speaks in several places of the believer's incorporation into Christ as a baptism into Christ that involves the believer directly in his death and resurrection. Through this baptism into Christ, the believer enjoys a fellowship with him that is nothing less than a resurrection (*Rom.* 6:3-4; *Col.* 3:1-3; *Eph.* 2:4-6).

These passages are especially pertinent because they clearly teach

that all believers, by virtue of their union with Christ, share in his resurrection and all its attendant benefits. The believer's resurrection in fellowship with Christ brings the reality of life from the dead, the assurance of
never-ending life, and the blessedness of sitting and reigning with Christ
in the heavenly places.

It is intriguing to note that though Revelation 20:1-6 seems to imply
that there is a second resurrection, it does not speak of a second resurrection. Only one resurrection is mentioned, and it is defined as the
first because it brings the benefits of the believer's reign with Christ and
immunity from the power of the second death.

This way of understanding the reference to the first resurrection in
this vision is perfectly consistent with the teaching of the Scriptures. Not
only does it remove the difficulty of separating by one thousand years of
time the resurrection of the just from the unjust, but it also appeals to
an important biblical teaching regarding the resurrection of believers in
union with Christ. Although all believers are baptized in Christ and share
in his resurrection, in John's vision in Revelation 20 this benefit is seen
in its peculiar application to those who have been translated upon death
into heavenly glory.

This reading finds further confirmation in the language concluding
the vision: 'The rest of the dead did not come to life until the thousand
years were completed. This is the first resurrection. Blessed and holy is
the one who has a part in the first resurrection; over these the second
death has no power, but they will be priests of God and of Christ and will
reign with him for a thousand years.'

The 'rest of the dead' refers to the unjust and unbelieving. Because
they have no part in the first resurrection, they remain subject to the
power of the second death. They share none of the privileges enjoyed by
the saints. The second death to which they are subject cannot be physical
death, the separation of body and soul as the consequence of sin, because
they have already suffered this death. It is a spiritual death that results
from separation from favour and fellowship with the living God. The first
resurrection is distinguished as first because it brings victory over spiritual
death. The second death is second because it means liability to punish-

ment in a spiritual excommunication from God's presence. The phrase 'second death' seems to confirm, therefore, that the first resurrection is not a physical resurrection.

In summary, Revelation 20:1-6 presents a vision of history between the first and second advents of Christ. This vision does not describe events that will occur after the return of Christ (with which the vision of Revelation 19 concludes), but events that cover the whole period of redemptive history from Christ's coming in the fullness of time until his return in glory at the end of the age.

The vision of the binding of Satan offers a behind-the-scenes glimpse of the triumphant gathering of Christ's church from among the nations. During these last days of fulfilment, the nations—no longer liable to the deceptive devices of Satan—are being discipled by the Spirit and word of Christ. Though Satan may not be absolutely constrained, even the 'little season' of Satanically inspired rebellion will quickly end in defeat. Nothing can prevent Christ's gathering and building of his church.

Echoing a theme sounded throughout the book of Revelation, the vision of Revelation 20 also teaches that, far from the death of the saints indicating defeat for the cause of Christ's kingdom, these saints fully share in the victory of Christ. This victory is not some earthly millennial reign after Christ's return, but a present reality.

The vision of Revelation 20 provides the church (to which it was first written and until Christ comes again) great consolation and encouragement in the face of trial and persecution. Believers, seeing history with the eye of faith, join John on the isle of Patmos and stand marvellously strengthened by this vision of the saints in glory, seated upon thrones, in the presence of God and the Lamb.

8

THE FUTURE OF THE KINGDOM: AN EVALUATION OF MILLENNIAL VIEWS

*W*e have seen that, although there are four primary views regarding the future of the Kingdom, they can be considered broadly as either premillennial or postmillennial. In this chapter, we will evaluate both the historic and dispensational premillennial and postmillennial views.

Evaluating Premillennialism

The common feature of all premillennial teaching is the claim that Christ's return will take place before the millennium. Whatever differences exist between Historic and Dispensational Premillennialism—and they are considerable—they have this teaching in common. Though a number of arguments are offered for a premillennial return of Christ, two biblical passages often cited in support are 1 Corinthians 15:23-26 and Revelation 20:1-6. The latter is the more important passage because without its teaching even some premillennialists acknowledge that 1 Corinthians 15:23-26 would not obviously suggest Christ's return before the millennium.

Since we have already discussed Revelation 20:1-6 at some length, our evaluation here will be restricted to two matters. We will consider the 'general analogy' of the Scripture and we will evaluate the appeal to 1 Corinthians 15:23-26, showing that neither supports the premillennialist position.

Would anyone argue for a premillennial return of Christ, were it not for the supposed teaching of the two passages just mentioned? Does the Bible anywhere else support this position?

Christ's Return: A Consummating Event

It is commonly acknowledged that the general analogy of Scripture has more weight in determining what the Bible teaches than one or two obscure or difficult passages. A general teaching of Scripture is confirmed when supported by texts throughout the Bible. When a general teaching is apparently contradicted by a relatively obscure text, it is appropriate to interpret the more obscure passage in light of the general analogy of Scripture.

The usual presentation of Christ's return in the Scriptures is as a consummating event at the close of the age. Christ's coming will be a public event that will bring about the salvation of God's people and the fullness of his kingdom (*Matt.* 24:27, 33; *Luke* 17:24; 21:27-28, 31). When Christ is revealed, he will bring rest for his beleaguered church and eternal punishment upon the unbelieving (*2 Thess.* 1:6-10). The return of Christ will bring the fullness of salvation; no further event will surpass it in redemptive significance (cf. *1 Cor.* 1:7, 8; *Phil.* 1:6, 10; *1 John* 2:28; *1 Tim.* 4:8; *2 Tim.* 4:1). When Christ returns, a rapture of the living and the dead will lead to the transformation of all believers and their un-interrupted communion with the Lord (*1 Thess.* 4:13-18). Christ's return will introduce the final state of a new heavens and a new earth (*2 Pet.* 3:13; *Rom.* 8:17-25). The resurrection of the just and the unjust alike will occur simultaneously (*Dan.* 12:2; *John* 5:28, 29; *Acts* 24:14-15; *Rev.* 20:11-15). The resurrection of believers will occur at the 'last day' (*John* 6:40; *1 Thess.* 4:16; *Phil.* 3:20-21; *1 Cor.* 15:23), the day that marks the close of this present age and the introduction of the final age.

These biblical teachings confirm that Christ's return will conclude history and introduce the final state. The pervasive testimony of the New Testament conforms to the Apostles Creed when it describes the return of Christ 'to judge the living and dead', which presumably will prepare the way for the 'resurrection of the body and the life everlasting', commencing the final state. Unless clear and compelling evidence from one or more biblical text supports the premillennialist view, it would seem that we should follow the rule that the general teaching of Scripture has more weight than one text, especially when the teaching of that text is not clear and undisputed.

1 Corinthians 15:20-28

Some defenders of the premillennialist view have argued that 1 Corinthians 15:20-28, especially verses 23-26, teaches three stages in redemptive history, including an interim period that is the millennium of Revelation 20:1-6. Though this argument can be defended on strictly grammatical grounds since the adverbs 'then . . . and then' can express a sequence in which a period of time could intervene ('Christ the first fruits, after that those who are Christ's at his coming, then comes the end'), this requires an unnatural reading of the passage. In all other instances where these words are found, they express events in the closest temporal connection, without any protracted period of time intervening (*Luke* 8:12; *Mark* 4:17; *John* 20:27). In the immediate context of 1 Corinthians 15:23-26, we find the same adverbs expressing a simple sequence of events (*1 Cor.* 15:5-7). The 'and then' is used alone in 1 Thessalonians 4:17 to express an immediate sequence of events. From context and ordinary usage, it is evident that these words express a simple sequence of events. The New Testament generally and the epistles of Paul particularly, show a close connection between the 'coming' (*parousia*) of Christ and the 'end' (*telos*). In 1 Corinthians 1:8, Paul speaks of the 'revelation of the day of the Lord' that is the end anticipated by believers. When Christ is revealed, the end will come and the need to persevere in hope will conclude (cf. *2 Cor.* 1:13-14; *Matt.* 10:22; 24:6, 13-14; *Mark* 13:7, 13; *Luke* 21:9; *Heb.* 3:6, 14; 6:11; *1 Pet.* 4:7). Treating the 'coming' of Christ and the 'end' in 1 Corinthians 15:23-26 as closely connected events follows the ordinary pattern found in the New Testament. The believer's victory over death in 1 Corinthians 15:54-55 occurs when believers receive resurrection bodies. This coincides with the description in 1 Corinthians 15:23-26 of both the 'coming' of Christ and the 'end', when the last enemy will be overcome.

Though a premillennial reading of this passage is grammatically possible, there are powerful biblical reasons to conclude that it is contextually and comparatively improbable. When 1 Corinthians 15:23-26 is read in its immediate context and in the more remote context of New Testament teaching, it corroborates the general analogy of Scripture: when Christ comes at the end of the age, redemptive history will close and the final state will commence.

A Pre-Tribulational Rapture?

The predominant view in premillennial Dispensationalism is pre-tribulational rapturism: the first phase of Christ's return 'for' his saints (the rapture) precedes a seven-year tribulation, and the second phase of Christ's return 'with' his saints introduces the one-thousand-year reign of Christ on earth.

Does the Bible teach that Christ's return will take place in two phases, separated by an intervening period of seven years' duration? And does the Bible teach that the first of these phases will be the rapture envisioned by Dispensationalism?

Earlier Dispensational Premillennialism suggested that the first of three common terms for the return of Christ (*parousia*—presence, coming) identified Christ's initial coming 'for' his saints at the rapture. The second and third terms (*apokalupsis*—revelation, and *epiphaneia*—appearance) indicated Christ's coming 'with' his saints at the end of the seven-year tribulation.

This claim, however, cannot withstand scrutiny. The New Testament clearly shows that *parousia* and *apokalupsis* are used interchangeably, as are *apokalupsis* and *epiphaneia*, to refer to the one return of Christ at the end of the age. In 1 Thessalonians 4:15, *parousia* describes the rapture, but in 1 Thessalonians 3:13, the same term describes the 'coming of our Lord Jesus with all his saints'. Similarly, in 2 Thessalonians 2:8, the term *parousia* refers to Christ destroying the 'man of lawlessness', an event which Dispensationalism places at the end of the seven-year period of tribulation. Most unsettling to the dispensationalist argument is that this passage uses two of the three terms for Christ's return in close proximity, as synonyms, when it speaks of how Christ will 'bring to nought' the man of lawlessness 'by the appearance of his coming'.

Both the terms *apokalupsis* and *epiphaneia* are used for what dispensationalists regard as the first and second phases of Christ's return. In 1 Corinthians 1:7, *apokalupsis* describes what would be called the rapture, since the believers in Corinth are 'waiting for the revelation of our Lord Jesus Christ'. However, in 2 Thessalonians 1:7-8, this term describes what dispensationalists regard as the 'revelation' or 'second' second coming of Christ. The same interchangeability is evident in 1 Timothy 6:14, where *epiphaneia* is used to describe the rapture, and in 2 Timothy 4:1, where it refers to Christ's coming as judge of the living and the dead. In its use of these terms, the New Testament offers no support for the idea that Christ's return will occur in two distinct phases.

Dispensationalists also insist that the church will not suffer the tribulation, including the great tribulation during the seven-year period between Christ's coming and his revelation. This insistence, however, cannot be sustained by appeal to the New Testament Scriptures.

In the Olivet Discourse recorded in Matthew 24, Jesus speaks of a severe tribulation prior to his coming that will be shortened for the sake of the elect (verse 22). This indicates that believers will not be raptured before the tribulation of those days. Dispensationalists maintain that the elect in these verses refers to the Jews and not to the church, noting that the term 'church' is not used in this chapter. This is an argument from silence, considerably weakened by the fact that the Gospels seldom use the term 'church'. The most evident reading of this passage is as a reference to tribulation that befalls the elect people of God (Jew or Gentile) before the return of Christ.

In this same passage, Christ indicates that the rapture will not only follow the period of tribulation, but also mark the close of the age. Matthew 24:31 describes what will occur after the tribulation: 'And he [the Son of Man] will send forth his angels with a great trumpet and they will gather together his elect from the four winds, from one end of the sky to the other.' This description is similar to 1 Thessalonians 4:16-17 and describes events at the time of the rapture: the descent of the Lord, the sound of the trumpet, the gathering of the elect. It is difficult to see why these passages should be taken as descriptions of different events. It is not difficult, however, to see why Dispensationalism is compelled to distinguish these passages. If Matthew 24:31 referred to the rapture, that would place the rapture after the period of tribulation rather than before it.

The same kind of difficulty confronts the dispensationalist when it comes to the teaching of 2 Thessalonians 2, with its description of the man of lawlessness. According to Dispensationalism, the events of this passage will occur during the period of tribulation—especially the great tribulation—between the time of the rapture and the time of Christ's revelation. However, this would undermine the point of Paul's teaching in this passage, which is to warn believers not to be deceived into thinking that the coming of the Lord has already occurred (verse 2), because the man of lawlessness and the great apostasy must occur first. Written primarily to Gentile Christian believers—and not Jewish believers, as dispensationalists commonly teach—this passage speaks of a number of events, including the tribulation and the Antichrist, that will precede the coming of Christ.

Unless the Bible reader brings to these passages a preconceived doctrine of two distinct phases in Christ's return, there is little prospect that such a teaching would be discovered from them. The biblical teaching is that Christ will return after the period of tribulation to grant his church relief and his enemies eternal destruction (*2 Thess.* 1). These consequences of Christ's return coincide and therefore do not permit the teaching of two distinct phases in the return of Christ.

1 Thessalonians 4:13-18

Furthermore, a careful study of 1 Thessalonians 4:13-18, which is the one passage in Scripture that directly describes the rapture, will show that it does not teach the pre-tribulational rapture advocated by Dispensationalism. This passage was originally written by the apostle Paul to

138

address the fear among the Thessalonian believers that those saints who had 'fallen asleep' in Jesus would not experience the blessedness accompanying the coming of Christ.

Four observations suggest that the dispensational interpretation of this passage is a classic example of finding something in a text that is not there.

First, when verse 16 states that the dead in Christ will rise first, it means that saints who have fallen asleep in Jesus will be raised before the living saints are caught up with them and the Lord at his coming. The dispensationalist teaching that this is the first resurrection, distinct from the second resurrection more than one thousand years later, is not found in the text and is not the point of the term 'first'.

Second, this passage speaks of all believers being caught up together to meet the Lord in the air. Dispensationalists maintain that this refers to a meeting in the air that leads to a return to heaven for seven years. But nothing of this is stated in the text. The word used in this text for 'meeting' typically means a meeting between a visiting dignitary and representatives of the city being visited. Such a meeting would occur outside the city, after which the visitor and welcoming party would return to the city. This word is used twice elsewhere in the New Testament (*Acts* 28:15; *Matt.* 25:6), in both cases referring to a meeting that takes place before the parties return to the place being visited. The meaning and use of this term suggests that in the case of the rapture, the saints who meet the Lord in the air will return with him, not to heaven, but to the earth.

Third, the result of this rapture is said to be the blessedness of being always with the Lord. This language best fits the circumstance of the final state in which believers will dwell forever in unbroken fellowship with the Lord Jesus Christ. Being always with the Lord is not limited to seven years in heaven or even one thousand years on earth. Rather, the simplest reading of this passage is to take it to be a description of the final state.

And fourth, several features of the description of this rapture do not fit well with the dispensationalist position. The coming of the Lord described in these verses is a public event, signalled by the descent of

Christ from heaven 'with a shout, with the voice of the archangel, and with the trumpet of God'. Other passages (cf. *1 Cor.* 15:20-24; *2 Thess.* 2:12) speak of Christ's return as a public event that will bring the present period of history to a close. In Dispensationalism, however, the first phase of Christ's return is said to be a secret rapture, in which believers will be suddenly snatched away without notice.

Thus, the teaching of a pre-tribulational rapture as understood within the framework of Dispensationalism is not founded upon the teaching of any biblical passage. Nor is it a teaching that can withstand careful scrutiny when measured against the general teaching of the Scriptures regarding the return of Christ. The Bible teaches neither that believers will be exempted from present or future tribulation nor that the rapture will be the event described by Dispensationalism.

The Dispensational Distinction between Israel and the Church

Classical Dispensationalism regards God's purposes in history to be twofold, corresponding to two distinct peoples, one earthly and the other heavenly. The line of separation that keeps Israel and the church apart in history will continue into the final state in which the earthly and heavenly natures of these peoples will correspond to salvation blessings that are distinctively earthly and heavenly.

The present age of the church, because it represents God's dealings with his heavenly people, is regarded as a 'parenthesis' period of history, a period between God's former dealings and his soon-to-be-resumed dealings with Israel in the millennial age to come. During the present age of God's dealings with the church, his dealings with Israel have been temporarily suspended, but when the time of fulfilment comes (preceded by the rapture), the prophetic promises will be fulfilled.

Does the Bible draw this kind of separation between these two peoples of God, Israel and the church?

In the New Testament, the church is commonly understood to be in direct continuity with the people of God in the Old Testament. The New Testament church is called the 'temple' of God (*1 Cor.* 3:16-17; *Eph.* 2:21-22), evoking the imagery and symbolism of the Old Testament temple.

Just as the temple was the place of fellowship between the Lord and his people, so the church is the place of the Lord's dwelling by his Holy Spirit. Accordingly, the church can also be identified with Jerusalem, the city of God, comprised of believers from every tribe and tongue and nation (*Heb.* 12:22-23).

Rather than being an interruption in God's dealings with Israel, the new covenant church is regarded as the fulfilment of the old covenant. Throughout the Old Testament, the Lord's dealings with Israel are never isolated from his promises of redemption for all the nations and peoples of the earth.

The simplest understanding is to see the church as God's new covenant people, in direct communion with Israel, his old covenant people. Though salvation may historically be 'to the Jew first and second also to the Gentile' (*Rom.* 1:16), the Lord is gathering to himself one people, Jew and Gentile alike. The biblical understanding of the church is not as a 'parenthesis'.

Closely linked to the idea that the church is a parenthesis in history is the dispensationalist claim that God's dealings with Israel have been postponed during the present time. This idea of the kingdom's postponement has several problems.

First, it suggests that the church is an afterthought in the purposes of God. This view of history seems to teach that Christ was frustrated in his original purpose for the establishment of the Davidic kingdom and was obliged to adjust the divine plan of redemption. Such a suggestion is consistent neither with the biblical presentation of God's sovereignty nor with the Bible's view of the church.

Christ's Great Commission to his disciples (*Matt.* 28:16-20) fulfils his earlier declaration regarding the church that he will build, against which the gates of Hades shall not prevail (*Matt.* 16:18-19). Far from being an afterthought or interim project, the church is described as the central accomplishment of the Lord Jesus Christ. This church, being gathered from all nations, can be understood only as a fulfilment of the promises God made to the Son of David, to whom the nations would be given as his rightful inheritance (see *Psa.* 2:22). Consequently, when Paul describes the church, he can speak of it as the 'fullness of him who fills all and all' (*Eph.* 1:22-23), through which the manifold wisdom of God is being made known 'in accordance with the eternal purpose which he carried out in Christ Jesus our Lord' (*Eph.* 3:8-11). None of these descriptions of the church suggest that it is anything less than the central instrument of God's final purpose of redemption.

Second, the dispensationalist idea of a postponement of the kingdom is based upon a misreading of Christ's preaching of the kingdom. It must not be forgotten that Jesus himself (the foremost member of the church!) was Jewish and that many of the Jews responded to him in faith. The twelve disciples, the nucleus of the New Testament church, were all Jewish. Christ and his apostles preached the gospel of the kingdom (e.g., *Acts* 20:28)—a kingdom that Christ proclaimed was 'among them' (*Matt.* 12:28), that would be built through the preaching of the gospel (*Matt.* 16:19). The idea that Christ offered the kingdom to the Jews, only to have them reject it, is contradicted by these realities and Christ's own testimony that they had misunderstood his kingdom (see *John* 18:36).

Third, the idea of a postponement of the kingdom implies that the crucifixion of Christ might have been delayed, even become unnecessary, had the Jews received him as their earthly king. Christ's own teaching, that he must first suffer and only then enter his glory, would have been invalidated (*Luke* 24:26). The uniform testimony of the New Testament Gospels and epistles, that Christ came in order to be obedient to his Father's will, including his death upon the cross, would be compromised.

The Gospel accounts of Christ's suffering and death frequently note that this occurred to fulfil Scriptures (e.g., *Matt.* 16:23; 26:24, 45, 56). Christ rebuked the men on the way to Emmaus because they did not believe in 'all the prophets had spoken' (*Luke* 24:25-26). John frequently testifies that Jesus Christ, the Word become flesh, came into the world for the express purpose of doing his Father's will, to be the 'lamb of God who takes away the sin of the world' (cf. 1:29; 2:4; 6:38; 7:6; 10:10ff.; 12:27; 13:1-3; 17).

In his sermon at Pentecost, Peter notes that Jesus was 'delivered up by the predetermined plan and foreknowledge of God' (*Acts* 2:23). Paul speaks of how 'Christ died for our sins according to the Scriptures . . . and that he was raised on the third day according to the Scriptures'. The writer to the Hebrews describes Christ's coming, priesthood, and sacrifice as a fulfilment of the old covenant types and shadows. Nothing in the New Testament is congenial to the view that Christ's death was occasioned primarily by the Jewish people's refusal to acknowledge him as their earthly king.

And fourth, the idea that the kingdom has been postponed does not correspond to the New Testament's insistence that Christ is now the King and Lord over all. In accounts of Jesus' death, resurrection and ascension, it is evident that Christ has been installed as king at the Father's right hand, where he rules over all things for the sake of the church.

Christ declared, 'all authority has been given to me in heaven and on earth' (*Matt.* 28:18). Peter claimed that with God's raising of Jesus from the dead, 'God has made him both Lord and Christ' (*Acts* 2:33-36). Christ is the Davidic King to whom the nations will be given as his rightful inheritance (see *Acts* 4:24-26). Paul describes the Lord as one who has been 'declared to be the Son of God with power by the resurrection of the dead' (*Rom.* 1:4). Christ has been given all rule and authority and power and dominion (*Eph.* 1:20-23; cf. *Phil.* 2:9-11). Therefore, he must 'reign until he has put all his enemies under his feet' (*1 Cor.* 15:25).

Though the present form and administration of the kingdom of Christ may not be earthly or physical in the dispensationalist sense of these terms, there is no escaping the biblical teaching that Christ now reigns upon the earth through his Spirit and word and manifests his kingly rule primarily through the gathering of his church. Serious injury is done to the biblical conception of Christ's kingship when Dispensationalism relegates it to some future period during which God's dealings are directed narrowly to the earthly people of God, Israel.

One Purpose of Salvation

The basic reason why Dispensationalism wrongly speaks of the church as a parenthesis in history and of the postponement of the kingdom, is that it fails to see that God has one purpose of salvation for his people in

143

the old and new covenants. Israel is the church, and the church is Israel. This can be illustrated in several ways from the New Testament.

The Apostle Peter defines the new covenant church with the exact terminology used in the Old Testament to describe the people of Israel (*1 Pet.* 2:9). Similarly, in Romans 9-11, Paul discloses God's purposes of redemption in the salvation of the Gentiles and subsequently of all Israel (*Rom.* 11:25) in a way that makes it unmistakably clear that the people of God are one, not two. All who are saved are saved through faith in Jesus Christ and are incorporated into the one fellowship of his church. This passage militates in the strongest possible terms against the idea of the existence of two separate olive trees or two separate purposes of salvation, a present one for the Gentiles and a future one for the Jews.

The earliest members of the church were drawn predominantly, though not exclusively, from the Jewish people. Since the incorporation of Gentile believers into the fellowship of the church was initially resisted, it is especially striking that Paul's preaching at the synagogue (note well!) in Antioch declares Jesus as the promised Davidic King through whom the promised blessings are now being fulfilled.

In Galatians, Paul emphatically opposes the false gospel of the Judaizers. Against this false gospel, he places the gospel of salvation by grace through faith in Jesus Christ, a gospel equally valid for Jew and Gentile alike. Illegitimate distinctions are not permitted between Jew and Gentile, circumcised or uncircumcised. This should not surprise us, coming as it does from the same apostle who reminded the church in Ephesus that Christ 'is our peace, who made both [Jew and Gentile] one, and broke down the barrier of the dividing wall' (*Eph.* 2:14). Dispensationalism seems to be in serious error in its distinction between Israel and the church.

The 'Literal' Hermeneutic of Dispensationalism

One of the characteristic features of Dispensationalism is its insistence upon a 'literal' reading of the Bible. Throughout its history many of its advocates have alleged that alternative millennial views reflect a low view of Scripture's authority. Dispensationalist authors differ considerably on a literal reading of the Bible with variations between early classic forms and more recent progressive forms, but two problems stand out with all forms of dispensational literalism.

The first problem is the tacit acknowledgement that a literal reading of the text need not exclude a spiritual meaning. In the original position of Scofield, a somewhat arbitrary distinction is made between the historical and prophetic texts in the Bible. This distinction allows for the possibility that the historical texts may have both a literal and a spiritual meaning. The possibility of non-literal elements in historical texts indicates that it is somewhat simplistic and misleading to insist that texts always be read literally.

A second and even more fundamental problem is the attempt to identify 'literal' with a grammatical-historical reading of the text, which is considered to be taking words in their normal or plain meaning. This approach begs the question of what 'literal', 'normal', or 'plain' strictly mean. To say that the literal meaning must always be the most plain, concrete, and obvious meaning is to prejudge the meaning of these texts before actually reading them according to the rules for the kind of language being used.

It has been common since the time of the Protestant Reformation to speak of a grammatical-historical reading of the biblical texts. This is one that takes the words, phrases, syntax, and context of the biblical texts seriously—hence, grammatical—and also takes the historical setting and timing of the texts into careful consideration—hence, historical.

The problem with dispensationalism's understanding of what is involved in a literal hermeneutic is evident in three problem areas: first, the relation between Old Testament prophecy and its New Testament fulfilment; second, the subject of biblical typology; and third, the oft-repeated claim that non-dispensationalists illegitimately spiritualise the biblical promises regarding the new earth.

Old Testament Prophecy

The first problem area is Dispensationalism's treatment of Old Testament prophecies and their fulfilment. Whatever the previous fulfilments

145

of Old Testament prophecy may have been, they reach their ultimate fulfilment in Christ, in whom all the promises of God have their 'yes' and their 'amen' (*2 Cor.* 1:20).

Dispensationalism fails to acknowledge the fulfilment of many of the Old Testament prophecies to Israel in the coming of Christ and the gathering of his church during this present age. Rather than allowing the New Testament's understanding of the fulfilment of prophecy to determine its viewpoint, Dispensationalism operates from the prejudice that no promise to Israel could, in the strict sense of the term, ever be literally fulfilled in connection with the church. But this is a prejudice based upon an unbiblical dichotomy between Israel and the church.

Biblical Typology

A second and related problem, the interpretation of biblical types and shadows, is in some ways the Achilles' heel of the dispensationalist's literal hermeneutic. Biblical types may be loosely defined as those events, persons, or institutions in the Old Testament that prefigure or foreshadow their New Testament realities. Many of the historical events, persons, and institutions which were integral to the Lord's administration of the covenant of grace in the Old Testament foreshadowed events, persons, and institutions in their new covenant reality and fulfilment. These are especially problematic for Dispensationalism.

For example, the dispensationalist insistence that the temple is an institution that pertains, in its literal form, peculiarly to Israel, fails to appreciate its typical significance in biblical revelation. The idea that the temple would be literally rebuilt and serve as a focal point for Israel's worship during the millennium represents a reversion to Old Testament types and shadows. Dispensationalism turns back the clock of redemptive history.

A similar misunderstanding of biblical typology also characterises the dispensationalist's treatment of 'Jerusalem' or 'Zion'. The literal Jerusalem of the old covenant is typical of the new covenant city of God, the church. The dwelling of the Lord in the midst of his people, the presence of the temple sanctuary, the throne of David—all of these find their

146

fulfilment and reality in the new covenant blessing and consummation witnessed by John in his vision on the isle of Patmos.

One further and closely linked instance of biblical typology is that of the sacrifices stipulated in the law of Moses, especially in the book of Leviticus. These sacrifices were symbols and types of the person and work of Jesus Christ, the high priest after the order of Melchizedek, who fulfils and perfects all that they foreshadowed.

The point exhibited in these biblical types constitutes the Achilles' heel of the dispensationalist claim for a literal hermeneutic. Not only does this claim fail to do justice to the New Testament's teaching regarding the fulfilment of Old Testament prophecy, but it also militates against the claim made by the inspired New Testament authors regarding the typological significance of the Old Testament sanctuary, priesthood, and sacrifice: the reality of the new covenant renders the shadow obsolete. The same principle holds for all of the types and shadows of the old covenant administration. Once this principle is conceded, Dispensationalism's insistence upon a literal reinstitution of the types and shadows of the old covenant is in serious conflict with the teaching of biblical typology.

'Spiritualising' Old Testament Promises?

The third problem area is the dispensationalist claim that a non-literal fulfilment of the biblical promises to Israel betrays a spiritualising that cannot do justice to the biblical texts. According to Dispensationalism, many promises to Israel cannot be accounted for unless they will be fulfilled literally during the period of the coming millennium.

Dispensationalists often cite Isaiah 11:6-10 and 65:17-25 as predictions of the millennium. According to Dispensationalism, these prophecies are compelling proof that the prophecies of the Lord to Israel can have only a literal, concrete fulfilment. A closer inspection of these two prophecies, however, does not support this claim.

Isaiah describes a beautiful picture of the kingdom of the shoot from Jesse. In this kingdom, the Lord declares that 'the wolf will dwell with the lamb, and the leopard will lie down with the kid . . . They will not hurt or destroy in all my holy mountain, for the earth will be full of the knowledge of the Lord as the waters cover the sea' (verses 6, 9). No mention is made of this being a period that will be limited in time, perhaps a period of one thousand years. More importantly, this passage speaks of a reign marked by universal peace and knowledge of the Lord. The millennium of dispensationalist expectation, by contrast, includes the presence of some people who do not acknowledge the Lord, and even a substantial rebellion at its close on the part of many against him (Satan's 'little season'). The description of Isaiah 11:6-10 better describes the universal peace of the final state.

Isaiah 65:17-25 is more difficult to interpret. In the New Scofield Reference Bible, the first verse, which speaks of the new heavens and a new earth, is taken as a description of the final state, but the remaining verses (verses 18-25) are taken as a description of the millennium. This reading has some plausibility, because death is mentioned in these verses and dispensationalists argue that they cannot accordingly refer to the final state.

If the language of this passage is pressed literally, it seems to conflict with the biblical teaching that death will not exist in the new heavens and earth. But perhaps the language is simply a way of poetically affirming the incalculably long lives the inhabitants of the new earth will live. Perhaps more significantly, these verses say that 'the voice of weeping and the sound of crying' will no longer be heard in Jerusalem, the very language used in Revelation 21:4 to designate the final state. The likeliest reading of these verses, therefore, is that verses 17-25 describe the joy, blessedness, and everlasting life that will be experienced by God's people in the new heavens and the new earth.

These and similar texts have an appropriate place within a non-dispensationalist reading of the Bible. It is simply not the case that all non-dispensationalists fail to take their description of renewed life on the new earth seriously. So long as it is understood that the final state requires a new heavens and a new earth, the richness and concreteness of the imagery in these biblical passages can be appreciated. It could even be argued that the dispensationalist millennium falls short of the blessedness of life in the new heavens and earth described in these passages. So long as non-dispensationalists properly insist upon the restoration of the earth in the final state, they need not concede the charge that they have illegitimately spiritualised the prophecies of Scripture regarding the final state.

The dispensationalist claim regarding a literal interpretation of the Scriptures is really the product of its insistence upon a radical separation between Israel, God's earthly people, and the church, God's spiritual people. Without this undergirding assumption there is no reason to deny the fulfilment of old covenant promises in the new covenant realities. Nor is there any reason to avoid the implications of biblical typology for the dispensationalist system.

Perhaps the most telling evidence against the dispensationalist hermeneutic is in Hebrews. The book of Hebrews is one sustained argument for the finality, richness, and completion of all of the Lord's words and works in the new covenant mediated by Christ. Dispensationalism wants to preserve the old arrangements intact for Israel, arrangements that will be reinstituted in the millennial kingdom. However, this would be tantamount to going back to what has been surpassed in the new covenant in Christ, reverting to arrangements that have been rendered superfluous because their reality has been fulfilled in the new covenant. The Mediator of this new covenant, Jesus Christ, is the fulfilment of all the promises of the Lord to his people.

Dispensationalism represents a continued attachment to the shadows and ceremonies of the old covenant and a failure to appreciate the finality of the new covenant. Its literal hermeneutic is not literal in the proper sense of the term, but a reading of the New Testament through the lens of its insistence upon a radical separation between Israel and the church.

EVALUATING POSTMILLENNIALISM

We noted earlier that the term 'postmillennial' simply means 'after the millennium', and this position teaches that Christ will return after the millennium at the end of the present age. Two distinct millennial viewpoints, golden-age Postmillennialism and Amillennialism, are commonly termed Postmillennialism and Amillennialism. Amillennialism—when it does not express a pessimistic view of the presence of Christ's kingdom—is the view that most satisfies the biblical teaching.

Our evaluation here will focus upon Postmillennialism in its narrower sense, which looks for a golden age between the times of Christ's first and second comings. This period will last a thousand years, not in a literal sense, but in the sense of a great and expansive period of time. At its conclusion, there will be a brief period of Satanic rebellion and apostasy, the 'little season' of Revelation 20.

Some postmillennialists suggest this golden age will commence gradually and increase. Others suggest that it will commence abruptly with a future conversion of the nations by an unprecedented working of the Spirit through the gospel. Opinions also vary as to the function of the civil magistrate in the realisation of this millennial kingdom. Complicating matters even further is the tendency today among some postmillennialists to identify the entire period between Christ's first and second advents as the millennium. Though this latter tendency amounts to a position all but indistinguishable from Amillennialism—though perhaps more optimistic—it retains the characteristic emphasis upon a coming golden age. There are several problems with Postmillennialism, which we will identify in terms of several questions.

When Does Christ Become King?

Golden-age Postmillennialism suggests that the kingship of Jesus Christ is not so much a present as a future reality. The coming of Christ in the fullness of time, though it inaugurated a new period in the history of redemption, did not by itself constitute the great turning point in history so far as the kingdom of God is concerned. Rather, it commenced a series of events that only in terms of subsequent developments lead to the millennial kingdom.

This construction compromises the testimony of the New Testament. The reign of Christ commences with his first advent and installation at the right hand of the Father. Though the manifestation of Christ's rule may vary throughout history, he has all authority during the entire period between his resurrection and his return (*Matt.* 28:16-20). The preaching of the gospel and the discipling of the nations, the great tasks of Christ's church, express his present rule as king.

The description of Christ's exaltation in Philippians 2:9-11 defines his present glory, not one that is reserved for the future. Ephesians 1:22-23 describes the present dominion of Christ in the strongest terms (see also *Col.* 1:15-18; *1 Pet.* 3:22). No suggestion is made that this present reign of Christ is to be divided into non-millennial and millennial phases, each distinguished from the age to come. Christ's reign both in the present age and in the age to come is affirmed, with no other age intervening.

The only passages in the New Testament that might appear to teach such a distinction between the inter-advental period and a golden-age millennium are 1 Corinthians 15:22-26 and Revelation 20:1-6. Careful study indicates, however, that neither passage teaches such a distinction.

The Corinthians passage teaches that after his resurrection from the dead, Christ was installed as king and presently reigns over all things. This reign will end when all of his enemies—including the last enemy, death—have been brought into subjection under his feet. There is no suggestion of a millennial reign that will intervene between his present reign and the final state, or of a golden age between the present age and the age to come. Rather, it teaches that the (millennial) reign of Christ encompasses the present period of history, to be concluded only by the final conquest of all Christ's enemies.

To support the view of a future golden age in history from Revelation 20, two things would need to be proved. The first is that the events depicted in Revelation 19:11-21 refer not to the second coming of Christ, but to a transitional period in history leading to the beginning of the millennium of Revelation 20. Revelation 19:11-21 seems clearly to refer instead to the return of Christ at the end of the present age. The second is that the events depicted in Revelation 20:1-6 must take place after the events recorded in Revelation 19:11-21. But, as was previously argued, this has not been proven and is unlikely.

There is, accordingly, no biblical support for the idea that Christ's kingship will enter a new and distinct phase with the inauguration of a future millennium or golden age. Christ is king now. And he has been king from the commencement of his mediatorial rule at the Father's right hand.

Is the Millennium Now or Future?

In reply to the claim that Postmillennialism's golden age compromises the present reality of Christ's reign, some present-day postmillennialists insist that the difference is not one of kind but only one of degree. According to these postmillennialists, the only basic difference between postmillennialist and amillennialist views is that the former has a more optimistic and biblical expectation of the gospel's success in this present age. They criticise the amillennialist for an unbiblical pessimism and lack of confidence in the promised success of the church's discipling of the nations.

Curiously, this argument abandons the 'chiliasm' of classic postmillennialist expectation: the millennium of Revelation 20 as a distinct period in history that begins some time after Christ's first advent. This is a major concession to Amillennialism. Indeed, it leads to a position that is formally amillennialist, identifying the millennium of Revelation 20 with the whole period between Christ's first and second advents.

Furthermore, this modified view actually undermines the very idea of the millennium as a golden age. If the entire period of history between Christ's first and second advents is the millennium of Revelation 20, the golden age of the millennium no longer seems so golden. On this view, Satan's binding coincided with the first advent of Christ and has characterised the history of the church from the first century. How, then, can advocates of this Postmillennialism continue to describe in the most glowing of terms the anticipated glory of a coming millennial era? Does the glory of this anticipated millennium tarnish and fade when considering the reality since the beginning of the new covenant era? If the millennium includes the nearly two thousand years of the church's history thus far, during which the church has experienced times of great prosperity as well as adversity, there seems little reason to expect this pattern will be

152

radically different in the future. Once the idea of a future distinguishable millennium is abandoned, no place remains for an expectation of a coming period of unprecedented blessing.

In some respects, this is the same difficulty faced by any chiliast doctrine that argues for a distinct millennial age in the history of redemption. A new age intrudes which is neither the present age nor the age to come in the biblical sense of these expressions. Perhaps this is the reason, when some contemporary postmillennialists describe the millennium, they alternate between descriptions echoing what the Bible ascribes to the new heavens and the new earth and descriptions that seem indistinguishable from what has been true throughout the present period of history.

What About the 'Signs of the Times'?

In our previous consideration of the Bible's teaching regarding these so-called signs, it was noted that in these last days of gospel preaching, believers will encounter several signs of opposition to Christ. Though there may be times when the believing church will experience great tribulation or apostasy, tribulation and apostasy are nonetheless typical signs of the gospel's presence in this age. The preaching of the gospel will provoke opposition and conflict between the kingdom of God and the kingdom of the evil one. The testimony of Scripture is that these signs will be the invariable experience of the believing church between Christ's first and second advents.

This suggests little likelihood, certainly no biblical expectation, that the circumstance of Christ's church will typically be one of blessedness during the present age. Golden-age Postmillennialism teaches that the millennium will be an extensive period in history during which the nations will be converted, the principles of God's law and gospel will govern the conduct of people, and undisturbed peace and prosperity will prevail throughout the world. However, the passages we have considered demand a more restrained and temperate view of the prospects for the kingdom and people of God.

Is a Servant Greater than his Master?

One of the great themes in the Scriptures relating to the Christian life is the theme of suffering. Believers incorporated into Christ not only share in all the benefits of his saving work, but also participate in some way in his sufferings. They are united with him in the likeness of his death, and raised with him in newness of life (*Rom.* 6:3-6). Just as he suffered the hostility and unbelief of the world, so will all those who are his.

The theme of the believer's suffering in fellowship with Christ was often emphasised in the writings of the great Reformers, Calvin and Luther. Calvin, in the *Institutes*, spoke of cross-bearing as a hallmark of the pilgrimage of every Christian. Luther likewise described biblical theology as a theology of the cross, not a theology of glory. Triumphalism, the idea that the believer will go from victory to victory in this life without suffering any distress, has no place. Just as in the experience of the early church, so in the experience of Christ's church through the centuries, it is only 'through many tribulations [that] we must enter the kingdom' (*Acts* 14:22).

This theme is woven like a thread throughout the New Testament's depiction of the Christian life. Jesus emphasizes suffering as an inescapable dimension of discipleship: 'If anyone wishes to come after me, let him deny himself, and take up his cross daily, and follow me. For whoever wishes to save his life shall lose it, but whoever loses his life for my sake, he is the one who will save it' (*Luke* 9:23-24; see also *Matt.* 10:38-39; 16:24; *Mark* 8:34; *Luke* 14:27). Jesus warned his disciples of the opposition they would inevitably face (*Matt.* 10:34-36). No disciple is worthy of the Master, unless prepared to assume the suffering service that marked his life. Greatness in the kingdom of God is measured, not by becoming the first, but by becoming the last (*Mark* 9:35; compare 10:43; *Matt.* 20:26). Jesus, in the context of teaching the disciples about his impending suffering, insisted that they too would drink the cup that he was appointed to drink and 'be baptized with the baptism with which I am baptized' (*Mark* 10:39).

Consistent with Jesus' teaching about the suffering service that will mark the lot of all his disciples, the apostles themselves often spoke of their participation in the sufferings of Christ. Paul admonishes the Corinthians for their arrogance and unwillingness to recognise that God magnifies his power through human weakness. Paul speaks of his and every believer's readiness to 'know [Christ], and the power of his resurrection and the fellowship of his sufferings, being conformed to his death' (*Phil.* 3:10; compare *Col.* 1:24). In the life of every believer, there is conformity to Christ's suffering, a participation in Christ that inevitably includes the elements of self-denial, shame, and loss.

Finally, Paul describes the whole creation in Romans 8 in the language of suffering. Echoing language used by Jesus in his Olivet discourse regarding the signs of the times (*Matt.* 24:8), this passage speaks broadly of the 'sufferings of this present time' which are 'not worthy to be compared with the glory that is to be revealed to us' (*Rom.* 8:18). What is striking about this passage is that the present age is typified by suffering, not only on the part of believers, but also on the part of the whole creation that 'travails' until the time of deliverance. Not until the close of this present age and the beginning of the age to come will this circumstance change. Suffering is an inescapable feature of this interval between the times of Christ's coming and his return in glory.

These passages do not state that every believer and church in this present age will suffer in the same way or to the same extent. Nor do they deny that at many times and in various places the cause of Christ's gospel and kingdom will enjoy wonderful success and blessing. They certainly do not teach that believers who enjoy prosperity and peace must be guilty of unbiblical compromise or accommodation. But they do teach that, in this present age, the believer and the church must expect and anticipate some fellowship in the sufferings of Christ. The preaching of the gospel and the advance of the kingdom always call forth a counter-gospel of unbelief and opposition. Believers learn obedience through their suffering, just as Christ their Lord and Master did (*Heb.* 5:8). They understand firsthand the meaning of Hebrews 13:12-14, 'let us go out to him outside the camp, bearing his reproach. For here we do not have a lasting city, but we are seeking the city which is to come' (compare *Heb.* 12:3).

Golden-age Postmillennialism mutes this biblical teaching about the fellowship in suffering between Christ and his disciples. No matter how it

155

is qualified or described, the millennium of postmillennialist expectation excludes this dimension of being a follower of Christ in the present age. Consequently, Postmillennialism betrays a triumphalist theology of glory that prematurely anticipates in history what will be the circumstance of God's people only in the day of their vindication. Only Christ's coming again will bring an end to the trouble that marks the Christian's pilgrimage in this life, anticipating the city that has foundations, whose builder and maker is God. The believer of today, like Abraham and the saints of the past, does not enjoy the promised rest in this life.

What is the Focus of the Believer's Hope for the Future?

The final objection against golden-age Postmillennialism is that it alters the focus of the believer's hope for the future. While the New Testament depicts the church in this present age as continually participating in the sufferings of Christ and eagerly awaiting his return at the end of the age, the postmillennialist view encourages an outlook that focuses on the millennium rather than the return of Christ.

The biblical focus is upon the return of Christ as the great event on the horizon of the future. In Romans 8:22-25, Paul speaks of the hope for the day when the sons of God will be revealed and their bodies be fully redeemed. The writer to the Hebrews speaks of the coming of Christ 'a second time for salvation without sin, to those who eagerly await him' (9:28). Peter wrote: 'But according to his promise we are looking for new heavens and a new earth, in which righteousness dwells' (*2 Pet.* 3:11-13).

A striking illustration of this expectation is found in 2 Thessalonians 1. Writing to a church that had known tribulation from its earliest beginnings (verse 4), Paul holds out the promise of rest at Christ's revelation from heaven:

> For after all it is only just for God to repay with affliction those who afflict you, and to give relief to you who are afflicted and to us as well when the Lord Jesus shall be revealed from heaven with his mighty angels in flaming fire, dealing out retribution to those who do not know God and to those who do not obey the gospel of our Lord Jesus (verses 6-8).

156

Nothing is said about a future millennial era that will end their present distresses. Only the revelation of Christ from heaven will bring them the salvation for which they long.

In these and other passages, the second coming of Christ is the blessed hope of the believing church (*Titus* 2:13; *1 Pet.* 1:3-7). As the believer faces tribulation and distress in this present age, as the church meets with opposition to Christ and his cause, the one great promise that brings unspeakable comfort is the promise of the return of Christ and the final vindication of his cause at the end of the age.

Throughout the New Testament, a contrast is drawn between the sufferings of this present age and the joy of the age to come. There is no millennial age between the two that might draw attention away from the return of Christ. Certainly no promise is held out for a period of uninterrupted and undisturbed blessedness in history prior to the revelation of Christ at the end of the present age.

Two Qualifications

Having raised several biblical objections to golden-age Postmillennialism, two qualifications to these objections need to be mentioned.

First, though golden-age Postmillennialism is inconsistent with biblical emphases, we have not argued that this position directly conflicts with the teaching of the Reformation confessions. The only Reformation confession that explicitly condemns some form of golden-age Postmillennialism is the *Second Helvetic Confession*, a historic standard of the Swiss Reformed churches, written by Heinrich Bullinger.

This should serve as a caution against any exaggerated criticism of the postmillennial view among those who hold to these Reformation confessions. Many who subscribe to the *Westminster Confession of Faith* advocate a form of postmillennial teaching. In doing so, they have not contradicted or compromised any part of the biblical system of doctrine summarised in this confession. Though the Reformation confessions are clearly incompatible with Dispensational Premillennialism and, to a lesser degree, with Historic Premillennialism, they are compatible with the two forms of Postmillennialism: Amillennialism and golden-age Postmillennialism.

The debate between amillennialists and postmillennialists is an intramural one. The differences between these views are differences of theological emphasis within a common confessional bond.

Second, these criticisms of golden-age Postmillennialism should not be construed as an argument for a pessimistic and limited expectation for the gospel or kingdom in this present age. The objections do not mitigate the legitimate insistence of postmillennialists for the greatest possible confidence in the victory of Christ's cause in history.

Too often the position known as Amillennialism has been associated with a pessimistic view that things will inevitably go from bad to worse throughout the course of history. Expectations for the growth and triumph of Christ's kingdom are diminished. Little attention is given to the claims of Christ as king in all areas of life.

However, there are ample biblical arguments for the most robust expectation for the success of the gospel. Christians ought to live under the banner of Christ's Great Commission. They ought to live out of the full expectation that Christ shall have dominion throughout all the earth; that the nations will undoubtedly be given to him as his rightful inheritance. They ought to seek the kingdom of God and its righteousness in every area of Christ's dominion. Nothing less than the bringing of every thought captive to Christ will satisfy. Nothing less than the subjection of all things to the will and reign of Christ will do.

9

THE FUTURE OF ALL THINGS: THE RESURRECTION OF THE BODY

*T*he time has come to take up the last part of general eschatology: the things that will accompany the return of Christ at the end of the age.

These events are aptly termed 'concomitants of the second advent' by Charles Hodge in his *Systematic Theology*. Though this term is rather abstract, it nicely captures the idea that we are looking at events which, according to the Scriptures, will accompany Christ's return at the end of the age. These events will close this age, consummate God's purposes in redemptive history, and introduce the final and enduring state of God's kingdom.

In the light of the word of God, we will consider: the resurrection of the dead, the final judgement of all human beings, the eternal punishment of unbelievers in hell, and the creation of a new heavens and earth.

THE RESURRECTION OF THE BODY

We have noted that the biblical expectation for the future of believers is not primarily focused upon the intermediate state. The spotlight of the Bible falls upon the resurrection of the body as restoration of the whole person, body and soul, in a renewed state of integrity within the context of a new heavens and earth.

This is one of the distinctive features of the biblical view of the future and of our salvation in Christ. The Triune God created Adam a 'living soul', formed from the dust of the earth (*Gen.* 2:7). Our creatureliness in its wholeness always includes the body, which originally was created good. Redemption from the curse of God addresses our whole need, body and soul. This is why the *Heidelberg Catechism* speaks of the believer's comfort in terms of belonging to Christ 'with body and soul'. Redemption does not deny the goodness of creation; rather it brings the healing and renewal of creation. The same Lord who forgives all our sins is the one who 'heals all our diseases', including that sickness of body and soul which leads to death (*Psa.* 103:3). No biblical picture of the believer's future may fail to include, as a central part, the promise of the resurrection of the body.

The Time of the Resurrection

Though Christian believers commonly acknowledge this expectation, the timing of the resurrection is often disputed. As we have seen, Premillennialism teaches at least two distinct resurrections: the resurrection of the just at the time of Christ's coming before the millennium, and the resurrection of the unjust after the millennium.

The most decisive objection against this separation is its incompatibility with the Bible's common association of the resurrection of both the just and the unjust. In one of the Old Testament's few direct references to the resurrection, Daniel 12:2, we read that 'many of those who sleep in the dust of the ground will awake, these to everlasting life, but the others to disgrace and everlasting contempt'. This passage closely links the resurrection of believer and unbeliever.

A similar linking is reflected in John 5:28-29, when Jesus speaks of one great event in which all of the dead will be raised for judgement. Though some premillennialists suggest that this passage's reference to an hour might include a long period of time—appealing to verse 25 where it refers to the period in which the spiritually dead shall be brought to life— its meaning in these verses parallels its common meaning in the Gospel of

John (see 7:30; 8:20; 12:23; 13:1; 16:21; 17:1). It refers to a distinct period in which God's purposes will be fulfilled. As in other Scripture passages (*Acts* 24:14-15; *Matt.* 16:27; 25:31-33; *2 Cor.* 5:10), this passage affirms that the resurrection of all the dead, believers and unbelievers alike, will occur at a single point of time in the future.

Even the passage most often cited by premillennialists in support of their view shows evidence that the resurrection and judgement will include all people, believers and unbelievers. In Revelation 20:1-15, the vision of the final 'great white throne judgement' that will occur after the millennium portrays 'the dead, the great and the small, standing before the throne' (verse 12). These dead include not only the great and small, but also all those 'given up' by the sea, death and Hades. All of these dead are then judged, 'every one of them according to their deeds' (verse 13). As a consequence of this judgement, anyone whose 'name was not found written in the book of life', is thrown into the lake of fire, the second death. The description of the resurrection and judgement in this vision implies that all people are embraced and only those whose names are written in the Lamb's book of life are saved from the lake of fire. Were the vision only describing the resurrection and judgement of those whose names were not written in the book of life, the language describing this vision would be confusing at best, misleading at worst.

Other passages teach that the resurrection of believers will occur on the last day, when Christ will be revealed from heaven and the sound of the trumpet will be heard. In John 6:40, Jesus assures his disciples that he came in fulfilment of his Father's will and purpose, and that it was his Father's will 'that everyone who beholds the Son and believes in him, may have eternal life; and I myself will raise him up on the last day'. In the passage which speaks of the rapture, 1 Thessalonians 4:13-18, the coming of Christ and the resurrection of believers are associated with the call of the Archangel and the sound of the trumpet (verse 16; see also *Matt.* 24:31; *1 Cor.* 15:52). According to these passages, when Christ comes and the dead in Christ are raised, this will close the present age and introduce the glory of the age to come (see *Phil.* 3:20-21; *1 Cor.* 15:23).

Those who insist upon two resurrections separated in time often will appeal to the language of 1 Thessalonians 4:16 and 1 Corinthians 15:23-24. These passages describe a certain order among the events of Christ's coming, the resurrection of believers, and the coming of the end of the age. According to the premillennialist, this order confirms the distinction between two resurrections. However, neither of these passages affords a convincing case for this position. When Paul in 1 Thessalonians 4:16 speaks of the dead in Christ rising first, he is not drawing a contrast between the resurrection of believers and of unbelievers, but rather between the resurrection of the dead, those who have fallen asleep in Jesus, and the rapture of believers who are still living at the time of Christ's coming. Far from being excluded from the benefit of Christ's coming, those who have fallen asleep in him will have pre-eminence—they will rise first. The order described in 1 Corinthians 15:23-24—'Christ the first fruits, after that those who are Christ's at his coming, then comes the end'—does not allow for an intervening period of one thousand years between Christ's coming and the end. The events described, though they occur in a definite order, are components of one great complex of events at the end of the age.

The Author of the Resurrection

The more important and difficult questions relating to the Bible's teaching regarding the resurrection have to do with its author and nature. Who will be responsible for raising the dead at the end of the age? What will be the nature of the resurrection body?

It must be admitted that the Bible does not provide a complete description to answer all of these and other questions. Some things are clearly taught to encourage and comfort believers. Others remain shrouded in mystery.

Though the Old Testament includes explicit references to the resurrection of believers (*Isa.* 26:19; *Dan.* 12:2), and though the expectation of the resurrection follows from all that the Lord promises his covenant people, it is only in the New Testament that the full light of the gospel promise of the resurrection shines. The biblical teaching and hope for the resurrection is securely founded upon the great redemptive accomplishments of Christ. Believers united with Christ enjoy him and all his blessings, most notably victory over death and the sure confidence of the resurrection of the body.

In spite of this focus on Christ's resurrection and the believer's share in it, the New Testament makes it clear that the author of this resurrection is the Triune God. Each Person of the Trinity plays an integral part in granting resurrection to those who belong to Christ. When Jesus responds to the Sadducean denial of the resurrection, he ascribes resurrection power to God: 'You are mistaken, not understanding the Scriptures, or the power of God. For in the resurrection they neither marry, nor are given in marriage, but are like angels in heaven' (*Matt.* 22:29-30). In 2 Corinthians 1:9, Paul describes believers as those who should not trust in themselves but 'in God who raises the dead'.

In other passages, the resurrection of the dead is ascribed especially to the power and work of Christ. In John 5, it is the Son of God who together with the Father calls the dead from their tombs and grants them life (verses 21, 25, 28-19). This authority to raise the dead is, according to the teaching of Christ, a prerogative granted to him by the Father and a fruit of his saving work (*John* 6:38-40, 44-45; 11:25-26). The Holy Spirit, who applies and communicates the benefits of Christ's saving work, gives believers a foretaste and share in the power of Christ's resurrection. The same Spirit 'who raised Jesus from the dead' dwells in believers and grants life to their 'mortal bodies' also (*Rom.* 8:11).

As believers share in the benefits of their fellowship with Christ, they are promised the gift of resurrection from the dead, a gift which the Father is pleased to grant through the Son and in the power of the life-giving Spirit.

The Nature of the Resurrection Body

This leaves us with the crucial question yet to be answered: what is the nature of the resurrection body, as disclosed to us in the Scriptures? If the return of Christ will be accompanied by the resurrection of the dead, the just and the unjust alike, and if the resurrection of believers in fellowship with Christ is a gracious work of the Triune God, what do the Scriptures teach about the character of this event?

We can arrive at an answer to this question in two ways. One way would be to focus upon the accounts of Christ's resurrection to see what they might tell us. Since the believer's resurrection body will be fashioned after the pattern of Christ's glorious body (*Phil.* 3:20-21), this is a legitimate way to proceed. Another way would be to consider those passages that speak directly of the nature of the resurrection body.

Careful study of Christ's resurrection and subsequent appearances allows us to draw some conclusions regarding the nature of the resurrection body. The accounts of the resurrection consistently witness to the fact that the tomb was now empty (*Matt.* 28:6; *Mark* 16:6; *Luke* 24:3, 6; *John* 20:1-10). The truth of the empty tomb authenticates that the resurrection was not a spiritual event separable from Jesus' body. There is genuine continuity between Jesus' pre-resurrection and post-resurrection body (not bodies).

Consequently, when the risen Lord appeared to his disciples after the resurrection, they were able (despite their perplexity and initial unbelief at times) to recognise him, identify the marks of his crucifixion, and even enjoy a meal with him (see *Matt.* 28:9, 17; *Mark* 16:9-14; *Luke* 24:11, 16, 31; *John* 20:19-23, 27-29). In the Gospel of Luke, all doubt as to the reality of the Lord's resurrection body is removed when we read the Lord's words of rebuke to his startled disciples who thought they were seeing a spirit: 'Why are you troubled, and why do doubts arise in your hearts? See my hands and my feet, that it is I myself; touch me and see, for a spirit does not have flesh and bones as you see that I have' (*Luke* 24:38-39).

Though we need to beware the temptation to draw too many conclusions from these accounts, it does seem clear that, whatever the differences between the glorified and pre-resurrection body of Christ, there is a substantial and real continuity between them.

In addition to these accounts of the resurrection of Jesus Christ, a few passages speak directly of the nature of the resurrection body. In 2 Timothy 2:18, Paul alludes to false teachers who taught that the resurrection had 'already taken place'. Apparently spiritualising the resurrection, these teachers were confusing believers. Paul makes an important comment in Philippians 3:20-21:

> For our citizenship is in heaven, from which also we eagerly wait for a Saviour, the Lord Jesus Christ; who will transform the body of our humble state into conformity with the body of his glory, by the exertion of the power that he has even to subject all things to himself.

This passage not only establishes the important principle that the believer's resurrection body will be conformed to Christ's, but it also contrasts the humble condition of our present bodies with the glorious condition that will be ours in the resurrection. Our present bodies exhibit all the marks of sin and God's curse—they are weak, decaying, fragile, and temporary. Our resurrected bodies will exhibit all of the marks and benefits of Christ's saving work—they will be strong, incorruptible, indestructible, and enduring.

In 2 Corinthians 5:1-9, the believer's present body is described as an 'earthly tent' that, after it is dissolved or torn down, is replaced by a 'building from God, a house not made with hands, eternal in the heavens' (verse 1). This passage continues with another metaphor. The present body compares to the resurrection body as being-clothed-with-mortality compares to putting-on-the-clothing-of-immortality.

1 Corinthians 15:35-49

The passage that draws the contrasts between the present body and the resurrection body most extensively is 1 Corinthians 15:35-49. Because of the importance of this passage to our understanding of the nature of the resurrection body, we will quote it in full and then make some observations upon it.

> But someone will say, 'How are the dead raised? And with what kind of body do they come?' You fool! That which you sow does not come to life unless it dies; and that which you sow, you do not sow the body which is to be, but a bare grain, perhaps of wheat or of something else. But God gives it a body just as he wished, and to each of the seeds a body of its own. All flesh is not the same flesh, but there is one flesh of men, and another flesh of beasts, and another flesh of birds, and another

165

of fish. There are also heavenly bodies and earthly bodies, but the glory of the heavenly is one, and the glory of the earthly is another. There is one glory of the sun, and another glory of the moon, and another glory of the stars; for star differs from star in glory. So also is the resurrection of the dead. It is sown a perishable body, it is raised an imperishable body; it is sown in dishonour, it is raised in glory; it is sown in weakness, it is raised in power; it is sown a natural body, it is raised a spiritual body. If there is a natural body, there is also a spiritual body. So also it is written, 'The first man, Adam, became a living soul.' The last Adam became a life-giving spirit. However, the spiritual is not first, but the natural; then the spiritual. The first man is from the earth, earthy; the second man is from heaven. As is the earthy, so also are those who are earthy; and as is the heavenly, so also are those who are heavenly. And just as we have borne the image of the earth, we shall also bear the image of the heavenly.

Recognising the complexity and richness of this passage, we nevertheless see several themes relating to the primary question with which Paul is concerned: 'with what kind of body do they come?'

First, Paul uses the metaphor of the seed and fruit to illustrate the connection between the present body and the resurrection body. However great the difference between the seed sown and the fruit that it eventually bears, the seed and the fruit are of one kind. The resurrection of the body is likened to the dying of a seed in order that it might come to life in the form of its fruit. This means that the resurrection body is of a distinctively human kind. When God raises believers from the dead, their bodies, however new and changed, remain distinctively and peculiarly human.

Second, a series of contrasts are drawn between this natural or earthly body and the spiritual or heavenly body. These do not contrast a body made up of 'material stuff' with one made up of 'spiritual stuff', as if to suggest that the resurrection body will be immaterial or non-fleshly. Rather, they distinguish sharply the present body as one belonging to the present age that is passing away and under the curse of God, and the resurrection body that belongs to the life of the Spirit in the age to come. The distinction is not between material and immaterial, but between two kinds of bodies that answer to the present age and the age to come. Paul bases his description of these two bodies upon the two respective heads of humanity: the first man, Adam, and the second man, Christ.

It is especially important to note the four contrasts between the natural and the spiritual body. The earthly body of this present age is sown perishable; the heavenly body of the age to come is raised imperishable. When death has been defeated and the consequences of sin and God's curse have been removed, the liability of the body to decay and corruption will be vanquished. The earthly body is sown in dishonour; the heavenly body will be raised in glory. In contrast to the tarnished and dimmed condition of the present body, the resurrection body will be splendid and striking. The earthly body is sown in weakness; the resurrection body will be raised in power. Fragility and vulnerability will be replaced by enduring and indestructible power. And finally, the present body is natural; the resurrection body is heavenly. These contrasts paint a striking picture of the glory of the resurrection body. This body will be of a human kind, but not like anything believers have seen or known in this life—a body no longer ravaged by sin and its consequences, a body that will be a fit and enduring building in which to dwell and enjoy unbroken (and unbreakable) fellowship with Christ and those who are his.

Third, in the closing section of this passage, Paul bases his description of these respective bodies upon the contrast between the two original bearers of these bodies—the first man, Adam, and the second man, Christ. There is an intimate and close correspondence between the first man, Adam, who is 'from the earth', and the earthly bodies of those who bear his image. Likewise, there is an intimate and close correspondence between the second man, Christ, who is 'from heaven', and the heavenly bodies of those who bear his image. Adam and Christ represent two humanities. The first humanity is under the dominion and liability of sin—subject to perishing, dishonour, weakness, and death. The second humanity is under the dominion and blessing of salvation—the recipient of imperishability, glory, power, and never-ending life.

This passage confirms the teaching of the Scriptures elsewhere on the nature of the resurrection. When Christ returns at the end of the age, the dead will be raised. The unjust and unbelieving will be raised unto judgement. The just and believing will be raised unto glory. The nature of this resurrection will be like a seed that is sown and dies, and is raised in newness of life. It will be a real body, material and fleshly, not immaterial and spiritual so as to deny the continuity between the present body and the resurrection body. However, this body will be so conformed to the image and glory of Christ that no vestige of the power and destructive effects of sin will remain. As Paul so eloquently puts it in 1 Corinthians 15:

> But when this perishable will have put on the imperishable, and this mortal will have put on immortality, then will come about the saying that is written, 'Death is swallowed up in victory. O Death, where is your victory? O death, where is your sting?' The sting of death is sin, and the power of sin is the law; but thanks be to God, who gives us the victory through our Lord Jesus Christ (verses 54-57).

The Resurrection and the Renewal of All Things

Another concomitant of the second advent of Christ is the renewal of all things, the cleansing of this sin-cursed creation and the re-creation of a new heaven and earth. The relation of the resurrection of the body to this renewal of the creation merits brief attention. The continuity between the pre- and post-resurrection body of the believer finds its counterpart in the continuity between the present and the renewed creation. Just as Adam was originally formed from the dust of the earth and placed within the creation-temple of God in which to serve and glorify the Creator, so also in redemption the new humanity will be restored to life and service under the headship and dominion of the second Adam, in a newly cleansed creation-temple.

For this reason, Romans 8:18-23 describes the creation as being under the same 'slavery of corruption' that afflicts believers in their present bodies of humiliation. The term used to describe the corruption of creation in Romans 8 is used in 1 Corinthians 15:42, 50 to describe the corruption of the body. The creation's groaning under the curse of sin mirrors the groaning of the believer. The creation waits eagerly for the revelation of the sons of God, because the redemption of God's children is a redemp

168

tion in which creation itself participates. The link between the resurrection of the believer and the renewal of the creation is an intimate one.

This intimate link between the believer's resurrection and the renewal of the creation allows us to see the unity between individual and general (or cosmic) eschatology. It joins together the salvation of the church and her members with the great events of cosmic renewal that will accompany Christ's return. The justification and sanctification of the believer find their parallels in the justification and sanctification of the heavens and earth in the new creation. Just as the Lord declared the first creation very good (*Gen.* 1:31), so the renewed creation will be worthy of the same judgement. And just as the first creation was perfect and holy in its consecration to the Lord, so the renewed creation will be one 'wherein dwells righteousness' (see *2 Pet.* 3:10-13). Justified and sanctified saints will dwell in a justified and sanctified creation. A people holy unto the Lord, a royal priesthood, will enjoy fellowship with the Lord in the sanctuary of his renewed creation.

Having come to the close of our consideration of the biblical teaching regarding the resurrection of the body, we can appreciate afresh the hope of which Peter speaks in 1 Peter 1:3-5:

> Blessed be the God and Father of our Lord Jesus Christ, who according to his great mercy has caused us to be born again to a living hope through the resurrection of Jesus Christ from the dead, to obtain an inheritance which is imperishable and undefiled and will not fade away, reserved in heaven for you, who are protected by the power of God through faith for a salvation ready to be revealed in the last time.

10

THE FUTURE OF ALL THINGS: THE FINAL JUDGEMENT

*L*ike the resurrection of the body, the final judgement is an end-time event that will accompany the return of Christ at the close of this present age. The writer to the Hebrews remarks: 'And inasmuch as it is appointed for men to die once and after this comes judgement, so Christ also, having been offered once to bear the sins of many, shall appear a second time for salvation without reference to sin, to those who eagerly wait for him' (9:27). Consequently, when Christians affirm their faith in the Apostles' Creed, they speak not only of the resurrection of the body but also of the return of Christ from heaven 'to judge the living and the dead'.

We will examine several themes regarding the final judgement before turning to the controversial subject of differing degrees of reward granted to believers.

THE TIME OF JUDGMENT

Among the first questions regarding the Last Judgement are its time and number. Historic and dispensational premillennialists speak of several judgements. The most common dispensationalist position speaks of four distinct judgements: the judgement of believers at the rapture; the judgement of Israel at the close of the seven-year period of tribulation;

the judgement of the nations; and the 'great white throne judgement' at the close of the millennial age (*Rev.* 20:11-15). The first three judgements precede the millennium and the last follows. Because Premillennialism distinguishes between the resurrection of believers before the millennium and the resurrection of unbelievers after the millennium, at least two distinct judgements are necessary.

Once it is acknowledged, however, that the return of Christ will occur after the millennium of Revelation 20, no occasion remains for claiming there will be more than one judgement. Just as we have seen that the resurrection will be an event at the end of the age which embraces believer and unbeliever alike (*John* 5:25-29), so the final judgement will include all people. As Paul says, 'For we must all appear before the judgement seat of Christ, that each one may be recompensed for his deeds in the body, according to what he has done, whether good or bad' (*2 Cor.* 5:10). When Christ describes the final judgement in Matthew 25, all the nations are judged together and the 'sheep' separated from the 'goats' (*Matt.* 25:31-46).

Though it is evident that the final judgement will occur as a single event after the resurrection, it is not as clear from Scripture whether it will precede or follow the transformation of the creation. Some passages seem to suggest that the judgement will take place before the recreation of the heavens and earth (e.g., *2 Pet.* 3:7). However, in other passages the final judgement is simply linked with the end of the present age (e.g., *Matt.* 13:40-43; 25:31-32; *2 Thess.* 1:7-10). Revelation 20:12 suggests that the judgement will immediately follow the general resurrection:

> And I saw the dead, the great and small, standing before the throne, and books were opened; and another book was opened, which is the book of life; and the dead were judged from the things which were written in the books, according to their deeds.

In the sequence of Revelation 20, the great white throne judgement is followed by a series of visions describing the new heavens and earth. Although the visions of Revelation are not arranged in a neat chronological order, the placement of the visions of the new heavens and earth after that of the great white throne judgement suggests this sequence of events: the resurrection, the final judgement, and the transformation of the creation.

On several occasions, the Bible speaks of the final judgement as a day of judgement (see *Matt.* 7:22; 11:22; *2 Thess.* 1:10; *2 Tim.* 1:12). This language, however, should not be pressed to mean a literal period of one day. It may only be a way of referring to the peculiar period for the purpose of judgement. Just as the Scriptures speak of the 'day' of salvation (*Heb.* 3:7- 19), a day is coming when all will be judged.

THE NECESSITY OF JUDGMENT

What necessity or purpose is served by the final judgement of those who have already been shown to be saved or lost?

This question treats the final judgement too much in terms of our ordinary understanding of a trial court with its process of reaching and pronouncing a verdict. The final judgement is a work of God, particularly a work of Christ, who has been appointed as judge. As a work of God, it cannot be understood as a process to determine guilt or innocence, but rather as an occasion to pronounce and execute with divine authority the sentence that God alone can pass with perfect justice. Since God knows all those who are his from eternity (see *Eph.* 1:4; *Rom.* 8:29), he is not discovering them by means of this final judgement. Rather, he is revealing his power and glory as the only one who has the prerogative to judge his creatures and declare their final destiny.

Scripture and the Reformation confessions confirm the final judgement as the occasion for God to manifest his glory. Note the *Westminster Confession of Faith,* Chapter 33.2:

> The end of God's appointing this day is for the manifestation of the
> glory of his mercy, in the eternal salvation of the elect; and of his justice,
> in the damnation of the reprobate, who are wicked and disobedient.
> For then shall the righteous go into everlasting life, and receive that full-
> ness of joy and refreshing, which shall come from the presence of the

Lord; but the wicked who know not God, and obey not the gospel of Jesus Christ, shall be cast into eternal torments, and be punished with everlasting destruction from the presence of the Lord, and from the glory of his power.

CHRIST WILL JUDGE

One prominent and clear teaching of Scripture is that Christ will be the judge. One of the prerogatives characterising Christ's rule at the Father's right hand is the prerogative to carry out the final judgement. In keeping with this biblical emphasis, the Apostles' Creed speaks of the return of Christ as his coming 'to judge the living and the dead'. The great work in which Christ will be engaged at his coming is the work of judgement, vindicating his people and the cause of the gospel, condemning all their and his enemies.

This authority belongs to Christ's office as king (*Matt.* 28:18; *Phil.* 2:9, 10). In John 5:22-23 we read, 'For not even the Father judges anyone, but he has given all judgement to the Son, in order that all may honour the Son, even as they honour the Father.' Later in the same chapter, Christ closely associates the resurrection of the just and the unjust with his 'authority to execute judgement' (verse 27). At the close of his sermon on Mars Hill, the Apostle Paul declares that God 'has fixed a day in which he will judge the world in righteousness through a man whom he has appointed, having furnished proof to all men by raising him from the dead' (*Acts* 17:31). Paul also speaks of the day of judgement as one on which all must appear 'before the judgement seat of Christ, that each one may be recompensed for his deeds in the body, according to what he has done, whether good or bad' (*2 Cor.* 5:10). Similarly, in the familiar description of the final judgement given in Matthew 25, the Lord Jesus Christ speaks of the time 'when the Son of Man comes in his glory, and all the angels with him' to sit on 'his glorious throne' (verse 31; compare *2 Thess.* 1:7-10). In these and other passages, it is unmistakably clear that the one who will judge and sit upon the throne of judgement is Christ himself.

The significance of this truth is captured well in the *Heidelberg Catechism's* answer to the question, 'What comfort is it to you that Christ shall come to judge the living and the dead?'

> That in all my sorrows and persecutions, with uplifted head I look for the very same Person who before has offered himself for my sake to the tribunal of God, and has removed all curse from me, to come as judge from heaven; who shall cast all his and my enemies into everlasting condemnation, but shall take me with all his chosen ones to himself into heavenly joy and glory.

Though the coming of Christ in glory and power to judge the living and the dead is a fearful prospect for the unbelieving, it is an unspeakable comfort to those who have believed in him. In the day of Christ's coming, the impenitent will be condemned. But the people of God will receive from the judge, who is also the Saviour previously judged in their place, their vindication and rest.

Some of the biblical descriptions of the final judgement suggest that believers and even the angels who serve the Lord will play a role. In 1 Corinthians 6:2-3, Paul, in the context of his rebuke to the Corinthians who take fellow believers to court, reminds them that 'the saints will judge the world' (verse 2). The vision of Revelation 20 also speaks of the 'judgement' that is given to those who reign with Christ during the millennium (verse 4). Similar descriptions of believers sharing in the work of judgement are found in other passages as well (e.g., *Psa.* 145:5-9; *Matt.* 19:28). What role do the saints and the angels play in Christ's work of judgement?

Certainly, because Christ is the Mediator and Head of his people, they share fully in whatever honour or glory belongs to him. On the principle that believers are co-heirs with Christ of all things (*1 Cor.* 3:21-23), it follows that they have some part in his work of judgement. What that part might be remains unclear. Nothing could be done independently of what Christ will do, nor could their activity add something that is lacking in his work. Perhaps it is best to note simply that they share in the victory and glory that belong to Christ in his role as the judge. It is best to restrict the involvement of the angels to a ministry that is auxiliary and

175

subordinate to Christ's. The angels are assigned the work of gathering the peoples together for the judgement and executing the judgement that is pronounced (e.g., *Matt.* 13:41-2; 24:31; 25:31; *2 Thess.* 1:7).

ALL WILL BE JUDGED

The fact that believers need not fear the final judgement because it will vindicate their faith and service to the Lord, does not mean that the final judgement will be only of those who are unbelieving and impenitent. The Scriptures teach that all will be judged, the just and the unjust. No one will be spared or excluded from this judgement when the books are opened and the verdict pronounced.

All believers will therefore be subject to judgement. Though it is not one that they need to fear, it is a genuine judgement for them nonetheless. When in 2 Corinthians 5:10 Paul speaks of 'we all' who must appear before the judgement seat of Christ, he is referring specifically to believers. Hebrews 10:30 states that 'the Lord will judge his people'. Writing to believers in Rome, Paul admonishes them for judging their brothers, noting that 'we shall all stand before the judgement seat of God'. James 3:1 speaks of a more severe judgement to be applied to those believers who are teachers. And in 1 Peter 4:17, believers are even warned that judgement will 'begin with the household of God'. This liability to judgement, however, does not contradict the clear biblical teaching that believers have already passed out of death into life (*John* 5:24). Nor does it conflict with the confidence expressed in Romans 8:1, that there is 'now no condemnation for those who are in Christ Jesus'.

Some Scripture passages suggest that the fallen angels will be liable to judgement (*2 Pet.* 2:4; *Jude* 6). One passage, 1 Corinthians 6:2, contains an intriguing reference to the judgement of angels, which does not specify whether these angels are obedient or disobedient. It seems possible that all angels will be liable to the final judgement. That seems to be consistent with the general teaching of Scripture regarding its purpose. In this way, the justice of God's verdicts regarding all of his creatures will be clearly revealed.

If all will be judged, what will be judged? The Scriptures are quite vigorous in their teaching that all will be judged for whatever they have done. 2 Corinthians 5:10 speaks very broadly of the 'deeds in the body, according to what he has done, whether good or bad'. Nothing is excluded. Matthew 25:35-40 specifically speaks of those things done to 'the least of these my brethren'. Revelation 20:12 speaks of the dead being judged 'according to their deeds' (compare *1 Cor.* 3:8; *1 Pet.* 1:17; *Rev.* 22:12). God will not overlook those works done in accord with his will (*Eph.* 6:8; *Heb.* 6:10). Nor will he overlook the idle words spoken (*Matt.* 12:36), or the deeds 'now hidden in darkness' (*1 Cor.* 4:5). Just as all are judged, so all that they have done will be subject to judgement.

The difficult aspect of this question relates to the works of believers. If believers are no longer liable to condemnation, then it seems implausible that all of their works should be revealed on the day of judgement. Would not that bring shame and embarrassment to believers whose sins are wholly covered and forgiven for the sake of Christ? And would not such shame and embarrassment be inconsistent with the believer's present confidence that his or her sins have been removed as far as east is from west (*Psa.* 103:12)?

In the following section, we will consider part of the Scriptures' answer to this question: the reward for good works granted in connection with the final judgement. Clearly, if there is greater or lesser reward for works done by believers while in the body—as 1 Corinthians 3:10-15 seems to suggest—then the recognition of greater and lesser obedience will play a role in the final judgement of believers. To be sure, the final judgement is not an occasion for undoing the confidence that believers now enjoy. But that believers' works will be judged is undeniable and may even serve as a legitimate encouragement for diligence and conscientiousness in fighting against sin in this life.

THE STANDARD OF JUDGEMENT

One critical aspect of the final judgement is the standard used to confirm the justice of the verdict. This will be the law and word of God so far as these have been revealed to those who are judged. The standard will not be the same for everyone, however, because of the important difference in the extent of what has been revealed. The principle will be that greater privilege brings greater responsibility. Much will be required of those to whom much has been given, while less will be required of those to whom little has been given.

This principle is set forth remarkably in Matthew 11:20-22. In this passage, Jesus severely rebukes the cities in which he had done many of his miracles:

> Woe to you, Chorazin! Woe to you, Bethsaida! For if the miracles had occurred in Tyre and Sidon which occurred in you, they would have repented long ago in sackcloth and ashes. Nevertheless, I say to you, it shall be more tolerable for Tyre and Sidon in the day of judgement, than for you. And you, Capernaum, will not be exalted to heaven, will you? You shall descend to Hades; for if the miracles had occurred in Sodom which occurred in you, it would have remained to this day. Nevertheless I say to you that it shall be more tolerable for the land of Sodom in the day of judgement, than for you.

These words do not mean that those to whom less has been given bear little responsibility for their unbelief and disobedience. All bear full responsibility for what God has given them. Some have enjoyed a richer disclosure of God's words and works and carry a greater responsibility. Because of the greater richness and blessing of the new covenant, disobedience and unfaithfulness in the new covenant situation becomes even more deadly than in the old covenant situation (*Heb.* 2:1-3; 12:25-29).

What will happen to those who have not had the opportunity to hear the gospel or be taught from the word of God? To answer this question, we need to remember that the standard will be the law and will of God so far as these have been revealed. In Romans 1:18-23 and 2:11-16, we are taught that all people, Jews and Gentiles alike, have been given some knowledge of God through the things he has made and the law whose work is written upon their hearts. No one can be excused before God on the basis of a plea of ignorance. To the extent that God has revealed himself to all, all are without excuse before him.

The *Belgic Confession*, one of the confessional documents of the Protestant churches, summarises in its last article the various aspects of the final judgement that we have considered:

> Finally, we believe, according to the Word of God, when the time appointed by the Lord (which is unknown to all creatures) is come and the number of the elect complete, that our Lord Jesus Christ will come from heaven, corporally and visibly, as he ascended, with great glory and majesty to declare himself judge of the living and the dead, burning this world with fire and flame to cleanse it. Then all men will personally appear before this great judge, both men and women and children, that have been from the beginning of the world to the end thereof, being summoned by the voice of the archangel, and by the sound of the trump of God . . . Then the books (that is to say, the consciences) shall be opened, and the dead judged according to what they shall have done in this world, whether it be good or evil. Nay, all men shall give account of every idle word they have spoken, which the world only counts amusement and jest; and then the secrets and hypocrisy of men shall be disclosed and laid open before all. And therefore the consideration of this judgement is justly terrible and dreadful to the wicked and ungodly, but most desirable and comfortable to the righteous and elect; because then their full deliverance shall be perfected, and there they shall receive the fruits of their labour and trouble which they have borne.

DEGREES OF REWARD?

Does God reward the righteous according to their deeds? How is the idea of God rewarding the righteous compatible with salvation based upon grace alone?

In the history of the discussion of these questions, a number of key passages have played an important role. In Corinthians 3:14-15, Paul describes ministers or teachers in the church, some of whom have built upon the foundation of Christ with 'gold, silver, precious stones', and others with 'wood, hay, straw'. The day is coming when these respective works will be tested by fire and their character revealed. Those whose works are shown to be worthy will receive an appropriate reward. Those whose works are shown to be unworthy will be saved, 'yet so as through fire'.

This passage seems to teach clearly that those who labour in the ministry of the word of Christ will be rewarded variously, depending upon the quality of their works. One group is rewarded and the other is not because of the difference in the kind of work.

In 2 Corinthians 9:6, Paul speaks not only of ministers of the gospel, but also of all who give generously in support of the Lord's work. He encourages the Corinthians by reminding them of the correspondence between sowing and reaping. If they sow sparingly, they will reap sparingly. If they sow generously, they will reap generously. This 'law of the harvest' applies also to the Christian life. Those who labour in a spirit of generosity and beneficence will reap a correspondingly greater reward.

It could be argued that this passage refers only to the experience of believers in this life. In a similar passage (*Gal.* 6:8) and others that use the common theme of harvest (e.g., *Matt.* 25:24), however, reaping coincides with the final judgement and the ingathering of the full harvest. Those who sow much will receive a greater reward than those who sow sparingly.

The parables of the talents and of the pounds suggest that God grants different gifts to his servants in this life and in the life to come. Citizens of the kingdom of heaven vary in the extent and nature of their responsibilities and privileges in the service of their king. In the day of reckoning, they receive correspondingly different rewards for their service.

In the parable of the talents, a man granted to one servant five talents, to another two talents, and to still another just one talent (*Matt.* 25:15). After a long time, the man returns to settle accounts with his servants. He grants a greater reward to the man who received the five talents than to the one who received two. By contrast, the man to whom one talent was given, because he had not wisely used what had been given to him, was deprived of all that he had earlier received and cast into 'outer darkness' (verse 30).

In the parable of the pounds, the unequal distribution of pounds and subsequent rewards is even more striking. Each of the nobleman's servants is given ten pounds. One servant is rewarded with responsibility for ten cities and another for five cities, but another is deprived even of the little he was given. This parable clearly emphasises the right of the nobleman to grant a diversity of gifts and rewards to his servants corresponding to their responsible use of what is entrusted to them.

The language used in these parables for the final reckoning and rewarding suggests that they describe the final judgement. The context in Matthew 25 explicitly refers to the final judgement and the separation between the righteous and the unrighteous. This is also confirmed by the language of harvest used to describe the master's reckoning with his servants upon his return. These parables appear to teach that Christ will distribute a diversity of degrees of reward to the righteous at the final judgement.

In addition to passages that speak of a diversity of rewards at the final judgement, other passages teach that in the final judgement certain privileges and responsibilities will be granted to some of the righteous but not to others.

In Matthew 8:11, we read that believers will sit down 'with Abraham, Isaac and Jacob in the kingdom of heaven'. When the rich man and Lazarus die, Jesus speaks of Lazarus being 'carried into Abraham's bosom' (*Luke* 16:22; compare *Rom.* 4:11-12). In the account of the Transfiguration, Moses and Elijah were present (*Matt.* 17:3) as representatives of the prophets of the old covenant. Christ, in his description of the 'regeneration' at the end of the age, declares that the apostles 'will sit upon twelve thrones, judging the twelve tribes of Israel' (*Matt.* 19:28; *Luke* 22:30). Similarly, when in the book of Revelation we are given a description of the foundations of the heavenly Jerusalem, the names of the twelve apostles are inscribed upon them (*Rev.* 21:14).

These passages suggest that the peculiar distinctions that the Lord has granted to his servants in this life are not lost in the life to come. The role played by the patriarchs, prophets, and apostles in the course of redemptive history is remembered perpetually. These distinctions are not ignored in the final state so that a flat 'egalitarianism' prevails among the people of God. The richness, diversity, and degree of responsibility in this life seem to find their correspondence and fulfilment in the life to come.

A number of biblical passages speak of a diversity of 'crowns' to be awarded to Christ's servants in the day of judgement. In some of these passages, the crown probably refers to the granting of eternal life—the common reward and joy of God's people (e.g., *1 Cor.* 9:25; *2 Tim.* 4:8). This is not always the case, however. In 1 Thessalonians 2:19, Paul speaks of the Thessalonians as his 'hope or joy or crown', in whom he will glory and rejoice in the presence of the Lord Jesus. Clearly this cannot mean any arrogant boasting. But it does mean that the Thessalonians will be an occasion for joy and thanksgiving when the work Paul performed among them is recognised in the day of Christ's coming. In James 1:12, we read of the 'crown of life' that will be given to the man who 'perseveres under trial' in the service of the Lord. Peter also encourages the elders in the churches by reminding them that, 'when the Chief Shepherd appears, [they] will receive the unfading crown of glory' (*1 Pet.* 5:4). This crown of glory is a special reward for the faithful ministry of those who serve as shepherds of the flock of God.

The diversity of gifts and callings among the people of God will not go unnoticed in the final judgement. Each will receive a reward in keeping with the service rendered. Christ will openly acknowledge and reward his faithful servants as they together enter into the joy of the Lord.

A REWARD OF GRACE, NOT MERIT

If we say that the good works of believers have their reward according to the quality of the works performed, how can we say that believers are saved by grace alone?

At least three approaches to this question could be—and often have been—taken in the history of the Christian church.

One approach insists that some notion of merit must be appropriate. In the Roman Catholic tradition, a distinction has been drawn between two kinds of merit: 'congruent merit' (half-merit) and 'condign merit' (true merit). Works of congruent merit are imperfect and not strictly deserving of the reward God grants to them. Works of condign merit, by virtue of God's grace infused into believers, genuinely merit the reward that God grants. In this understanding, merit plays a legitimate role in the Christian life.

A second approach opposes the whole idea of a diversity of rewards as incompatible with the doctrine of grace. This approach assumes that God does not variously reward the righteous for their good works, because that requires merit as its corollary and salvation is wholly by grace. Those who take this approach frequently appeal to the parable of the labourers equally rewarded for different amounts of work in the vineyard (*Matt.* 20:1-16). This parable, it is argued, clearly teaches that the law of the kingdom is a law of grace, not of merit. God subverts the ordinary law of justice by graciously granting the same wages to all of the labourers.

The third and best approach maintains that the idea of rewards is consistent with the biblical teaching regarding salvation by grace alone, provided the rewards are of grace and not of merit. Nothing the believer receives from God is deserved, either in the strict or lesser sense of condign or congruent merit. When God rewards the righteous for their good works, he only adds grace to grace, rewarding believers for those deeds that he himself works in them by his Spirit (*John* 15:1-17). In no sense whatsoever does any believer receive from God what is deserved. The Christian who obeys God perfectly—which, of course, cannot be the case—would be no more than an 'unprofitable servant' who had only done his or her duty (*Luke* 17:7-10). All of the gifts of God's grace are just that—gifts—unmerited favours granted for the sake of Christ.

The wonder of God's grace in the life of the believer includes God's gracious reward of those (imperfect and undeserving) good works that the believer does by the powerful working of the Spirit. Like a loving father, the heavenly Father takes pleasure in the deeds of his children.

AN ENCOURAGEMENT, NOT THE MOTIVE

One objection to the idea of diversity of rewards is the worry that this will pollute the stream of Christian service with a self-seeking spirit. The radical teaching of God's grace is threatened by the introduction of the performance-orientated and commercial spirit that so often corrupts contemporary life and culture in North America.

It is interesting to notice that the *Heidelberg Catechism*, after having declared God's rewards to be 'not of merit but of grace', goes on to say that 'it is impossible that those who are implanted into Christ by a true faith should not bring forth fruits of thankfulness' ('Lord's Day' 24). While acknowledging that good works are rewarded, this confession recognises gratitude as the only proper motive for Christian obedience. It does not follow, therefore, that any teaching of rewards for good works must lead to an improper emphasis upon rewards as a motive. That this may occur, no one would deny. That it must occur, or that it is inherent in the very idea of varying rewards, does not follow.

Perhaps a distinction between motive and encouragement may be helpful here. Though the prospect of rewards may not serve as a motive or the basis for Christian obedience, it certainly might function as an encouragement. The prospect of rewards encourages the believer to understand that no labour is in vain in the Lord. Christians are properly encouraged to know that their service will be graciously and abundantly acknowledged by Christ at his coming.

Some question if degrees of rewards are compatible with the perfect blessedness of the final state. Would that not suggest the strange, perhaps self-contradictory, idea of degrees of perfection? And how could a believer enjoy the fullest blessedness, knowing that he or she falls short of others in the life to come?

Two of the most helpful answers in the history of Christian theology stress the diversity among believers as well as the communal joy of the final state.

The final state of God's kingdom will be characterised by a diversity of giftedness, office, and capacity for service and joy that mirrors the diversity among God's people in this life. Though no one will experience less blessedness and joy, the capacity for and the quality of these may differ considerably. To use a quantitative analogy, one vessel may be larger than another and therefore of greater capacity. If each vessel—the larger and the smaller—is wholly filled, however, it enjoys a fullness or perfection commensurate with its capacity. So perhaps it will be in the new heavens and earth.

The diversity in the final state of God's kingdom, far from being the occasion for regret, will also be the occasion for greater joy. On the principle that perfect holiness excludes every possibility for envy or contention among the people of God, this suggestion argues that the greater rewards enjoyed by some will only engender further thankfulness among all. Since it is already true in this life that all things belong to all believers, and all believers belong to Christ, and Christ belongs to God (*1 Cor.* 3:21-23), this principle will presumably also hold in the kingdom to come. How could there then be any sense of loss or impoverishment among the people who belong to Christ, when some are distinguished from others in gifts and rewards?

We have seen that the good works of the righteous will be rewarded in the day of judgement. These rewards are not of merit but of grace. The prospect of such rewards, though an encouragement to God's faithful children, is not the motive for the Christian life; the great motive for all Christian obedience is gratitude for God's grace in Christ. Rather than an inequality that would diminish perfect blessedness, degrees of rewards will be a further occasion to rejoice in God's goodness. All things in Christ belong to all believers; whatever gain one may experience in the life to come will only be gain for all.

11

THE FUTURE OF ALL THINGS: THE DOCTRINE OF ETERNAL PUNISHMENT

*T*oday the biblical teaching about the eternal punishment of the unbelieving in hell is either neglected or disapproved. In the environment of western post-Christian and post-modern culture, most people find the doctrine of eternal punishment abhorrent.

Due to the unpopularity of this doctrine and the frequent attempts to revise it, even within conservative evangelical contexts, it is necessary to begin with a brief statement of the historic position of the church on the subject of hell.

THE HISTORIC POSITION OF THE CHURCH

The traditional doctrine teaches that, subsequent to the resurrection and the final judgement, all those persons whom God does not save through the work of Christ will be consigned to hell. Though its exact nature and location remain somewhat uncertain, hell will be a place of unending punishment for God's enemies. Those who have lived in enmity against God will find themselves forever banished from his blessed presence, in a state of conscious awareness of his disfavour. Among the Reformation confessions, the following statements represent well the traditional Christian understanding of hell:

187

And therefore the consideration of this judgement is justly terrible and dreadful to the wicked and ungodly, but most desirable and comfortable to the righteous and elect; because then their full deliverance shall be perfected, and there they shall receive the fruits of their labour and trouble which they have borne. Their innocence shall be known to all, and they shall see the terrible vengeance which God shall execute on the wicked, who most cruelly persecuted, oppressed, and tormented them in this world, and who shall be convicted by the testimony of their own consciences, and shall become immortal, but only to be tormented in the eternal fire which is prepared for the devil and his angels. (*Belgic Confession*, Art. 37)

The end of God's appointing this day is for the manifestation of the glory of his mercy, in the eternal salvation of the elect; and of his justice, in the damnation of the reprobate, who are wicked and disobedient. For then shall the righteous go into everlasting life, and receive that fullness of joy and refreshing, which shall come from the presence of the Lord; but the wicked who know not God, and obey not the gospel of Jesus Christ, shall be cast into eternal torments, and be punished with everlasting destruction from the presence of the Lord, and from the glory of his power. (*Westminster Confession of Faith*, Chap. 33:2)

Though these confessional statements set a proper standard of sobriety and reserve in what they say about hell, and though their focus remains primarily fixed upon the comfort that God's people derive from the gospel, they clearly affirm a doctrine of eternal punishment. Echoing the Scriptures, the language underscores the horror of hell as a place of unceasing, consciously felt punishment. With an economy of words, these confessions affirm what the orthodox Christian church has always taught. Though they do not attempt any detailed description of hell, they clearly affirm its reality.

Two Alternative Views

The chief alternatives to this historic doctrine are universalism and annihilationism.

Universalism is the teaching that, in the end, all human beings will be saved. No human being will ultimately fail to enjoy the fullness of salvation, by whatever means that salvation is obtained. Broadly speaking, universalism can take one of two forms: pluralistic or Christian. Pluralistic universalism teaches that the Christian faith is one of many ways of salvation, each of which is legitimate. Christian universalism teaches that Christ is the one and only Saviour by whom all will ultimately be saved, either in this life or in the life to come.

In its Christian expression, universalism affirms that no one will obtain salvation apart from the saving work of Christ. However, this saving work is universal in its scope; no one will suffer eternal punishment in hell. Some of those who advocate a Christian universalism include the provision for a second opportunity for salvation after death, or they may speak of a period of purgatory during which some are fitted for the enjoyment of salvation as they suffer temporary punishment for the sins committed in this life.

Annihilationism is the view that, although the saved enjoy everlasting life, all the lost will be annihilated ultimately. They will not suffer unending torment, but extinction. The punishment is eternal in the sense of result, but not in the sense of experience.

Annihilationism is clearly the most tempting and therefore dangerous alternative to the traditional doctrine of hell among evangelicals today. In the form called 'conditional immortality', it has captivated an increasing number of evangelical theologians, some of considerable ability and influence. Conditional immortality teaches that only those who meet the conditions for benefiting from Christ's saving work—however those conditions are understood—will obtain immortality. All others will be annihilated, either immediately upon death or subsequent to a limited period of punishment after death. In its most common evangelical form, the annihilation of the lost will take place after they have endured some kind of punishment for their sin and disobedience. Conditional immortality denies any doctrine of unending conscious torment of the wicked.

COMMON OBJECTIONS

Among contemporary advocates of conditional immortality, several common objections are expressed to the traditional doctrine of hell. Though these may not be stated in the same way or be given the same degree of importance by different advocates of this position, they tend to recur in their writings.

The first and perhaps most important objection is the claim that the Bible speaks of the ultimate destruction of the wicked (e.g., *Phil.* 3:19; *1 Thess.* 5:3; *2 Thess.* 1:9; *2 Pet.* 3:7). The idea of destruction, it is argued, suggests the 'ceasing-to-be' of the wicked, rather than their continued existence in a situation of torment. The word 'destruction' usually means the cessation of something's existence. The destruction of the wicked after the final judgement means simply that they are removed from existence.

A second and related objection appeals to the biblical imagery used to describe this punishment. Just as the language of destruction implies complete cessation of existence, so the imagery of fire implies a process whereby the sinner is completely consumed. Like the burning of the chaff at the return of the judge in Matthew 3:12, so the burning of the wicked at the last judgement will utterly destroy them.

The third objection takes advantage of the apparent ambiguity in the word 'eternal'. In the history of the church, the parallel between 'eternal' life and 'eternal' punishment in a passage like Matthew 25:46 has been a basis for arguing that hell is a place of unending punishment. However, many advocates of annihilation maintain that in the case of eternal punishment, this need only mean that the punishment has an unending result. Annihilation is an eternal punishment only in the sense that its consequences never end.

In addition to these objections argued from biblical material, others are of a more theological nature. These raise questions about the consistency of the doctrine of eternal punishment with other doctrines clearly taught in the Bible.

One of these theological objections (and the fourth in our list) argues that the doctrine of hell is incompatible with what we know of the love of God. Those who raise this objection insist that God could not possibly punish the sinner in hell eternally, were he a God of love.

The fifth objection is similar to the fourth; it argues that this doctrine is incompatible with what we know of the justice of God. If justice in its most basic meaning has to do with receiving one's due, then eternal punishment in hell outweighs the crime. The doctrine of hell, it is objected, teaches that a limited offence will receive at the hands of God an unlimited penalty, and this is manifestly unjust.

The sixth and last objection argues that the existence of hell would mar the perfection and glory of the eternal state. It suggests that the redemptive work of God will fall short of bringing about the fullness of blessing and joy. The eternal joy and perfection of God's kingdom will have to compete with the jarring reminder of sin and sin's consequences. The consummation of God's purposes in history would be a bit like a story without an altogether happy ending. The joy of heaven would be muted by the weeping of hell.

ANSWERING THESE OBJECTIONS

Since no teaching of Scripture labours under a more severe burden of proof than the historic Christian doctrine of hell, our approach to the doctrine of eternal punishment will be to answer these common objections.

1. The word 'destruction'

A common biblical argument against the doctrine of eternal punishment appeals to the language of destruction. The terms in the New Testament for 'to destroy' or 'destruction', according to this argument, simply mean to cause to cease to exist, or the state of no longer existing.

When Herod plotted to kill the newborn babies in Bethlehem in order to get rid of Jesus, he sought to 'destroy' him (*Matt.* 2:13). Jesus instructed his disciples not to be afraid of someone who can only 'destroy' the body, but of the one 'who can destroy both body and soul' in hell (*Matt.* 10:28). The straightforward meaning of 'destruction' seems to be an act that causes something or someone to cease to exist. In two passages where a different term for 'destruction' is used (*1 Thess.* 5:3; *2 Thess.* 1:9), the implication seems to be that this destruction involves an annihilation or cessation of the existence of those who experience it.

When this same term is used in the intransitive form, meaning 'to perish' or 'to die', a similar idea is expressed. In Luke 15:17, we read that the prodigal son came to his senses when admitting, 'I am dying here with hunger.' Paul, describes the fate of the Israelites who tested the Lord as being 'destroyed by the serpents' (*1 Cor.* 10:9). These passages speak of a physical perishing. However, several passages also speak of an eternal perishing in connection with hell. The well-known verse, John 3:16, describes those who believe as those who 'shall not perish but have everlasting life'. In describing the judgement upon those who have 'sinned without the law', Paul speaks of their perishing without the law (*Rom.* 2:12). In 1 Corinthians 15:18, he insists that a denial of the resurrection of the body for believers means that they will have 'perished'. The Lord who is not slow regarding his promise is said not to wish that any should perish (*2 Pet.* 3:9).

Though this argument appears plausible, it does not stand up well under cross-examination. As several of the cited references show, the term 'destruction' can describe cessation of existence. But in other instances, it describes something rather different.

In the well-known parables of the 'lost' coin or the 'lost' son in Luke 15, the term Jesus uses is the same term used for 'to destroy' in the passages cited above. No one would conclude that the coin or the prodigal son ceased to exist. Likewise, in Matthew 9:17 the term used to describe the 'bursting' or the 'ruining' of the wineskins is the common term for 'to destroy'. The destruction of these wineskins is their ceasing to be useful for their intended purpose. When the disciples rebuked the woman who anointed Jesus with costly ointment, they declared her excess a 'waste', the same term translated elsewhere as 'destruction'.

Due to this diverse use of the term 'to destroy', it is too simplistic to argue from it for a doctrine of annihilationism. If annihilationism is to be demonstrated, then it must be shown that the word 'destruction', when describing the destiny of the unbelieving, means their ceasing to be. It would also have to be shown that in other biblical passages that speak of the final state of the unbelieving, the idea of ongoing existence is not affirmed.

2. The language of a 'consuming fire'

A second and similar argument against the doctrine of everlasting punishment appeals to passages that use the image of a 'fire that consumes'. This language, together with other common images for the final state of the wicked, suggests that the final outcome of God's judgement upon the unbelieving is their extinction or annihilation.

This argument can be answered at two levels. The first is hermeneutical: is it permissible to take the word fire in such a literal, non-metaphorical way and draw the conclusion that fire must utterly consume its object? The second level is more textual: do the texts employing this imagery lend any support to the position of the annihilationist?

At the hermeneutical level, it would seem that annihilationists fail to take seriously the metaphorical language of the Scriptures. To say that these descriptions are often metaphorical in no way diminishes the reality of hell. But the descriptions of hell in the Scripture can hardly be pressed literally. Imagery of a consuming fire—bespeaking God's holy punishment and judgement of the wicked—is frequently coupled with imagery of the 'worm that does not die' (e.g., *Mark* 9:48; compare *Isa.* 66:24). Insisting upon a literal fire that consumes would seem incompatible with a worm not liable to death.

If the literal meaning of fire is that of a force that consumes its object, then that includes a rapid process. Many annihilationists, however, want to allow for a period of time during which the wicked undergo differing degrees of punishment prior to their eventual annihilation. The idea of a period of time, however, seems incompatible with the way literal fire rapidly consumes its object. Moreover, once a literal fire has consumed its object, it can no longer be sustained. In the biblical imagery and descriptions of the fire of hell, however, the fire is explicitly described as 'eternal' (*Matt.* 18:8). Like the worm that does not die, it is a fire that is never extinguished. Indeed, in Jesus' unforgettable description of hell in Mark 9:47-48, we read of those who are thrown into hell where *'their* worm does not die, and the fire is not quenched' (emphasis mine).

Another example of the metaphorical imagery regarding hell is the language of 'darkness' or 'outer darkness' that is often used in the Scriptures. In Matthew 8:12, Jesus warns that the 'sons of the kingdom shall be thrown into the outer darkness; in that place there shall be weeping and gnashing of teeth'. The guest at the wedding banquet without the appropriate garment in Matthew 22 is cast into 'outer darkness' (verse 13). This motif of hell as a place of darkness is commonly found in the Scriptures (e.g., *Matt.* 25:30; *2 Pet.* 2:17). Darkness represents the absence of the light of God's favour and countenance. Remarkably, in one passage the imagery of an 'eternal fire' and 'black darkness' are used in the same context (*Jude* 7, 13). Insisting upon a literal reading of this imagery would be incoherent. The differing images represent differing dimensions of hell. Hell is not only a place where the unbelieving suffer God's holy displeasure (fire), but it is also a place where the unbelieving experience exclusion from his blessed presence (darkness).

3. An eternity of result or experience?

Do the biblical texts support the claim of the annihilationist that the wicked are ultimately destroyed? According to annihilationism, the only sense in which the punishment is eternal is in the sense of result. If the wicked are destroyed, this result endures throughout eternity, but not in the sense of any ongoing awareness of God's judgement.

Several biblical texts, however, militate against this view. These texts speak not only of hell as a place of fire and judgement, but also of the unending nature of these realities.

Matthew 25:46 concludes Jesus' account of the final judgement and separation of the sheep and the goats: 'And these [the goats] will go away

194

into eternal punishment, but the righteous into eternal life.' Not surprisingly, annihilationists attempt to take the language of eternal punishment in this text to mean something other than an everlasting experience of God's judgement. Either the adjective 'eternal' is taken qualitatively to mean a kind of punishment, or it is taken temporally to refer to the ongoing result of God's annihilation of the wicked. The first interpretation seizes upon the root of the term for 'eternal' in this text, aeon or age, and says that Jesus is therefore speaking of a punishment that corresponds to the coming age. However, this interpretation neglects the inescapable temporal aspect of the coming age, that it is an age having no end. In the Gospel of Matthew, this term always has a temporal meaning, referring to an unlimited period of time.

The second interpretation appeals to the fact that Jesus does not define the nature of eternal death in this text and it could mean either conscious torment or irreversible destruction. But there is considerable difference between a possible reading of the text and the likeliest reading of it. Three features make the annihilationist reading most unlikely. First, the text is preceded in verse 41 by a description of hell as 'the eternal fire which has been prepared for the devil and his angels'. This description, like the one in verse 46, clearly teaches the presence of a fire that has no end. Second, verse 46 speaks of an eternal punishment in strong language that suggests the awareness of God's displeasure. And third, the parallel and contrast in this verse is between 'eternal' punishment and 'eternal' life. A straightforward reading of this text indicates an everlasting experience—of punishment on the one hand, of life and blessing on the other.

Another important text answering annihilationism is Revelation 14:10-11, in which those who worship the beast are described as being 'tormented with fire and brimstone in the presence of the holy angels and in the presence of the Lamb. And the smoke of their torment goes up forever and ever, and they have no rest day and night . . .' This text is especially troublesome to the annihilationist because it speaks emphatically of the ongoing torment of the wicked in language that hardly seems compatible with extinction.

The most common annihilationist interpretation of this passage introduces a sequence first of suffering, then of total annihilation, and then of the 'memorialising' of that annihilation. However, this sequence is something that has been introduced into the text in order to avoid its clear implications. Revelation 14:10-11 does not say that the punishment of the wicked occurs in a sequence of steps, beginning with torment and leading to annihilation. It says, in clear and terrible terms, that the wicked will experience unending torment without rest throughout all eternity. Though it may be convenient to take the various images of this and other texts—of punishment, of fire, of destruction, of exclusion—and order them chronologically, the biblical texts commonly use these images as diverse ways of referring to the same reality.

Still another important text in this connection is Revelation 20:10-15, which describes the final judgement of all the dead and the living at the end of the age. It also describes the state of the wicked subsequent to this judgement in hell or the 'lake of fire' in terms that speak unmistakably of an ongoing experience of torment. The language could not be more emphatic: the devil, the beast, and the false prophet 'will be tormented day and night forever and ever'. According to the annihilationist's view, others who are thrown into the lake of fire will eventually be consumed; they will cease to exist. This posits a sharp difference between the experience of the devil and the wicked who are thrown into the same lake of fire. A more obvious reading of this text would conclude that all—the devil, the beast, the false prophet, and the wicked—will experience the same destiny.

4. Incompatible with the love of God?

The most common and compelling argument against the doctrine of eternal punishment, is the claim that it contradicts what we know from the gospel about the love of God. That God would pour out his wrath upon the wicked by excluding them from his grace seems incompatible with the biblical portrayal of God's abundant love and unfailing mercy. If God so loved the world that he gave his only begotten Son to save the world (*John* 3:16), how is it conceivable that he should punish the wicked everlastingly in hell?

According to this criticism, it seems needlessly vindictive that God's displeasure with the unbelieving should continue throughout the endless final state. How can this comport with the scriptural testimony, often repeated and dramatically manifested in the Lord Jesus Christ, that his God and Father does not repay us according to our iniquities; that he is slow to anger and abounding in love; and that like an earthly father, he takes pity upon us and remembers that we are dust (*Psa.* 103:8-14)?

Though it may seem too concessive at first hearing, we must acknowledge in response to this objection that there is a significant difference between God's love and his wrath. Whereas the former is his natural and delightful work, the latter is his alien and reluctant work (*Ezek.* 23:23, 30-32). God delights to save in a way that must be distinguished from his holy reluctance to punish. The Scriptures teach that God purposed from all eternity to save the elect alone (*Eph.* 1:4-6) and that God has chosen not to save others (*Rom.* 9:6- 13); however, they do not teach a perfect symmetry between God's sovereign purposes to save and not to save.

The doctrine of hell has been needlessly burdened by defenders who neglect this difference between God's joy in the salvation of sinners (*Luke* 15:7, 10, 20-32) and his holy reluctance to punish the wicked. When the biblical theme of God's patience with sinners (*1 Tim.* 2:9; *2 Pet.* 3:9) is minimised, the doctrine of hell suffers distortion. Similarly, when professing Christians exhibit nothing of God's love toward his enemies, but take a perverse delight in the punishment of the wicked, then God is mocked and his gospel corrupted. Defenders of the biblical doctrine of hell who do not share Christ's sorrow over the unbelief of his fellow Israelites (*Luke* 19:41-44), who do not understand Paul's agony over the unbelief of his countrymen (*Rom.* 9:2-3; 10:2), bring the grace of God into disrepute and encumber the biblical teaching about hell.

The doctrine of hell has nothing to do with a divine cruelty that delights in condemning the wicked. Those who through sin and disobedience forfeit any claim upon God's favour should look only to themselves to find the occasion for their punishment in hell. Their exclusion from God's presence is a consequence of their unwillingness to seek him while he was to be found, to call upon him while he was still near (*Isa.* 55:6-7).

This objection tends to isolate the attribute of God's love from other features such as God's justice or his holiness. In the process, significant dimensions of the Bible's teaching are diminished or rejected outright. The love of God is redefined in ways inconsistent with any doctrine of divine retribution. The love of God becomes sentiment, making no demands and imposing no penalty.

In the biblical doctrine of God, however, God's holiness and justice are emphasised as well as his love. Each attribute of God's nature discloses who he is, so that it is impermissible to play one attribute off against another. God's justice is not incompatible with his love. God is loving in his justice, and just in his loving.

5. Incompatible with the justice of God?

Another related theological objection is that the doctrine of everlasting punishment is unjust. If the punishment should fit the crime, then the doctrine of eternal punishment involves a form of punishment that outweighs the crime.

Defining justice and, in particular, the justice of God, is no simple task. One place to begin is with the *lex talionis*, the law of retribution in the well-known 'eye for eye' passage of Leviticus 24. The principle in this passage is one of due proportion between offence committed and punishment exacted. The perpetrator must, by means of a corresponding punishment, be brought to acknowledge and pay for the offence.

Justice is one of God's defining attributes. Because God cannot deny himself, he always deals with sin in a manner that upholds the strictest rule of justice, including appropriate retribution. Though this dimension of God's nature often receives short shrift in contemporary theology, the Scriptures are full of references to his unwillingness to permit sin to go unpunished and his role as judge. What human conscience and the law demand, by acknowledging wrongdoing and suffering its consequences, only reflect the justice of God. God is the supreme lawgiver and the vindicator of the right (*Psa.* 119:137-8; 145:17; *Jer.* 12:1; *1 John* 2:29). He maintains righteousness and finally vindicates the moral order he has established (*Psa.* 99:4; *Rom.* 2:6, 7).

This understanding of God's justice underlies the biblical teaching about the final judgement. It also provides the necessary context within which to comprehend the atoning work of Jesus Christ on behalf of his people.

According to the biblical descriptions of God's judgement, all those who are judged will be brought to recognise what they have done, whether it be good or bad. The secret things, including the motives of the heart, will be revealed in the presence of God (*1 Cor.* 4:5; *Rom.* 2:16). Each person will receive at the hands of God what he or she has deserved (*2 Cor.* 5:10; *Psa.* 62:12; *Jer.* 17:10). No one will be able to escape this judgement (*Acts* 17:30ff.; *Isa.* 29:15ff.). All will be called to give an account of their lives and actions (*Matt.* 25:31-46). The purpose of this judging and the exacting of an appropriate penalty will be the vindication of God's justice, the revelation of his authority in maintaining the right (*Rev.* 16:1-7; 19:1-6; *Psa.* 82:1, 8).

How can God be just in pardoning sinners? All will acknowledge their sin and unworthiness, but those who by the working of the Holy Spirit have trusted in Christ and repented of their sins will be openly declared acceptable to God and the recipients of the rewards of his grace. Christ, by virtue of his life of obedience and his atoning death, met the demands and the penalties of the law on behalf, and in the place, of his own people. All those who are beneficiaries of Christ's saving work as their Mediator are restored to favour with God and made acceptable to him. The work of Christ displays equally the mercy and the justice of God. As Paul describes it in Romans 3:21- 26:

> But now apart from the Law the righteousness of God has been manifested, being witnessed by the Law and the Prophets, even the righteousness of God through faith in Jesus Christ for all those who believe; for there is no distinction, for all have sinned and fall short of the glory of God, being justified as a gift by his grace through the redemption which is in Christ Jesus; whom God displayed publicly as a propitiation in his blood through faith. This was to demonstrate his righteousness, because in the forbearance of God he passed over the sins previously committed; for the demonstration, I say, of his righteousness at the present time, that he might be just and the justifier of the one who has faith in Jesus.

199

One interesting consequence of this biblical emphasis upon Christ's atonement as a demonstration of God's justice is what it tells us about the seriousness and gravity of human sin. The common objection to the doctrine of eternal punishment—that the punishment outweighs the crime—would seem to hold with equal force against the justice of Christ's suffering and cross. Why would God be just in exacting an infinite penalty—the death of his own Son—were the offence limited in its seriousness? The justice of God in exacting the price of Christ's atoning death would be imperilled, were some lesser price adequate to meet the need of sinners. To estimate the seriousness of human sin apart from a consideration of Christ's cross and work of atonement would be to call into question the justice of God's provision for our need.

To state the matter more concisely: that Christ suffered the agony of hell to atone for our sins teaches us that hell is what we sinners deserve. This penalty for sin was infinite in its price precisely because human sin offends against the infinite majesty and worth of God himself.

Though it is often assumed that the unbelieving and impenitent cease to sin at the judgement of God, it seems more probable that they continue to sin and live in hostility toward God throughout the final state. When God delivers the impenitent over to hell, he can be said to give them not only what they deserve but also what they perversely continue to desire. To live apart from God is the epitome of hell's suffering. But this is precisely what the impenitent sinner seeks even in hell. If this is the case, the ongoing punishment of the lost will correspond to their ongoing sin and rebellion. This likelihood cannot be conclusively demonstrated; however, it seems to fit the biblical data better than the contrary assumption that the lost begin to live in full conformity to God's will (*Matt.* 8:12).

Those who contest the justice of hell either fail to estimate properly the gravity of sin against God or to respect God's justice in dealing with it. There can be no escape from God's justice: either Christ suffered it for us at the cross or we shall suffer it ourselves.

6. A blemish upon the final state of things?

The last objection to the doctrine of everlasting punishment appeals to the perfection of the final state. If God's redemptive and re-creative purposes in Christ find their ultimate fulfilment in the consummation of all things, then the continued presence of the wicked in hell would constitute a blemish upon the otherwise pristine state of the new creation.

To put the matter a bit more prosaically, objectors insist that hell would deprive God's plan in history of a happy ending. When all of God's purposes in Christ will have reached their fulfilment, the presence of sin and sinners will still remain within the realm of God's creation. The loose thread of the presence of hell will mar the beautiful tapestry of God's redemptive purpose.

Of all the objections to the biblical doctrine of hell, this one is the most difficult to answer, not because it is so persuasive, but because it is so speculative. For the argument to work, it has to be assumed that the reality of hell represents a failure on God's part to realise his purposes of grace. Hell would, on this view of things, be an insuperable obstacle to the complete victory of God's gracious work through Christ. The reach of God's grace would be bounded. The embrace of God's love would be frustrated at the borders of hell.

Contrary to these assumptions, the biblical understanding of hell includes the conviction that even in the punishment of the unbelieving, God's purposes will be vindicated. Every mouth will be stopped. All will be held accountable to God, and no one will have reason to complain against the justice of his judgements (see *Rom.* 2:19-20; 9:17, 22-24). All those for whom Christ shed his blood will be saved. Not one will be lost or snatched from his hand. Not one of his own will fall outside of the reach of his gracious purpose to save (*John* 10:14-18, 27-29).

This last objection rests upon an assumption that is nowhere in Scripture. It is a disguised form of universalism, since it asserts that all who are not redeemed by the grace of God must be annihilated. However, God's will and purpose are triumphant in both the salvation of his people and in the condemnation of the lost.

CONCLUDING OBSERVATIONS

The biblical teaching regarding hell and the eternal punishment of the lost is difficult to maintain in the face of many assaults upon the doctrine today. Never in the history of the church has this dimension of the Bible's teaching been more obviously on trial.

Rather than close our consideration of this doctrine on a defensive note, however, I would like to conclude with a few general observations.

First, the doctrine of hell is a true test of our willingness to stay within the boundaries of Scripture when it comes to the subject of the last things. At no point in our consideration of the Bible's teaching about the future are we more inclined to allow our own opinions to take precedence over the Bible's teaching and the church's historic understanding. What we do with the subject of hell is a litmus test of our readiness to follow the way set out in the Scriptures, even when that way proves difficult.

Second, the doctrine of hell has immense significance for the manner in which the church proclaims the gospel. If the biblical teaching about hell is true, then it is scarcely possible to exaggerate the importance of seeking the Lord while he may be found, calling upon him while he is still near. The ramifications of this doctrine for the Christian believer or the mission of the church are transparent and undeniable. The seriousness with which believers 'work out their salvation with fear and trembling', and the urgency with which the church preaches the gospel to the nations, are a fair measure of conviction regarding the doctrine of eternal punishment. Ironically, perhaps one of the reasons this doctrine is so little believed and confessed is the failure of many ostensibly orthodox Christians to live in a manner consistent with its truth.

And third, an inappropriate fascination with the biblical imagery has often encumbered the doctrine of hell. Fuelled by the lurid imagery of Dante's poetic descriptions and over-zealous preaching, this fascination can easily become an unnecessary stumbling block. Biblical imagery conveys something of the reality of hell, but ought not be taken literally. We should think soberly and carefully about the reality to which this imagery points us: the reality of being banished from the blessed pres-

202

ence of God, being under the felt impression of his everlasting displeasure, and being subjected to the perpetual frustration and fury of sinful, but futile, rebellion against his will.

12

THE FUTURE OF ALL THINGS: THE NEW HEAVENS AND EARTH

*N*o one would be so bold as to think that the reality of heaven could be described in more than the most inadequate of words. Here one can only stammer like a little child. When it comes to the subject of the new heavens and earth, it may be said without exaggeration, 'Things which eye has not seen and ear has not heard, and which have not entered the heart of man, all that God has prepared for those who love him' (*1 Cor.* 2:9).

While acknowledging heaven's unspeakable mystery, we must be wary of false modesty and ingratitude that prevent any discussion. Not only do the Scriptures provide us with a window upon the glory of heaven, but they also teach us that believers even now taste something of the glory that awaits them (*1 Cor.* 2:10). Without considering heaven, a study of the promise of the future would be incomplete for at least two reasons.

First, we must acknowledge that the Bible does reveal, albeit in symbolic and rudimentary language, something of the splendour of the final state of believers. We must avoid going beyond what the Scriptures disclose, while echoing what they reveal.

Second, the new life in the Spirit which believers presently enjoy is of a piece with the fullness of immortal life yet to come (*2 Cor.* 5:4-5). The future is a reality whose first-fruits are the present experience of those who share fellowship with the risen Christ. Though we know in part, we truly do know something of what awaits the child of God. 'For now we see in a mirror dimly, but then face to face; now I know in part, but then I shall know fully just as I also have been fully known' (*1 Cor.* 13:12).

Christian understanding and popular piety tend to view the final state in a way that almost suggests a denial of creation's goodness. Life in the new creation is portrayed in terms so unlike life in the present creation that all continuity between the present and the future is denied. In a considerable body of Christian hymnody, the portrait of heaven is so ethereal that it has a barren, almost sterile, quality. A familiar picture is of believers in white robes flitting about in an indefinable space, singing and playing harps. The expectation for the life to come is so radically other than the richness and concreteness of life now experienced that heaven takes on a surreal, even dreamlike, quality.

However, the Bible speaks not only of 'heaven', but also of the 'new heavens and the new earth' (*2 Pet.* 3:13). If 'paradise lost' will become 'paradise regained', what is the relation between God's first creation of the 'heavens and earth' and his work of re-creation?

THE MEANING OF 'HEAVEN'

Undoubtedly, some popular portraits of heaven have been shaped by the imagery of Scripture. But they do not adequately reflect the biblical understanding of heaven and the promise of the life to come. They often show a failure to understand how the term 'heaven' is used in the Scriptures. It is commonly used in at least three ways.

First, 'heaven' is often used with 'earth' to describe the fullness of creation. Heaven in this sense is a part of creation, distinguishable from the earth but nonetheless a place that God has created. Genesis 1:1 says that 'in the beginning God created the heavens and the earth'. In the Gospels, frequent references to 'heaven and earth' confirm that heaven is a dimension of God's creation corresponding to, but distinguishable from, the earth. In this use, 'heaven' constitutes an essential part of the created cosmos.

Second, 'heaven' can be used as a synonym for God himself. In Matthew, the kingdom of God is referred to as the 'kingdom of heaven', probably reflecting deference to Jewish readers reluctant to use the name of God. When the prodigal son returns and confesses his sins before his father, he says, 'I have sinned against heaven and in your sight' (*Luke* 15:18, 21). In Matthew 21:25, Jesus asks the Pharisees whether the baptism of John was 'from heaven or from man'. And in John 3:27, John the Baptist declares that a 'man can receive nothing unless it has been given him from heaven'. In these passages, heaven is simply another way of referring to God.

The third and most significant use refers to the place of God's dwelling. Though God fills heaven and earth and cannot be restricted to any particular place, he has purposed to draw near to the creation from his special dwelling in heaven. Jesus taught his disciples to address God as 'Our Father who art in heaven' (*Matt.* 6:9). He often spoke to them of 'your Father who is in heaven' (*Matt.* 5:16, 45; 6:1; 7:11; 18:14) and of 'my Father who is in heaven' (*Matt.* 7:21; 10:32, 33; 12:50; 16:17; 18:10, 19). The same idea is expressed by the phrase 'heavenly Father' (*Matt.* 5:48; 6:14, 26, 32; 15:13; 18:35). Because God's dwelling is in heaven, the Scriptures also speak of Christ's first or second coming 'from heaven' (*John* 3:13; *2 Thess.* 1:7). The angels are likewise commonly described as being in or coming from heaven (*Matt.* 28:2; *Luke* 22:43; *Isa.* 6:1-6; *Psa.* 103:19-20).

Just as the totality of creation comprises heaven and earth together, so the work of redemption embraces heaven and earth together. Sin has disrupted the harmony and peace between God and his creatures, a disruption that encompasses heaven and earth. The rebellion of the creature against the Creator began in heaven and spilled over to earth. When God's work of redemption reaches its consummation, not only will every rebellious creature be cast out of heaven, but the earth itself also will be cleansed of every vestige of sin. Heaven and earth, rather than being estranged from each other, will be reunited in a new heaven and new earth in which righteousness dwells (*2 Pet.* 3:13).

The future of the believing community will be one in which the original harmony between heaven and earth is restored. Heaven, the place of God's special dwelling, will come down to earth and God will dwell in the midst of his people. The promise of the future for believers finds its focus in heaven, but it does not exclude the earth. All things will be united in Christ, whether things in heaven or things upon the earth (*Eph.* 1:10).

The whole creation will undergo renewal and transformation, being wholly sanctified, cleansed of every stain and remainder of sin. The new heavens and the new earth will be more glorious and resplendent of God's power, wisdom and grace, than creation at its beginning. In a surpassing way, the creation will be a temple fit for the dwelling of God with his people, a place suitable for the enjoyment of communion and friendship between the Creator and the creature.

THE CONTINUITY BETWEEN THE FIRST AND NEW CREATION

Will the new creation be radically unlike the present creation? Or will it be substantially like it though having undergone a transformation?

In the history of the church, both views have had advocates. Some have argued that the new heavens and earth will be altogether new; the present creation will be destroyed, and a new creation—quite unlike the present—will take its place. Others have maintained that the new heavens and earth will be this creation made new, similar in substance to the present. The second of these views seems more likely for several reasons.

First, just as the resurrected body represents the transformation of the present body of the believer, so the new creation represents the transformation—not annihilation—of the present creation. Like the seed that must die before it produces fruit, so the dissolution of the body is a prelude to its glorification (*1 Cor.* 15: 35-49). In the biblical understanding, the future of the believer (individual eschatology) corresponds to the future of the creation (general or cosmic eschatology). The resurrection the believer undergoes parallels the resurrection that creation will undergo at the consummation of all things.

Second, if the new heavens and earth will be substantially unlike the present heavens and earth, we would have to conclude that God's redemptive work discards rather than renews all things. God's original pronouncement that the created heavens and earth were 'very good' would have no longer have any significance after the fall into sin. Such an implication seems incompatible with the doctrine of the integrity and goodness of creation, however much it has been corrupted and distorted through sin. It would even imply that the sinful rebellion of the creation had so ruined God's handiwork as to make it irretrievably wicked, beyond God's capacity to restore and redeem.

Advocates of the view that the new creation will be altogether different from the present creation appeal to a number of passages in the Scriptures. The language used in Old Testament prophecy regarding the new heavens and earth seems to imply the destruction and removal of all things. In Psalm 102:26, the old heavens and earth are compared to a garment that wears out and perishes: 'Even they will perish, but thou dost endure; and all of them will wear out like a garment; like clothing thou wilt change them, and they will be changed.' Isaiah describes the wearing away of the host of heaven as being like a leaf that withers from the vine or the fig tree (*Isa.* 34:4). Like the vanishing of smoke, the sky will vanish and the inhabitants of the earth will die (*Isa.* 51:6). When the prophet goes on to speak of the new heavens and earth, he speaks of them as something God will 'create', 'the former things shall not be remembered or come to mind' (*Isa.* 65:17; compare 66:22). In a similar way, New Testament passages that describe the work of recreation employ the imagery of perishing or wearing out like a garment (*Heb.* 1:11), of a fire that consumes (*2 Pet.* 3:10), of a changing of all things (*Heb.* 1:12), and of the present order of things passing away (*Matt.* 5:18; 24:35; *2 Pet.* 3:10; *1 John* 2:17; *Rev.* 21:1). These images seem to imply that the present world will be extinguished to make way for something altogether new.

However, the vivid imagery of these passages ought not to be pressed too literally. Though they convey a radical renovation, they do not require the conclusion that this will mean a complete annihilation of the present cosmos. Some Scriptural passages require the alternative—that this renewal will involve a process of purification—making all things new, but not all new things. Two of these passages deserve particular attention.

Romans 8:18-25

Romans 8:18-25 not only illustrates the analogy between the resurrection of the believer and the resurrection-renewal of the whole creation, but it also confirms the new creation's substantial continuity with the present creation.

> For I consider that the sufferings of this present time are not worthy to be compared with the glory that is to be revealed to us. For the anxious longing of the creation waits eagerly for the revealing of the sons of God. For the creation was subjected to futility, not of its own will, but because of him who subjected it, in hope that the creation itself also will be set free from its slavery to corruption into the freedom of the glory of the children of God. For we know that the whole creation groans and suffers the pains of childbirth together until now. And not only this, but also we ourselves, having the first fruits of the Spirit, even we ourselves groan within ourselves, waiting eagerly for our adoption as sons, the redemption of our body. For in hope we have been saved, but hope that is seen is not hope; for why does one also hope for what he sees? But if we hope for what we do not see, with perseverance we wait eagerly for it.

First, this passage reminds us that sin has affected not only the human race but also the whole creation. As the apostle expresses it, the creation has been subjected to 'futility', to 'vanity' or 'pointlessness', because of the sinful rebellion of God's image-bearers. Without becoming unrelievedly evil, sin has brought corruption to the entirety of God's handiwork. The fabric of creation has been torn and broken, corresponding to the humility and weakness that now affect the human body (*1 Cor.* 15; *Phil.* 3:21).

Second, the redemption for which the children of God eagerly wait and the redemption of the creation itself are intimately connected. Individual eschatology and cosmic eschatology are so joined together that what is true for believers holds true for creation. When the children of God are revealed in glory and freedom, a similar glory and freedom will be granted to creation. Its present corruption and distortion will be removed. Its torn fabric will be mended. Remarkably, the language describing the restoration of creation corresponds exactly to the language describing the restoration of the children of God. The same process of renewal that will transform the believer's present bodies of humiliation into bodies of glory will transform the creation itself.

And third, the metaphor of childbirth that dominates this passage suggests that the transformation of the creation will be in substantial continuity with its present state. The creation groans, according to this passage, like a woman in childbirth prior to the delivery of her child. So the new creation, born of the old, will bear a resemblance and similarity to the original. To suggest that the new creation will be radically other than the former creation would violate the clear implication of this passage.

2 Peter 3:5-13

Another passage of special importance is 2 Peter 3:5-13, in which Peter answers those mockers who conclude that the promise of Christ's coming is untrue:

> For when they maintain this, it escapes their notice that by the word of God the heavens existed long ago and the earth was formed out of water and by water, through which the world at that time was destroyed, being flooded with water. But the present heavens and earth by his word are being reserved for fire, kept for the day of judgment and destruction of ungodly men. But do not let this one fact escape your notice, beloved, that with the Lord one day is as a thousand years, and a thousand years as one day. The Lord is not slow about his promise, as some count slowness, but is patient toward you, not wishing for any to perish but for all to come to repentance. But the day of the Lord will come like a thief, in which the heavens will pass away with a roar and the elements will be destroyed with intense heat, and the earth and its works will be discovered. Since all these things are to be destroyed in this way, what sort of people ought you to be in holy conduct and godliness, looking for and hastening the coming of the day of God, on account of which the heavens will be destroyed by burning, and the elements will melt with intense heat. But according to his promise we are looking for new heavens and a new earth, in which righteousness dwells.

The gist of Peter's answer to these mockers, who disputed the expectation of Christ's return, is clear. The Lord will indeed fulfil his promise, but in his own time and in accord with his desire to grant all an opportunity for repentance. In his patience and mercy, the world continues so that the gospel might be preached and the day of salvation prolonged. No one, however, should misjudge the Lord's patience and conclude that the day of his coming will not arrive. Two features of this passage speak about the present and future state of creation.

First, Peter compares the destruction of the world in the great flood with the future destruction of the world at the 'day of God' (verses 6-7, 10-12). When God's judgement fell upon the world at the time of the flood, the world was destroyed only in the sense that its inhabitants were subjected to judgement and the earth cleansed of wickedness.

And second, imagery drawn from the field of metallurgy suggests a process of refinement and purification, but not of utter annihilation. The language of this passage suggests a process of extraordinary power and destructiveness by which the present creation is refined and left in a state of pristine purity. Just as the refiner's fire is used to produce the highest and purest grade of gold or silver, so the refining fire of God's judging this sin-cursed creation will yield a holy and pure heavens and earth.

An interesting confirmation of this reading is found in the seemingly odd expression in verse 10, 'and the earth and its works will be discovered'. Many of the later Greek manuscripts use the verb, 'burned up', to conform to verse 12 and the working of fire. However, the word in older and better manuscripts conveys the idea of a process that does not so much destroy or burn up, but uncover or lay open for discovery. In the same way the refining process 'discovers' or 'lays bare' precious metal in all of its purity, so God uncovers the beauty and glory of the created order by removing every impurity.

These two passages confirm that God's powerful and redemptive work will involve the renewal of all things, not the creation of all new things. This creation will undergo cosmic sanctification, and all of God's renewed creation-temple will be holy unto the Lord (*Zech.* 14:20-21), suitable for his dwelling with his people and their service to him.

THE BLESSINGS OF LIFE IN THE RENEWED CREATION

Considering the substantial continuity between the present and new creation, it follows that the life to come in the new creation will be as rich and full of activity in the service of the Lord as was intended at the beginning. Just as humankind was originally placed in God's creation-temple to fulfil a particular office and calling, so the new humanity, in union with Christ, the second Adam, will live in unceasing joy in the presence and service of God.

The blessings of the life to come for the redeemed people of God will be a consummation of those enjoyed already in fellowship with Christ. What believers now know and experience only in part will then be theirs in fullness. Those who today can praise God that their 'cup overflows' (*Psa.* 23) will in the life to come drink unendingly from the inexhaustible riches of their inheritance in Christ.

Among these blessings are such things as: perfection in holiness (*Rev.* 3:4, 5; 7:14; 19:8; 21:27); the complete experience of the joy and benefit of adoption (*Rom.* 8:23); the fullness of salvation from sin (*Rom.* 13:11; *1 Thess.* 5:9; *Heb.* 1:14; 5:9); unbroken and unbreakable fellowship with God and his Christ, together with all the saints (*John* 17:24; *2 Cor.* 5:8; *Phil.* 1:23; *Rev.* 21:3; 22:3); conformity to Christ (*Rom.* 8:29; *1 John* 3:2; *Rev.* 22:4); eternal life (*Matt.* 19:16, 29); and the glory of full redemption (*Luke* 24:36; *Rom.* 2:10; 8:18, 21; *2 Thess.* 1:10). Believers who presently bless God for 'every spiritual blessing in Christ' (*Eph.* 1:3), will enter into the perfection of these blessings in the life to come. Every vestige of sin will be utterly expunged. Every obstacle to fellowship with the Triune God will be removed.

Believers will also enjoy the blessings of freedom from every effect of the curse. Life within the renewed creation will be freed from culpable ignorance and error (*John* 6:45), from the fear and reality of death (*Heb.* 2:15; *1 Cor.* 15:26; *Rev.* 2:11; 20:6, 14), from every form of futility and frustration, from sickness and affliction, from hunger and thirst, cold and heat (*Matt.* 5:4; *Luke* 6:21; *Rev.* 7:16-17; 21:4), and from all weakness, dishonour and corruption (*1 Cor.* 15:42). Believers in glorious resurrection bodies will stand in the presence of God and all his people, unbowed by the burden of sin's devastation. The God who forgives all the sins of his people, who heals all their diseases (*Psa.* 103:3), will renew their youth and strength. Believers will 'take up wings like eagles' and experience the exhilaration of never growing weary in well doing.

Even though the language tells more about what will not mark the life to come, John's vision in Revelation 21:1-4 stirs longing in the hearts of God's people:

> And I saw a new heaven and a new earth; for the first heaven and the first earth passed away, and there is no longer any sea. And I saw the holy city, new Jerusalem, coming down out of heaven from God, made ready as a bride adorned for her husband. And I heard a loud voice from the throne, saying, 'Behold, the tabernacle of God is among men, and he shall dwell among them and they shall be his people, and God himself shall be among them, and he shall wipe away every tear from their eyes; and there shall no longer be any death; there shall no longer be any mourning, or crying, or pain: the first things have passed away.

No child of God who has felt deeply the pain and brokenness of sin and the curse—in sinful indifference to God and others, broken relationships, the terror of crippling disease, the boredom and barrenness of life without God, the injustice among people and nations, and so much more—can read these words without being stirred. They fan into flame an eagerness and longing, like that of a little child who waits expectantly, even impatiently, for the fulfilment of a parent's promise.

Unlike hell—a place of utter isolation, separation from God and others—life in the new creation will be marked by friendship and love, perfect fellowship with God and those who belong to him. The beauty of the marriage relationship, of self-denying love between a man and a woman, will be surpassed by the beauty of the marriage between Christ, the bridegroom, and the church, his bride. Whatever loss of loved ones that loyalty to Christ may bring in this life will be more than matched by an increase of spiritual brothers and sisters, not only in this life, but also in the life to come (*Mark* 10:29, 30; *Matt.* 12:50; *Heb.* 12:22-24). When the Psalmist exults, 'How good and how pleasant it is for brothers to dwell together in unity' (*Psa.* 133:1), he leads the people of God in singing of their future experience. When all of God's people dwell together in the most intimate and rich communion, the second table of the law will be fulfilled. The sinful brokenness and division that so often mar the beauty of Christ's bride in this present age, will give way to the glory for which Christ prayed, when he asked the Father for the oneness of his people, even as he and the Father are one (*John* 17:21).

Though the Scriptures plainly teach that in the kingdom of heaven they will neither marry nor be given in marriage, they nonetheless use imagery that suggests many ordinary pleasures will characterise life in the new creation. Some of the most common imagery speaks of the saints eating and drinking, enjoying table fellowship with God and others. In the prophetic descriptions of the Old Testament, life in the new heavens and earth is depicted as a rich banquet, lavishly furnished with the best of foods. Isaiah pictures the day of redemption as one in which 'the Lord of hosts will prepare a lavish banquet for all peoples on this mountain; a banquet of aged wine, choice pieces with marrow, and refined, aged wine' (*Isa.* 25:6). This picture is drawn in a context that clearly refers to the final state when 'the Lord God will wipe tears away from all faces, and he will remove the reproach of his people from all the earth' (verse 8). Jesus, on the occasion of the institution of the Lord's supper, spoke of the time when he would drink anew with his disciples from the fruit of the vine in the kingdom (*Matt.* 26:29). Revelation 19:9 speaks of the coming 'marriage feast of the Lamb'. We also are told in the Gospels that Christ, after his resurrection, not only appeared to his disciples but also enjoyed eating and drinking with them (*Luke* 24:43; *John* 21:9-14).

Just as our eating and drinking today is to be done to God's glory (*1 Cor.* 10:31), so it may well be in the new heavens and earth that the blessings of food and drink, sanctified through the word of God and prayer (*1 Tim.* 4:5), will be the occasion for worshipping and serving the living God. It is wise not to be too dogmatic on this question one way or the other. Nevertheless, life in the new creation will undoubtedly be like a rich banquet at which the saints of God will sit down together and enjoy the richest of foods. The joy and happiness that we have known in this life on the occasion of the wedding of a man and woman is but a foretaste of the joy and happiness that will be ours when Christ receives his bride on his wedding day. The wine Christ served at the wedding of Cana is surely a foretaste of that best of wines that he will furnish on that day.

A LIFE OF WORSHIP

When describing the blessings of the life to come, we face the danger of losing sight of what is central to every aspect of that life—the worship and service of the Triune God. The blessings enjoyed by the children of God in the new heavens and earth have meaning only within the context of the worship of God. True life for the child of God is first and foremost a life of worship. So it will be in the life to come.

One prominent way this is emphasised throughout the Scriptures is the promise of a Sabbath rest for the people of God. At the conclusion of his work of creation, God rested (*Gen.* 2:2-3). That rest was not inactivity, but active pleasure in the work of his hands and communion with his image-bearers. The dominion that Adam and Eve were to exercise over the creation, under God and in his service, was to be a life of worship, an unending and full-orbed offering of loving obedience to their Creator and Friend, the living God.

Sin radically broke these bonds of fellowship between God and his people. The Sabbath rest of God and the *shalom* of his people were disrupted. The care over the creation assigned to God's image-bearers degenerated into a state of sinful misuse and cultural development in the service of the creature rather than the Creator.

The work of redemption promises a renewal of rest and *shalom* in the relations between God and his people, and between his people and the creation under their care. The ordinance of Israel's Sabbath was a sign of this renewed fellowship and service. The rest promised to Israel in the land that the Lord gave to her was only a prefiguration of the eternal rest that awaited her at the consummation of God's saving purposes in Christ. Canaan was a type of the true promised land, the new heavens

216

and earth wherein righteousness dwells. Israel never entered fully into the promise (*Heb.* 3:11, 18). Joshua, an Old Testament type of Jesus, was unable to bring God's people into the promised rest.

> There remains therefore a Sabbath rest for the people of God. For the one who has entered his rest [Jesus Christ, the Mediator of the new covenant] has himself also rested from his works, as God did from his. Let us therefore be diligent to enter that rest, lest anyone fall through following the same example of [Israel's] disobedience' (*Heb.* 4:9-11).

The rest that God's Old Testament people enjoyed in their Sabbath day worship and festivals was only a foretaste of what God's New Testament people enjoy in their Lord's Day worship. Even the Lord's Day, when the people of God gather for worship and praise, resting in the finished work of the crucified and risen Saviour, remains a promissory note of the Sabbath rest that still awaits them. The worship of the Lord's Day is but a foretaste of the eternal Sabbath yet to come, an emblem of eternal rest.

Revelation's visions of the life to come are full of the imagery of worship and praise. What Isaiah glimpsed in a vision of the Lord, surrounded by the seraphim and the host of heaven unceasingly declaring his holiness (*Isa.* 6), John witnessed again and again in his visions of heaven. In Revelation 4, he describes the throne of God as surrounded by twenty-four elders and the four living creatures. Representing the whole company of God's people and every living creature, this heavenly assembly falls before God in worship, saying, 'Worthy art thou, our Lord and our God, to receive glory and honour and power; for thou didst create all things, and because of thy will they existed, and were created' (verse 11). An equally vivid picture of the worship of God is given in Revelation 19:

> And I heard, as it were, the voice of a great multitude and as the sound of many waters and as the sound of mighty peals of thunder, saying, 'Hallelujah! For the Lord our God, the Almighty, reigns, for the marriage of the Lamb has come and his bride has made herself ready' (verses 6-7).

When the new Jerusalem descends from heaven to earth, the whole creation will become a dwelling place for God in fellowship with his people.

217

There will be no temple there, for the Lord God himself and the Lamb will be in the midst of the people (*Rev.* 22:22). The sanctuary in which God dwells and in which he is served and worshipped will be the new heavens and earth.

This worship will surely include the two facets that characterise worship now. In the Scriptures, the worship of God includes not only the worship of the *cultus* but also the worship of the whole of life. God's people assemble at specific times and places for official worship. In obedience to God's command and in gratitude for his saving work, God's people gather in worship to acknowledge the Triune God's worthiness to receive the thankful praise of all creation.

This does not exhaust the worship or service of the people of God, however. In the two tables of the law, commanding love for God and for neighbour, the life of God's people is described as a life of worship. As royal priests, believers in union with Christ respond to God's mercy and grace by offering their selves wholly to God (*1 Pet.* 2:9; *Rom.* 12:1). No legitimate activity of life—whether in marriage, family, business, play, friendship, education, politics, etc.—escapes the claims of Christ's kingship. In fellowship with Christ, the second Adam and obedient servant of the Lord, the redeemed of God are renewed unto the service of their Creator in every area of life. Though we are not told what life as worship in the new creation will involve, certainly those who live and reign with Christ forever will find the diversity and complexity of their worship of God not diminished, but enriched, in the life to come.

Will the people of God not become weary, perhaps even bored, in a life that has no end? It is difficult to imagine a life of worship, whether in the narrow or broad sense, that ceaselessly continues. However, we lack the imagination necessary to grasp with any adequacy the richness and texture of the life to come. If the Sabbath rest of God's people, far from being an inactive and listless passing of time, is full of activity in the worship of God, we have the beginning of an answer to this puzzle. In our present experience, we know what it is for time to pass with painful slowness. On the other hand, when we are engaged in an exhilarating activity time seems to fly. No child of God need fear that the life to come will end in boredom or tiresome repetition. Though the language is poetic and somewhat general, the hymn writer, John Newton, well expressed it—'When we've been there ten thousand years . . . we've no less days to sing his praise'.

The inexhaustible glory of their God will be more than enough to furnish the praise of God's people in the life to come.

THE RICH INHERITANCE OF THE RENEWED CREATION

Consistent with our argument that the life of the redeemed in the new creation will be rich and diverse, one of the descriptions in the book of Revelation speaks of the rich inheritance that awaits God's people. In Revelation 21, John envisions the nations walking together by the light that is the Lamb, and 'the kings of the earth will bring their glory into it [the holy city]' (verse 24). The rich diversity of peoples, together with the works and accomplishments of those who have been among the leaders of the nations, will contribute significantly to the splendour of the new heaven and earth.

It has been plausibly suggested that this describes the way the new creation will receive all the appropriate fruits of human culture and development produced throughout the course of history. Every legitimate and excellent fruit of human culture will be carried into and contribute to the splendour of life in the new creation. Far from being an empty and desolate place, the new creation will be enriched with the sanctified fruits of human culture. Nothing of the diversity of the nations and peoples, their cultural products, languages, arts, sciences, literature, and technology—so far as these are good and excellent—will be lost upon life in the new creation. Life in the new creation will not be a starting over, but a perfected continuation of the new humanity's stewardship of all of life in the service of God.

Though some have argued that this reading of John's vision is speculative, the language of Revelation 21:24 can scarcely be read otherwise. The alternative—denying that life in the new creation will be enriched by the presence of these fruits of human culture—seems unlikely and problematic. Life in the new creation will not be a repristination of all things—a going back to the way things were at the beginning. Rather, life in the new creation will be a restoration of all things—involving the removal of every sinful impurity and the retaining of all that is holy and good. Were the new creation to exclude the diversity of the nations and the glory of the kings of the earth, it would be impoverished rather than enriched, historically regressive and reactionary rather than progressive. To express the point in the form of a question: Is it likely that the music of Bach and Mozart, the painting of Rembrandt, the writing of Shakespeare, the discoveries of science, etc., will be altogether lost upon life in the new creation?

ENJOYING GOD FOREVER

The *Westminster Shorter Catechism*, one of the better-known Reformed catechisms, begins with a justifiably famous question and answer: 'What is the chief end of man? Man's chief end is to glorify God, and to enjoy him forever.' If our lives find their chief end in glorifying and enjoying God, then the epitome of life in the new heaven and earth will consist in the worship and enjoyment of the true God. The life to come, because it will bring the fruition of human blessedness, will consist in finding joy in God, living before his face.

In the traditional language of Christian theology, the joy of heaven will consist essentially in the contemplation, knowledge, and enjoyment of God. When believers see God in the life to come and know him even as they are known, their joy in God will have no measure or end. Indeed, remove the joy of God's presence and the sight of his face, and all of the blessings of the life to come that have been described would amount to very little. For the confession of every believer is that of the Psalmist, 'Whom have I in heaven but thee? And besides thee, I desire nothing on earth' (*Psa.* 73:25). The restlessness of the human heart finds no end, unless we find our rest in God (Augustine). The deepest longing and thirst of every image-bearer of God can be quenched only by God himself (*Psa.* 42:1-2; 63:1-2).

220

When the Bible speaks of the believer's future, it is this enjoyment of God, this 'seeing God face to face' that is most emphasised. Whereas sin brought shame upon the human race so that we cannot look upon God's face without averting our eyes (*Gen.* 2:7-11; *Luke* 18:13), redemption promises the restoration of direct communion between God and his people. The work of Christ as Mediator, not only in justification but also in sanctification, restores those who are united with him to favour with God (*1 Cor.* 1:30; *Rom.* 8:1, 33). Sanctified by the work of Christ and his indwelling Spirit, Christ's people are enabled to see God (*Heb.* 12:14). When the work of redemption is completed, believers will stand unbowed before God, confident in his presence that they are acceptable to him (*Heb.* 10:19-22). The smile of God's countenance will shine upon the glorified members of Christ throughout all eternity. The pure in heart will see God (*Matt.* 5:8). Those who have purified themselves even as he is pure, will be like him for they shall see him as he is (*1 John* 3:2).

As with other dimensions of the life to come, this joy of seeing God stands out in the depictions of the new heaven and earth in the book of Revelation. In the last chapter of the Bible, John sees a vision of this enjoyment of God. Using language drawn from the picture of paradise in Genesis, he writes:

> And he showed me a river of the water of life, clear as crystal, coming from the throne of God and of the Lamb, and in the middle of its street. And on either side of the river was the tree of life, bearing twelve kinds of fruit, yielding its fruit every month; and the leaves of the tree were for the healing of the nations. And there shall no longer be any curse; and the throne of God and of the Lamb shall be in it, and his bondservants shall serve him; and they shall see his face, and his name shall be upon their foreheads. And there shall no longer be any night; and they shall not have need of the light of a lamp nor the light of the sun, because the Lord God shall illumine them; and they shall reign forever and ever (*Rev.* 22:1-5).

Central to this vision of the future is the believer's direct communion with God, basking in the light of his presence and favour, enjoying fellowship with him in the midst of the splendour of the new creation.

221

THE 'VISION OF GOD'

That the vision, knowledge, and enjoyment of God stand at the centre of life in the new creation is undeniable. But how we are to understand this vision of God is a more difficult matter. In the history of the church, particularly in the Roman Catholic doctrine of the beatific vision and the Eastern Orthodox doctrine of *theosis* or deification, this vision involves an unmediated knowing of God's being. Though Roman Catholic and Eastern Orthodox teaching differ on the nature of this vision of God, common to these traditions is the idea of an immediate participation in God's essence. In the Roman Catholic understanding of the beatific vision, believers will know God as he is in his innermost being. In the Eastern Orthodox understanding of deification, believers will become so much like God as to be, in some sense, participants in his divine life. Believers, indeed, will become 'god-like'. Just as God became man in the incarnation, so through mystical union with Christ believers will become partakers of the divine nature. In each view, it is claimed that believers will no longer depend upon any creaturely medium or Mediator in order to see God. The vision of God will be a literal seeing of God as he is in his essential nature.

Those who teach this idea of an immediate vision of and participation in the being of God often appeal to 2 Peter 1:4. In this text, Peter declares that God 'has granted to us his precious and magnificent promises, in order that by them you might become partakers of the divine nature, having escaped the corruption that is in the world by lust'. This text seems to lend support to the view that redemption ultimately involves a separation from this world in order to participate directly in the being of God. Upon first reading, this strange text seems to suggest the idea of an absorption into the being of God himself.

Two considerations, however, lead me to reject the teaching of an immediate seeing of the being of God in the life to come. The first relates to the meaning of the language of 2 Peter 1:4. The second has to do with the broader issue of the difference between God as Creator and all creatures, a difference that renders suspect any teaching of an immediate participation in the being of God.

222

The key to the interpretation of 2 Peter 1:4 lies in the three Greek terms that are commonly translated 'partakers of the divine nature'. The second term used in this phrase is a noun whose common meaning is that of 'partner' or 'companion'. The first and second terms, usually translated abstractly as 'the divine nature', might better be translated concretely as 'of the deity'. Peter is speaking of the promise that the redeemed people of God will become his 'partners' or 'companions'. This is covenantal language. The goal of our redemption, consistent with the general teaching of Scripture, is covenantal fellowship with the Triune God. Rather than conveying the strange idea of a commingling of the being of the creature and the Creator, this language conveys the idea of communion between God and those who are his. Redemption will find its consummation in the restoration of perfect friendship between God and his people.

This translation and understanding of 2 Peter 1:4 corresponds to the teaching of Scripture of an unbridgeable difference in being between the Triune Creator and the creature, even the creature bearing God's image. For the creature to know and enjoy God, God must take the initiative and condescend to the level of the creature. Throughout the entire course of creation and redemption, God is the one who comes to us, speaking language we can understand and appearing in a creaturely form within our reach. Accordingly, when God in the fullness of time comes to dwell with us (*John* 1:14), he does so by way of a Mediator, the Word become flesh. The miracle of the incarnation is not that we climbed up to God. The miracle is that God came down to us, assuming our flesh and blood. Through all of his acts of condescension, and chiefly through the incarnation of his beloved Son, God can be known and loved by the creature. However, at no time does the creature know and enjoy God immediately, that is, apart from any creaturely means of communion. God manifests his power and wisdom, not directly or immediately, but through the means of his handiwork (*Psa.* 19; *Rom.* 1:18ff.). God manifests his mercy and grace through the person and work of Jesus Christ, the Mediator. To see God one must see his glory in the Son (*John* 1:18; 14:9; 17:24).

In the same way, when God's fellowship with his people in the new heaven and earth is complete, God will be God and his people will still be creatures. The people of God will not be absorbed into or partake in an immediate way of the being of God. In order to do so, they would have to cease to be who they are as creatures. Nor will they know God with a perfection that knows no boundaries. Though their knowledge and enjoyment of God will be perfected, untainted by the culpable ignorance of sin, it will not be a knowing that fully exhausts who God is in his incomprehensible greatness. To know God even as he knows himself will ever remain outside of the reach of the creature.

How are we to understand, then, what it will be for God's people to see God? If it does not mean that we become as God is, knowing him as he alone knows himself, then what is meant by the expression, 'they shall see his face'?

Though believers have only a small inkling of what this means, what they do know is full of the promise of the future. To see the face of God means at least this: that believers will dwell in God's presence without any hint of fear or shame. In the new heaven and earth, God's joy in his people will be reciprocated by their joy in him. But more than that, God's people will see him without any of the sinful limitations of the present. No sin-induced stupor, no failure of hearing, no blindness of vision will obscure the beauty of God from their knowledge. Though believers will still be creatures, limited in their capacity to know God, their knowledge of God will be pure and undiminished by sin. Though God's majesty, splendour, holiness, love, wisdom, and all that he is, surpass the knowledge of any creature in inexhaustible richness, still believers will see God as they have never seen him before. This seeing will be of one piece with what they have already seen in this life (2 Cor. 4:6), but it will be so much richer and fuller as to leave room only for unending praise and thanksgiving.

Such is the great promise of the future for which the children of God wait—to dwell in God's blessed presence, glorifying and enjoying him forever.

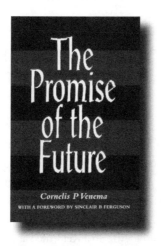

THE PROMISE OF THE FUTURE

CORNELIS P. VENEMA

ISBN-13: 978 0 85151 793 3, 560pp. clothbound.

A major new study of what the Bible teaches about the future. The chief note sounded is one of hope. 'The future is bright because it is full of promise, the promise of God's Word.'

'Dr Venema's fine study is both comprehensive and careful. He is thoroughly biblical; he is also honest and fair in dealing with the variety of eschatological positions that are current in the Christian church . . . his background in pastoral ministry guarantees that his exposition even of complex issues is expressed in a way that the average Christian should be able to follow.'

From the Foreword by Sinclair B. Ferguson

WHAT THE REVIEWERS SAID ABOUT

THE PROMISE OF THE FUTURE

For over 20 years, the standard amillennial textbook in Reformed colleges and seminaries has been Anthony Hoekema's classic work *The Bible and the Future*. This state of affairs may soon change because of the recent publication of a new book by Cornelis Venema entitled *The Promise of the Future*. Dr. Venema, Professor of Doctrinal Studies at Mid-America Reformed Seminary, has given the church a well-written and comprehensive textbook on eschatology from a Reformed and Amillennial perspective . . . All Christians should benefit from Venema's work.

Ligonier Ministries

If all of today's most popular books on the end times were suddenly raptured, *The Promise of the Future* would likely be among those left behind. This new work by Cornelis Venema . . . is everything its more popular counterparts are not: theologically substantial, careful in its exposition of Scripture, pastoral in approach, confessionally Reformed, highly critical of dispensational premillennialism, and nonsensational—hardly the stuff of which eschatological best-sellers are made.

Venema informs us . . . this book originated as, and to some degree remains, 'a study aimed at the biblically and theologically informed lay person'. No one should infer from that, however, that it cannot be read with profit by those with formal theological education. It should prove to be a highly useful tool for seminarians in training, for ministers in their preaching and pastoral care, and for theologians in their teaching and writing. Lay persons, pastors, and professors alike can be assured that this is the finest survey of Reformed eschatology to come on the market in the last twenty years. At the end of your next visit to the bookstore, make sure that this volume is not left behind.

Calvin Theological Journal

Occasionally one reads a new book and feels instinctively that this book will become a classic. Here is such a book. The subject is eschatology (the doctrine of the last things). It is a comprehensive treatment, sanely written, thoroughly biblical, and spiritually edifying. It is a clear, easy and enjoyable book to read. The language is amazingly non-technical for a modern theological book. But then if what one is writing is thoroughly researched and well thought out, one does not need to try to impress with jargon.

Free Church Witness

If you want your mind stretched on the subject of the Second Coming of the Lord Jesus Christ then *The Promise of the Future* would be a sound investment. It introduces you to the full range of biblical teaching on the subject of 'The Last Things' in a way that is both intellectually stimulating and spiritually rewarding. Important topics covered include: The Future between Death and Resurrection, The Future Marked by the Signs of the Times, Observations about Tribulation; The Antichrist, What about Revelation 20? Degrees of Reward in the Kingdom of Heaven, The Doctrine of Eternal Punishment, as well as a complete overview of the various millennial positions. This is an area which often generates more heat than light. Venema does not fall into that trap and you will greatly benefit from this book.

Evangelical Movement of Wales

Dr Venema . . . has produced an excellent study of 'eschatology', dealing with matters such as death and the intermediate state, resurrection, the return of Christ and the new creation . . . His position is 'Amillennial' . . . Venema's critique of other views is always gracious and his treatment throughout is thoroughly biblical and very readable. This will undoubtedly become a standard study of Reformed, amillennial eschatology.

The Covenanter Witness

The doctrine of the last things (eschatology) has both fascinated and divided Christians, and led to numerous debates among theologians. In this volume, Professor Venema . . . has provided us with a clear guide through the maze of current opinions . . . this is a volume worth having and studying. It covers a great deal of ground, and yet is surprisingly easy to read.

The Monthly Record

This major new examination of biblical teaching on the future of the individual, of the church and of the universe as a whole will be useful both to theological students and to informed non-specialists. Ranging over the whole field, it interacts extensively with recent literature on disputed issues, such as the nature of the intermediate state, the millennium of Revelation 20 and the doctrine of eternal punishment, always seeking to answer the fundamental question: 'What do the Scriptures clearly teach?' The Christ-centered nature of biblical teaching on the future is emphasized, as is the importance of the church's historic confessions for an understanding of eschatology. The chief note sounded is one of hope: 'God's people eagerly await Christ's return because it promises the completion of God's work of redemption. The future is bright because it is full of promise, the promise of God's Word.'

An outstanding volume—one of the best works in Biblical Theology we have seen in years. This is must reading—especially for those working through issues in New Testament eschatology.

www.discerningreader.com